PEASANT POLITICS

Johns Hopkins Studies in Atlantic History and Culture

Richard Price and Franklin W. Knight, General Editors

PEASANT POLITICS

STRUGGLE IN A DOMINICAN VILLAGE

Kenneth Evan Sharpe

The Johns Hopkins University Press
Baltimore and London

HD
430
.H34
S47

Copyright © 1977 by The Johns Hopkins University Press

All rights reserved. No part of this book may be
reproduced or transmitted in any form or by any means,
electronic or mechanical, including photocopying,
recording, xerography, or any information storage and
retrieval system, without permission in writing
from the publisher.

Manufactured in the United States of America

The Johns Hopkins University Press, Baltimore, Maryland 21218
The Johns Hopkins Press Ltd., London

Library of Congress Catalog Card Number 77–4782
ISBN 0-8018-1952-0

Library of Congress Cataloging in Publication data
will be found on the last printed page of this book.

To the Memory of Kalman H. Silvert

CONTENTS

CHARTS

TABLES

ACKNOWLEDGMENTS

Many people have helped me in the course of writing this book, and I would like to thank them. This project would not have been possible without the help and *confianza* of the people of Jaida Arriba. They warmly welcomed me into their homes, patiently answered my unending questions, came to trust me with some of their deepest thoughts, and gave freely of their valuable time to teach me about peasant life and struggle. Monseñor Roque Adames, "El Padre," officials in the Instituto de Café y Cacao, and many others in the Dominican Republic were also of great help. I want to give special thanks to Fidel and his wife. Their house was always a home to me, their constant friendship and enthusiasm were a great source of strength. Fidel's rare knowledge of peasant life and profound understanding of the difficulties faced by peasant organizations were invaluable to my work.

I am deeply grateful to my two major research advisers, Robert Dahl and Sidney Mintz, both for their excellent guidance and for their confidence in me and their respect for what I wanted to do. Their constant openness, their persistent refusal to force me into rigid molds of past research, and their critical efforts to help me do better what I sought to do are rare and valuable traits of wise teachers. I am also grateful to Alfred Stepan who never tired of asking me pointed questions about my research and who helped me see some of the broader implications of my work.

Douglas Bennett and Morris Blachman have been particularly helpful. During the many years and drafts behind this project, they were my hardest critics and my warmest supporters. I cherish their friendship.

I owe a great intellectual debt to Frieda and Kalman Silvert. They were the first to fire my interest in the study of politics, and later they helped to shape my ideas about what good theory and good research looked like. Kal's moral posture in the discipline will always serve as a guide. I also want to acknowledge a debt to two men I have never met, Clifford Geertz and Eric Wolf. Their work on ideology and on peasants helped create my initial interest in this project and later was important in formulating my approach to it.

Henry Y. K. Tom at The Johns Hopkins University Press provided much friendly editorial help far beyond his official responsibilities. I am also grateful to a number of friends for their critical comments and careful reading of research designs and chapter drafts. These include Edward Harris, Steven Hellman, Douglas Rosenberg, Rand Rosenblatt, and Oscar Cañicares. I am particularly indebted to Loli and Jerry Murray for their skillful and sensitive assistance in translating the peasant quotes from the colloquial Dominican Spanish, and to Olga Olavarrieta, Libby Sharpe, Richard Valelly, and Madeleine Kahn for their painstaking editorial assistance and advice.

I would like to give special thanks to two dear friends, Madeleine Thomson, who persistently but warmly encouraged me to struggle against mediocrity and toward excellence, and Bonnie Sharpe, whose sensitive pictures of peasant life in Jaida Arriba prodded me to be more sensitive in trying to capture in words the meaning of peasant life.

A number of organizations made this book financially possible. In January and February of 1970, an invaluable preliminary visit to the Dominican Republic was made possible by a grant from the Latin American Studies Council at Yale University. The actual research was funded by a grant from the Foreign Area Fellowship Foundation. Bryce Wood, Michael Potashnik, and the staff at the Foundation were always enthusiastic about and supportive of my work. The generous funds provided by the Foundation helped remove the financial burdens that plague many doctoral candidates. I am also grateful to the Universidad Católica Madre y Maestra and the Centro Belarminio for making their facilities readily available to me, and to Swarthmore College for helping to defray the preparation costs.

INTRODUCTION

> I conceive that there are two kinds of inequality among the human species; one, which I call natural or physical, because it is established by nature, and consists in a difference of age, health, bodily strength, and the qualities of mind or of the soul; and another, which may be called moral or political inequality, because it depends on a kind of convention, and is established, or at least authorized, by the consent of men. This latter consists of the different privileges which some men enjoy to the prejudice of others; such as that of being more rich, more honoured, more powerful, or even in a position to exact obedience.
>
> —Jean-Jacques Rousseau, *The First and Second Discourses*

If there are forms of inequality created by man, not by God or nature, then man may also be capable of changing them. How men come to believe that they can and should change the "moral and political inequality" they experience, and create the power to do so, are the central problems of this book.

The particular kind of inequality I am concerned with is inequality of power—that some men are "more powerful" than, or "even in a position to exact obedience" from, others. These differences in power mean that some men may have better life chances at the expense of the life chances of others. My concern is not simply that such inequalities exist. Man-made inequality may be a permanent feature of human societies. My concern, rather, is with how men can change the particular form or degree of inequality that exists. More specifically, my major interest is in how groups of men who live under a particular form of control that defines and limits their life chances come to believe in the possibility and desirability of collective action to change that control.

This book examines a particular case: how a group of Dominican peasants in Jaida Arriba came to believe that they could and should take action against the economic control exercised over them, and how they did so. My focus is on the control exercised by the middlemen (*compradores* [buyers] or *comerciantes* [dry goods store owners]) over peasant harvests through the control of capital and marketing given them by their positions in the local, national, and international economic system. By lending or advancing money to peasants in the months of no harvest, these middlemen met basic needs the peasants had in tending to their families and crops. But to repay the middlemen, the peasants had to bear high interest rates and to sell their coffee at prices far below its open-market value. These middlemen also were able to exercise control over this central cash crop through a virtual monopoly of access to the marketplace.

Before 1967, no attempt at collective action against this economic control had been made. Late that year, through the Catholic church—the bishop, the local priest, and a lay volunteer—an effort was begun to organize a cooperative among the peasants. Its underlying purpose was *concientización* (the creation of consciousness), creating an awareness of the importance of living true Christian ideals through collective struggle here and now to help oneself and others in the community. The specific task of the cooperative was to make the peasants conscious of the injustice of middleman power and the need to act together against it. The cooperative sought to wrest control over capital and marketing from the hands of these men.

The major purposes of this book are to use this case to explore a set of substantive issues of interest to those both academically and practically concerned with peasants and to focus attention on certain fundamental political and theoretical problems.

Much attention is placed on important topics in peasant studies: rural social stratification, the distribution of economic power in marketing and credit systems, the role of the middleman (broker, comprador), patron-client relations, the political and economic structures (local, national, international) that enmesh peasants and shape their life possibilities, and the kinds of difficulties a peasant struggle faces in creating the power needed to change the quality of peasant life and life chances. A particular concern, however, is the process of concientización, "creating a consciousness"—how did the peasants come to think of the middlemen as a problem and of their control as unjust; how did they come to accept an ideology calling for action against these men; and what was the relationship between "creating consciousness" and creating the power to act upon the consciousness? A cooperative movement is a relatively tame form of social action through which to explore concientización and the creation of power; but for the peasants of Jaida Arriba, the cooperative was a dramatic, tradition-breaking, and often risky struggle. As did many progressive elements of the Dominican Catholic church, I first went into the field with some vague notion that "creating consciousness" was *the* problem, that consciousness led to effective action: if only the oppressed could be "made to see" the injustices they suffered and "made to feel" the strength of their collective numbers, then they would organize and struggle and create new life chances for themselves. Creating such consciousness, I found, was indeed important in creating the power needed to challenge the middlemen; but the road from consciousness to control was far longer and more tortuous than the direct link I naively had imagined.

Another theme in this book is "community development." This case focuses attention not only on the practical problems involved but on the possibilities of success. Community development schemes, such as cooperatives, are seen as important programs in Latin America by a number of groups: progressive Catholic clergy, certain political parties of a Christian Democratic bent, populist groups, and the Peace Corps. Some view them as promoting socioeconomic change (improving economic conditions, developing local communities, stemming the tide of urban migration, improving production, forming a foundation for regional agricultural growth); others as harbingers of particular beliefs and attitudes (teaching the importance of Christian-based collective action, establishing support for particular political parties, encouraging anticommunist or prodemocratic ideologies). Although this study concentrates on only one case, a careful understanding of the difficulties encountered is telling for those in international agencies (FAO, AID, Peace Corps) and national organizations that seek to foment community development and local self-help projects. An important argument of this book is that beyond often-recognized organizational difficulties are critical structural problems that so seriously limit the scope of action of local economic organizations that the value of such undertakings within existing social structures must be seriously reconsidered.

There is an important theoretical intent behind this study, too: an exploration of the debate between "conflict" or "coercion" theories and the "integration" or "functionalist" approaches (Dahrendorf 1966:159ff; Rex 1963: 115ff; Lockwood 1964:246ff; Sutton et al. 1956). I will use this case study to argue that there are great costs in simply deciding in advance to use one *or* the other approach; the choice cannot be made a priori. The alternative, however, is not merely to "use both." The two conceptions of the world, of man, of the roots of social order and change are too different simply to "add" them together. Although this study does not present a comprehensive new theory integrating Marx and Parsons, a limited attempt is made to work out a synthetic approach in one specific area: the study of ideology.

This framework, initially presented in Chapter 6, provides the guidelines for exploring an important area little touched upon by anthropologists, sociologists, or political scientists studying peasants and peasant movements: how peasants come to believe that their world can be changed through collective struggle. With the exception of some important, often historical, case studies (Huizer 1972; Friedrich 1970; Womack 1970; White 1969; Handelman 1975) few have carefully analyzed the actual processes by which such movements have come about. There has been some excellent discussion of the social determinants of peasant movements (see, for example, Hobsbawm 1959; Wolf 1969; Moore 1966; Cotler 1970) and of the obstacles posed to action by peasant culture (Foster 1967; Erasmus 1968; Huizer 1972). But relatively little has been done systematically to link class situations, institutional structures, and cultural factors to the actual ideology and struggles of peasant movements. A number of authors do induce often insightful generalizations from their particular cases; but few of them try to present an explicit framework which they then apply to their cases. The theoretical framework developed in this study attempts to analyze why new ideologies are created and accepted and to explore related questions often left in need of careful examination. What are the obstacles peasants face in clearly defining their problem and formulating ideologies? Why are ideologies often "imported" into the countryside? Why do peasants accept or reject such ideologies? Is there a relationship between the peasants' class situation at a particular historical time and their acceptance or rejection of an ideology? How are the oft-cited obstacles to peasant organization and action (fatalism, mistrust, ignorance) actually overcome? What are the obstacles to creating the alliances between peasant and urban groups that some think are important if social revolutions are to occur (Huntington 1968:301−2)? What role do vertical, patron-client ties play in hindering horizontal, class-based action? How is the role of individual leaders to be understood in the context of social and cultural determinants of peasant movements? What are the obstacles to successfully organizing a peasant movement even when the peasants are conscious of the need for action?

Approaching such questions demanded more than good heoretical guidelines: I needed to use certain methods that rarely are a part of a political scientist's toolkit. Applying anthropological techniques of participant observation, I lived and worked in Jaida Arriba for eighteen months, from September 1970 until March 1972. I came to understand how the peasants viewed their world and how this view had come to change, leading them to organize a struggle to try to improve their life chances. I was able to piece together the complex history and causes of a movement that had begun over two years before I arrived and to gain the trust needed to uncover the often-sensitive issues of power, injustice, suspicion, and mistrust that I was exploring. Observing how the peasants handled other "outsiders" convinced me of the limitations and questionable validity of investigations based on one-shot interview questionnaires—a format most Dominican social scientists (modeling themselves on their North American colleagues) believe is the necessary and sufficient condition for being scientific. These limitations are particularly severe when one is studying attitudes and ideologies; but thirty years of the Trujillo dictatorship has made their use in proving even simple facts (land owned, kind of production, family size, income) problematic: the census takers of Trujillo used such information to set taxes in past times not soon forgotten. I do not mean to deny the critical importance of structured questions, systematically asked. They were an important part of my methodological toolkit and a source for a newly minted addage in Jaida Arriba: "If you want to learn anything, you've got to be a big questioner like Ken." I spent many weeks with each battery of questions I formulated in search of the missing pieces of unsolved problems. I would interview my "sample"— often scattered over dozens of miles of steep, muddy trails—as we worked, walked, rode, or sat around the kitchen fires. Although most of my questions were open-ended, seeking to explore complex changes in attitudes and deeply rooted political and economic problems, at one point I did find a short, systematic questionnaire useful (see Chapter 8, Acceptance of the Cooperative: Four Years Later).

There is another leitmotif in this study: the importance of theory in doing case studies. As such it is a response to many of my students who want to know why "all this abstract theoretical stuff is important" in interpreting, or acting upon, the world, and to certain friends in anthropology who insist that a careful, detailed, ethnographic study (gathering "all the facts") avoids the need for complex theoretical eyeglasses which may put all-too-narrowing blinders on their observations. Any theoretical framework puts blinders on what is conceived and seen (even the ones implicitly used by the best barefooted empiricists). But without such theory we risk being blinded by the darkness of a cave filled with unrelated facts, missing much for not having asked the right questions.

A few specific notes might be helpful to the reader. This book is concerned with events that took place before and during my field work in the Dominican Republic (1970—72). It does not consider changes in the international or domestic situations that have occurred since that time. The names of the local communities and of those involved with the peasant movement are fictitious. Only a few key Spanish words have been left in the text; these are italicized only the first time they are used. There is a short glossary at the end of the book. The first-person quotations in the text were drawn from a wide and representative sample of peasants in Jaida Arriba. Because the reader would not recognize the names of these people, the quotations usually are unidentified. I have used the symbol $ to indicate Dominican *pesos*. At the official exchange rate, one peso is equal to one United States dollar. The term "cents" will be used to refer to *centavos;* there are one hundred *centavos* in one *peso*.

The first half of this book (Chapters 1—5) explores life among the peasants in Jaida Arriba: the quality of their existence, the dilemmas they faced, the kinds of economic control exercised over them, and the efforts made to organize a movement to take control of credit and marketing away from the local middlemen. Chapters 6—10 take a more theoretical approach: they encourage us to ask questions and to look in directions which reveal much that was missed in the earlier descriptions of the cooperative movement. Chapters 7, 8, and 9 are organized around three central questions suggested by the theoretical approach in Chapter 6: (1) Why did no ideology or movement aimed at collective action either to alleviate existing economic difficulties or to struggle against the control of the middlemen arise in Jaida Arriba before 1967? (2) When the cooperative ideology was introduced into Jaida Arriba, why was it accepted by some peasants and rejected by others? (3) How was the cooperative able to create the power necessary to break the control of the middlemen?

DRAMATIS PERSONAE

Antonio, a peasant leader

Arturo, a middleman-merchant

Chaguito, a middle-holder peasant

Colín, a small-holder peasant

The bishop, the bishop of the diocese

El Padre, the parish priest

Fidel, an urban cooperative organizer

Francisco, a middleman-merchant

Isidro, a middleman-merchant

Mamón, a large-holder peasant

Manuel, a middleman-merchant

Mélida, Chaguito's wife

Padre Miguel, a Jesuit priest, instructor in cooperative organization

Padre Rodolfo, a Jesuit priest, active in peasant *promoción social*

Pablo, a peasant leader

Pedro, a former middleman-merchant

Pucho, a peasant leader

Puro, the major peasant leader

Ramón, a day laborer

Salvador, a peasant leader

PART ONE

STRUGGLE IN A DOMINICAN VILLAGE

CHAPTER 1

A DAY IN THE LIFE OF A PEASANT

The gray predawn light filters through the roughhewn pine planks and shingles into Chaguito's sleepy eyes. The September morning coolness on his face and the pleasant warmth of his wife Mélida huddled close under their single wool blanket tempt tranquillity. By Mélida's side is their two-week-old baby. In the opposite corner in a single bed sleep four boys (eleven, five, four, and three years old); another bed embraces the two daughters (twelve and nine) and two more sons (six and two), the heads of the two boys by the feet of the two girls. I am sleeping in the next room on a bed usually used by the children. In the rocking cradle by Chaguito's side is their baby boy of eighteen months. It is just before 5:00 A.M.

Chaguito, eyes still half shut, begins to *rezar la primero* (to pray the morning prayer): "Holy Mary, mother of God, pray for us sinners. . . ." Mélida's voice and those of two sleepy children respond. A moment of silence follows. Then an impatient, but not harsh, call to his twelve-year-old daughter: "C'mon, Gilda, c'mon." Gilda shakes her nine-year-old sister and, still dressed in yesterday's worn frocks, they tumble out of bed. Bare arms folded over their chests to ward off the damp chill, they scurry through the adjacent room and outside into the kitchen, a small tin kerosene lamp lighting the way with its smoky yellow flame. Moments later, eleven-year-old Chepe patters out in tattered shorts, leaving sounds of giggling of his brothers still in bed. Leaping into the semidarkness of the kitchen he yells: "Here comes the bogeyman!" Soon a dull thudding mixes with the singing of the waking birds as Gilda lifts the heavy two-foot pestle and begins pounding the roasted coffee beans into a fine powder at the bottom of the wood mortar. The sounds of wood being split join the morning chorus as Chepe chops firewood, which his younger sister gathers to light the breakfast fires on the earthware hearth. From the bedroom, the announcer on Radio Santa María's program, "Wake Up, Dominicans," reads off early morning messages sent in by listeners. Each one is punctuated by someone knocking on a door: "Wake up Antonia

3

Rodríguez de Serraso to fix the coffee . . . get out of bed María de Jesús Pérez and haul in the water. . . ."

Chaguito carries the radio into the kitchen. He has on a fresh pair of cotton trousers, worn but still patchless, and a threadbare, yellow short-sleeved shirt, stained and slightly torn from work. Sitting in one of his two loose-jointed cane-bottom chairs, he calls to Chepe: "Go get me my shoes." Chepe reappears with two black, vinyl shoes, patched with strips from an older pair. Barefooted children crowd into the kitchen; they shiver in their short pants from the cold of the clay floor and morning air. They laugh and tease, gathering around the warmth of the cooking fires. The mornings are cold now, but the winters (December through February) are worse: the temperatures often settle into the mid-forties (degrees Fahrenheit), and the rain-bearing clouds drift through the open doors and cracks in the walls.

Gilda fills an old, quart-sized, tomato paste can with water and places it within the water now boiling in a blackened pot. Into this improvised double boiler she spoons the ground coffee, mixes it, and then filters the hot, dark, black liquid through a large flannel filter into another can below. The first cup is for her father, the next for me, and the third immediately brought in to Mélida. Mélida customarily gets up to make the coffee once the water is boiling, but she is still in her rest period after childbirth. Gilda returns, cradling her eighteen-month-old brother, and hands him to Chepe to nurse on a plastic baby bottle of warmed, sweetened, clove and cinnamon tea. Bare-bottomed Chelo, the four-year-old, and his nine-year-old sister clutch papa's legs as he sips his coffee and both shout their claims "Daddy belongs to me." "No! He belongs to me!" Chaguito calms the crescendo by putting Chelo between his legs. Wriggling free proves impossible for little Chelo. Chaguito kiddingly questions him as he struggles: "Who do you belong to, Chelo? Who do you belong to?" From around the hearth one of the kids shouts: "Listen to the pheasants! Listen to the pheasants!" There is a moment of silence to hear the distant singing.

At 6:00 A.M., the radio broadcasts the morning prayer and then a *padre* reflects: "There's so much bitterness and hatred among us . . . when in fact, love is the only thing that should reign among us."

Mélida enters the kitchen dressed in a blue and white cotton dress and a tightly knit dark blue sweater, both from Chaguito's parents in New York. A towel wrapped around her hair guards against the morning chill. While she peels the green skins off about thirty small bananas and places them in boiling water, Chepe goes out to milk the cow.

Standing on a rock near the house, he emits the familiar call. No response. Then he goes off into the pasture to search among the boulders, underbrush, and grass. His younger sister and five brothers are all waiting at the barbed wire fence when the cow finally emerges from the dense growth. Chepe close behind, urging it on. In unison, they break into the cheer: "There it is, there it is!"

Chaguito carefully squeezes milk from each udder into a small can and empties it into an old one-gallon Alliance for Progress soybean oil can. Soon his five-year-old son manfully drags the stubborn month-old calf to its mother's side. Chaguito explains that "the cow and the calf belong to Papa who's up in New York. But he lets me milk it so I can give milk to the children." The cow gives about a quart a day; all of it goes to the eighteen-month-old. "But, there's not always milk. When there's no milk you may find someone who'll give you some. But most of the time you have to buy it. I always used to buy two bottles every day; I paid eight cents a bottle. When Mélida stopped nursing one of the kids to give birth to another I couldn't find any cow's milk anywhere. So I had to buy powdered milk—over twenty cans at $1.40 each!"

In the smoke-filled kitchen, breakfast is almost ready with the help of Ramona, a sixty-year-old, white-haired neighbor who has been coming daily to assist Mélida with the meals and housework since Mélida gave birth. Breakfast is spaghetti with tomato sauce, boiled plantains and green bananas, hot chocolate, and two special treats for today's guest: boiled, store-bought potatoes with onions and a fifteen-cent can of sardines. Chepe wins a short tussle with his brothers for the right to lick the leftover sardine oil. The children eat around the warm hearth, sitting, standing, gobbling off tin plates with big metal spoons. Mélida stands eating near the hearth, sipping her hot chocolate from a big metal mug.

The dawn's streaming rays cut bright paths through the kitchen smoke. Cracks in the walls hold Chaguito's tools: a *machete* (broad-bladed tool for weeding), a *colín* (what North Americans commonly call a machete), and two small, curved saws for pruning his coffee trees. Near the door hang the halter and reins and straw saddle for his mule. Scattered on shelves around the kitchen are empty cans, old bottles filled with store-bought peanut oil and kerosene, juice from the "bitter orange" used as vinegar, various local and purchased remedies, and a can of Real-Kill to disinfect cows. Fresh water cools in a seven-gallon clay jug on a low, wide shelf. A five-gallon kerosene can for hauling the water is nearby. Soiled dishes and pots are piled in a basin on the sink platform. The enclosed pantry holds sugar, rice, and other foodstuffs protected from marauding cats, dogs, chickens, and mice. Pantry door hinges are made with old rubber shoe soles, themselves originally cut from worn tires. A branch broom leans against the wall near three sacks of newly arrived fertilizer for the coffee.

Chepe and his younger sister bound into the kitchen with scrubbed faces, combed hair, and small book pouches hanging from their shoulders. Mélida quickly inspects them before they go off to school. Both are still in the first grade after two years and are unlikely to pass on to the second this year. "What's the use?" shrugged Mélida, "they're changing the teachers all the time. Why, just in this year they've already changed the teachers five times!" Gilda has missed school for the last two weeks to help Mélida around the house. But Mélida, concerned, hopes that the daughter of one of Chaguito's *compadres* (ritual coparents) will soon arrive to help in Gilda's place.

It is 7:30 when Chaguito and I leave for his old *conuco* (small, cultivated plot). Plantain suckers have to be uprooted and transplanted to a newly cleared plot. The old two-acre plot looks almost too steep to stand on. We walk silently, our pants soon brushed wet with early morning dew, the sun warm on our backs. Voices greet us as we emerge from the underbrush onto a main trail. Colín, a neighbor, is approaching on foot, his wife Juana following on a mule.

"Hola compadre!" calls out Chaguito. "How are you this morning?"

"Feeling better, compadre, thank God," answers Colín.

"Look who's here," says Juana stretching out her hand to clasp my forearm. "What brings you here?" she asks, teasing.

"Oh, lots of things," I say, smiling. "Where are you coming from?"

"From Santiago. We went to the doctor's yesterday. Juana felt like she was dying, she could hardly breathe. And what a fever she had! And last night we slept in El Río at mother's house, because the river was still a little swollen and we didn't want to try to cross it in the dark, especially since Juana had that fever."

El Río is the small village on the jeep road, over two hours by mule or foot from Jaida Arriba. Three rivers, treacherous after heavy rainstorms, must be forded to reach the Land Rover jeeps that leave for town in the early morning hours. Packed with people, with chickens, pigs, and plantains squeezed inside or tied on top and latecomers often clinging to the back or bouncing on the luggage rack, these jeeps are one of the few links with the outside world. The nearest doctor is in the municipal capital, San Juan de La Sierra, two hours from El Río; the nearest city with specialized medical care, hospitals, major food warehouses, markets, and large stores is Santiago, where the jeeps arrive in about three hours. They stay for a few hours while passengers make purchases, see doctors, visit relatives, and do errands. The jeeps return late in the afternoon. Many from Jaida Arriba hike or ride back at night, arriving home at 7:00 or 8:00 P.M.

"What's with the money? Did you talk to Salvador?" Chaguito asks. Chaguito is a member of the coffee cooperative administered by Salvador and is anxiously awaiting the arrival of a loan from Idecoop, the government cooperative agency, which should have come two months earlier. Money needs are becoming urgent: coffee pickers, like Colín, will have to be paid when the harvest begins in a month; more immediately, food and medicine must be bought.

t yet," answers Colín. "He'll be going to the capital the day after
ow. Maybe something will come our way this week. God only knows!"
d what are they paying for coffee now?" asks Chaguito.
ll. I'm not really sure. Supposedly they're paying $28 and $30 now."
guito shakes his head disapprovingly. They had sold coffee at $36 and
few months before and he does not understand why the prices have
ed. He is sure, however, that it was the fault of the *grandes* (the
erful men) in the exporting houses and in the government.
'e all clasp hands good-by.
Go with God."
May he stay with you."
Chaguito and I crawl under a barbed wire fence and head on up toward the
nuco. In the distance we hear a deep, sonorous voice as Chaguito's neighbor
ddenly breaks out into song as he works in his conuco. It is a *décima,* a
ong-poem form once popular in many parts of the country, often sung as
neighbors worked together on exchange labor teams.[1]

We come upon Chaguito's newly cleared plot, about an acre in size. Here
the plantain suckers will soon be planted. Blackened tree trunks and brush
still lie where they were felled and burned only a few weeks before. Chaguito
kneels and shows me the small blades of corn just breaking through the soil.
The rows, eight feet apart, cut diagonally up across the steep slope, the green
shoots marking the lines between which Chaguito will plant the new plantains. Chaguito formerly planted vertically, straight up the slope, as his father
had done. It was easier to work in the conuco: during planting, weeding, or
harvesting, one could move straight up and down the rows. But in a "social
progress" program four years ago a Jesuit priest taught Chaguito that planting
diagonally helps check erosion of the thin soil cover. Such improved planting,
however, is only a palliative. "The little bit of good soil they used to have on
them, it's disappeared," says Chaguito, sweeping his hand over the depleted
land that barely supports the weeds and underbrush reclaiming it. "The land
is just too steep around here. The rains wash it all away. A piece of land will
produce well maybe for two or three years. You can get three bean crops
from it, but with plantains or sweet potatoes, one crop is the most. Maybe
that new chemical fertilizer would help, but who's got the money? I can
barely feed my family with the harvests." For two years Chaguito has had to
buy plantains and sweet potatoes. Paying cash for such staples cut severely
into his already meager income. The first family land he worked in another
sector of Jaida Arriba "has had it."

The erosion and depletion of the soil pose a continual dilemma for
Chaguito and the other peasants: where to find new land to clear. Jaida
Arriba was once heavily forested and open for settlement, but there is little
such state land left. Further, the government now prohibits not only the
clearing and settling of state lands, but even the clearing of land already

settled. This "law of the forest" seeks to protect the country's watersheds. But the peasants see it differently. Because they are dependent on pine for building their houses, and on clearing new lands for feeding their families, the law threatens their survival. The collision comes with the government foresters and the rural police who patrol the region and can grant permission to cut where they feel water sources are not threatened or can use fines and prison sentences to enforce the law. In practice, the system is based on bribes. Indeed, for many foresters and soldiers, their official, low-salaried positions are also sinecures for transforming official "permission" into private profit. The peasant strategy is either to cut wood "on the sly" and risk a fine, a summons, or a last-minute bribe; or to seek official permission, which usually means a bribe of rum, coffee, or money.

Chaguito had little trouble getting permission for his newly cleared plot because he had maintained "good relations" with the forester: mealtime hospitality, occasional presents of a few pounds of coffee beans, a bottle of rum, or a few pesos "for cigarettes." The poorer peasants—men with a critical need for access to new lands—often suffer most because they lack the resources for such "good relations." But all greatly resent both the forestry law and the foresters and rural police "who walk the land in search of bribes." Chaguito is particularly resentful when prohibited from cutting trees on his own land.

"What's wrong with farming around here is that you're not free—you may want to clear a little piece of land, but they won't let you clear it. The forest ranger has to come by and decide if he's going to let you clear ground. He doesn't seem to know that you have to work so you can eat. This is one of the biggest problems around here. If we were free to clear ground . . . frankly, I really think things would get better around here. But now, you're under someone else's control. You're just not free. If you own the land, if you own the property, they should let you do what you want. But what the government has up its sleeve is to use the pine trees to pay off its debts to the U.S."

"Where does that law come from?"

"It came from the government, because it's the government who pays the forest rangers. Now, I'm not saying that they should let you chop down trees on the government's land. But on your own land, they should. I live on this land, and I'm sure as heck not going to do anything to harm the water. But I have to clear land to live."

"How come if the government creates so many problems for you, there are so many people that still vote for it?"

"Well, I hope this government stays in power. I'm for Balaguer. And I'll always be for Balaguer. But . . . on election day, that doesn't necessarily mean that I'm going to vote for him."

The problems with the foresters are only one manifestation of the more central dilemma in Jaida Arriba: the shortage of land suitable for planting. In the face of this dilemma, Chaguito is twice blessed. Because his father (one of the first settlers in Jaida Arriba) squatted on or bought a total of 1600 *tareas* (a tarea is one-sixth of an acre), Chaguito still has some small piece of forest land to clear and plant. But three out of four households in Jaida Arriba have no more new land. Like Colín, they may attempt to replant depleted soil after letting it lie fallow for three or five years, but the yields are small. Sometimes, after continued use, the land yields little more than the seeds sown. Although about 95 percent of the peasants in Jaida Arriba have some land, over half are forced to work at least part time for low cash wages to feed their families.

Chaguito's second blessing is coffee. Its cultivation keeps him and his family alive without the need to sell their labor to others. The land from Chaguito's father is ideal for coffee. Each time Chaguito slashed and burned and planted subsistence crops, he placed small coffee seedlings between the rows of plantains. The broad leaves of the quick-growing plantains provided the needed protection from the sun while the slower growing *guama* trees grew to give permanent shade in the amount needed. In four or five years, with careful weeding, the coffee trees began producing. When the coffee matures, its roots hold the soil, checking erosion. And if it is tended carefully, it provides an annual cash crop. One coffee grove in Jaida Arriba still produces after thirty years.

Leaving the new clearing, Chaguito and I continue steeply upward. I break the peaceful morning silence with a question:

"Chaguito, what's the thing you most worry about in life, the thing you're most afraid of?"

Chaguito is not at all startled by such a question at such a time and place. We have known each other for over a year. He knows that Ken is a "big questioner" and is writing a book on peasant life and problems. And he knows that I have come today with many questions.

"Well, I'm afraid . . . the thing you're most afraid of around here is that you won't be able to take care of your kids the way they have to be taken care of."

He pauses in the trail and turns toward me. "We get by any way we can. Just so these children can grow up, so we can smooth the way for them. So that they won't have to end up living the way we're living. Though I really don't complain. Still, it's a lot of hard work. And now, the tiny plots of land that we have aren't enough for these boys to farm in the future. Because when the time comes to divide up all the land, we won't have hardly anything for ourselves. Just a little bit. And how will they get by with just a tiny bit? The only hope you have is to try and see if you can give them a little education. And if you give them a little education, they maybe can even find a job right here in the cooperative. When we can help them become accountants, agronomists, or some type of office worker, that's when we'll be leaving something worthwhile for our children."

"How many years of schooling do you think they should have?"

"I really can't tell. You have to have at least twelve years of schooling before you can get a job. If the cooperative keeps working well and if we keep supporting the cooperative, if we don't let it fail, I think that by ten years from now we should be saving some money and we'll have funds for all these things. My sister wants to take Gilda to New York, that is, if I let her. That would help me out."

"How can you give your children education here in the Dominican Republic?"

"Here in the Dominican Republic—maybe the cooperative can help us get different types of scholarships, and maybe that's how we can move ahead a little. Also, you can try to approach people that you're in with, people that are good friends of yours. You send them a child of yours, and maybe they'll receive him as though he were a member of their own family. That's if he has already had two or three years of schooling here in the *campo*—but if we could have a fourth or fifth grade here in the local school, we could do that right here."

"Are you planning to send all your children to school?"

"That depends. Right now, I don't really know how many I can send to school."

As we walk on, I ponder: only a three-grade school in Jaida Arriba, his hope to get a child or two out of the village so that they can be educated and have some chance in life. Perhaps he can do it. With the cash he earns from his coffee and saves in the cooperative, he might pay for city clothes and books and for the wages of someone to take that child's place. And he does have family connections with people in the city who, though poor, might take in one of his children. But what of someone like Colín? With no cash crop, with no connections, what chance does he have to educate even one of his nine children? For a moment I imagine what I would do if I were Colín or Chaguito. I feel trapped.

The cool forest shade had cut out the morning sun as we walked, and arriving at the old conuco, I am warm but not too tired. Its steep slopes overlook Chaguito's toylike house and the valleys and mountains that spread below. Chaguito takes up his machete and begins uprooting the plantain stumps. He cuts away the dirt around them, often digging with his fingers, and then yanks out the bulbous root stem. I watch for a moment and begin. He watches me out of the corner of his eye and soon hints that the plantains will grow stronger and better if only healthy suckers are chosen and if I do not slice them in half with my machete as I cut them out of the ground.

The sun on the open slope gradually changes from warm to hot to scorching as we work on into the morning, plunging our machetes into the ground and hoping they will sink easily into the damp soil and not come clanging to a stop against the rocks below the thin soil surface. My arm soon tires. The wooden machete handle finds a noncalloused spot just below my thumb and begins its blistering work.

"Chaguito, what do you think about farming?"

"Well, it's not that you get that much from farming. But, I've always liked farming because you're planting food for your own family. You're thinking about your children that are still here with you." He is quiet for a moment as his hands move swiftly, deftly removing the suckers and throwing them in a pile on a more level piece of ground below him. "But, if I can find some other job besides farming, some other way of earning my bread, I'm not going to keep on farming, no sir!"

"And what's the type of job in farming that you least like?"

"There's no type of work that I don't like. When you set out to farm, you've got to do everything. What I most like doing is planting, because there's where your hope is, in what you plant."

"Tell me, don't you ever get pains while you're working?"

"Well, yes, I do. Sometimes when I'm planting I get a pain here [he points to his shoulder blades with his machete] right between the shoulders. I can't stand it, and I have to lie down on the ground to see if it'll go away. Also, when I'm sawing: sometimes I get some really bad pains right here in my back, and I can't even lift up my arms. And also, a little while back, my knees used to get tired when I was walking. And my arms used to hurt me, from here [elbows] to here [shoulders]."

Our conversation is suddenly interrupted when my machete strikes a wasps' nest hidden in the underbrush, a discovery I make only after I have been bitten vengefully in the ear and on my forearm. With a brave face trying to cover my chagrin and painful winces, I watch contentedly as Chaguito gathers dry brush and burns them out, telling me all the while morale-bolstering stories of his childhood bites. He then sits down, takes his rolled cigarette from behind his ear, and lights up.

There is a moment of quiet and then the shouting and laughter of his children playing around the house below ring through the air. We both laugh. I ask Chaguito if Chepe yet works with him in the fields.

"Well, for the time being, I let them do what they want. When they're eight years old they begin to do small little jobs, picking up sticks, fetching the cow. When Gilda was ten years old, she began lighting the fire in the mornings. And maybe when Chepe is fourteen years old, I'll take him with me to work in the conuco. But before that, they may come to the conuco and do small little things like—whatever they want. That's how they learn to be willing to work—they become more willing. So by the time they really have to work, they're used to it. Sometimes they'll begin picking up the small grains of coffee which the rats drop in the coffee groves." He is quiet for a minute and then continues: "Colín's children were working from the time they were little kids. I can remember that when his little boy was only eight years old he was already working side by side with him in the conuco. And by the time he was ten years old, he was already working for money, together with his father. He had to. To help support his family."

"I could never understand, Chaguito, how you people can support so many children."

"It's not easy. We have too many children here in the campo. Sometimes we raise them like animals. Sometimes I begin to think. You hear people say that God will provide your children with food. But they don't say he's going to provide them with education. So what kind of heritage can you leave your children? Things are pretty tight around here now. There's no land; and there's no way of educating so many children."

"Isn't there anything you can do?"

He looks at me and says knowingly, "Well, they say that the best way to stop having children is to take three nails from a donkey's paw, boil them well, make them into an herb tea, and drink it. What do you think of that?"

A good anthropologist must understand the local customs. And knowing of the strange brews concocted by local curers, I maintain a serious and inquisitive expression, shrugging my shoulders and looking back questioningly. But then I catch a slight twinkle in Chaguito's eyes. His seriously set lips break out into a broad smile, followed by a roar of laughter from both of us. The sensitivity of the topic of birth control has vanished.

"But haven't you ever thought of something a little better that you can do to plan your family?"

"My opinion always was—and I used to spend all the time asking the priests about this. They say that you're not supposed to avoid children. So, when I already had about six kids, I kept on having them, so as not to be disobedient. The only method I used was to withdraw. So, I went back and spoke to the priests again. And they told me that that was absolutely forbidden. So I just didn't tell them anything else. When they told me something like that, I didn't dare argue with them. So I went back, and I stopped doing it. I placed myself at the will of God. But, when Mélida had another child, I went back to withdrawing, coming outside again.

"About four years ago, I began with the method of counting the days. But that didn't work. That's kind of hard when your wife is not completely regular, and she has occasionally been more than a month without having anything. The priests say that's the method you're supposed to use. But I never dared tell them the problem my wife had. When you're blind, you're ashamed to talk about this type of thing. You think those people know more than you do.

"Right now, I made up my mind, even if it's only for five years, I'm planning to avoid having children during that time. Mélida has made up her mind too. With our poverty—now, ten children is enough. But if you keep on having children, and you raise them up like donkeys, that's not the way to be a Christian. And I began thinking, I'm responsible for all those children. It's better to avoid having some of them than see them have a hard time and go hungry. If I had had my way, we wouldn't have had more than six. But back then I never wanted to go against what the priests said."

"You prefer boys or girls?"

"I've always preferred boys. The fact is that with girls, you always have to be more on your guard. They can't go out alone without somebody to accompany them. A girl who goes around alone can create problems for you. You don't know what she's going to end up being. But that's not the case with boys. They go out alone without any problems."

Our conversation is interrupted by a chorus of children's voices below: "Daddy! Daddy! Dad! Dinner's ready!"

While Chaguito and I had been working and talking, the women had been busy too. Ramona and Gilda had spent most of the morning doing the wash in the nearby stream. They boiled many of the dirtiest clothes in an old, blackened five-gallon kerosene can over a small fire by the stream, soaped them with a big bar of laundry soap, scrubbed the clothes hard in a flat wooden basin, rinsed them in the cold running water that swirled around their knees, then soaped, scrubbed, and rinsed again and again until the clothes were clean. Mélida worked on lighter chores: sweeping, washing the breakfast dishes and pots, changing the baby's wet clothes, and preparing powdered milk for the eighteen-month-old. Mélida sees her own life as "a really hard life—scrubbing the hearth every day [with a paint made of white clay], scrubbing the kitchen once a week, ironing all the clothes—even work clothes—washing, cooking, sweeping out the house and the kitchen, and having all these children on top of you all day long."

About 9:30, Mélida had started the fires in the hearth and put the beans up to cook. Later she had put the large pots of water on to boil for the plantains, green bananas, and rice. All is steaming hot when Chaguito and I walk through the open kitchen door into the tumbling, screaming, running children. We wash our dirt-caked hands in an aluminum basin filled with cool, clear water. One of the kids runs into the house and comes back with a towel for me before I even finish washing.

Mélida places the food in common bowls in front of us; I remember the distance felt toward me when I first visited many months before and I was given my own separate plates of everything. Another can of sardines sits on the table, and I chide Chaguito about his promise to do nothing special for my visit; we both laugh. (Had I not been explicit, they would have killed a chicken to serve for lunch, a custom of hospitality even in an impoverished house with only one chicken remaining. But had I not been close with Chaguito, telling him not to kill a chicken might have been insulting.) The three young boys sit on a small bench, eagerly swallowing their food off plates resting on the hearth. Chepe spreads an old burlap coffee fertilizer sack on the floor and sits down with his plate. The others eat standing.

The kitchen seems strangely quiet as the clinking of spoons on metal plates replaces the voices of hungry children. In the distance, there are low rolls of thunder. I marvel quietly at the quantity of rice and boiled green bananas that Chaguito rapidly devours. My appetite does not compare, and I worry lest Mélida think I dislike her cooking or feel embarrassed that there is nothing better to give their guest from New York. The dog and chickens anxiously search the floor, snapping up bits of rice or bananas the children drop.

Eating finished, the action begins again. Chepe teases the dog, faking throws with a leftover piece of banana. Gilda lays the eighteen-month-old on a sack and, to his giggling delight, tickles his bare belly while cooing softly. The braver chickens leap onto the hearth and into the pots, but Mélida waves them away and the boys pelt them with pieces of uneaten banana.

The thunder is louder now but no one takes notice: the children have spotted Chaguito taking a wedge of locally made guava paste out of the paper bag I brought. "Candy! Candy!" they yell, swarming around the table. "Me, daddy, me!" Chaguito carefully cuts off thin slivers, passing them to the waiting hands. The rain now begins to patter on the thatched kitchen roof. "Let's go inside the house." calls Chaguito. "The thatching is old and we'll get wet here in the kitchen." The kids run shouting into the house, Gilda carrying the eighteen-month-old and Mélida following, a towel held over her head. Chaguito and I bring in the two chairs and bench. I sit on a chair, Chaguito on the bench, his foot propped up on the empty chair. Mélida sits down next to him, resting her head just above his raised knee. The rain beats heavily but softly on the wood shingles, so unlike the din on the tin roofs of many newly built houses which makes conversation impossible.

The children romp on the wood plank floor, except barebottom Chelo who wanders off toward us. The noise of the playing children seems to drown out the rain. Chaguito, nodding toward them, says: "When they're playing like that you've got to let them go on playing. But sometimes, when they get too fresh, you have to speak firmly to them." Turning to four children now jumping and shouting in front of us to get our attention, he says with mock sternness: "Go get me a rope, I'm going to take care of these kids." Screaming and laughing, they all stampede through the open door into the rain and on into the kitchen. Turning to me again, he says, "When one of them gets too fresh I'd give them a few whacks with a little piece of rope or with my cap." One of them, grinning, peers cautiously through the door, a small rope in his hand, but runs screaming back into the kitchen when we look toward him. "Some people," continues Chaguito, "hit them too hard. Maybe they're not aware that children have rights too. Sometimes you have to hit them, but not to kill them. I hardly ever have to hit them because I make a face, and they know." Two small ones bound back into the house, one chasing the other into the bedroom.

The rain now patters intermittently on the roof, its softness broken by flashes of light and now more distant claps of thunder. Little Chelo comes back from the kitchen and seats himself on Chaguito's lap. One by one the others wander back too. Chaguito and Mélida begin pointing at various parts of the body as Chelo tries to remember the words for his teeth, hair, feet and ears. The others whisper the answers and laugh with amusement at his strange pronunciations. But within a few minutes they are all leaping on the wood floor and chasing around the small room. Chaguito frowns: "Bring me the rope!" And they all bound for the door again.

Mélida smiles. "Sometimes, when I think they've fallen down from something I get nervous. About a week ago, Gilda spilled a kettle of hot milk on herself. She really burned herself here." She points toward her stomach. Chaguito adds: "I was out in the conuco and when I heard the screams I thought she was dying, and I went running home. Thank God it wasn't too serious."

I ask Mélida if the kids often fall sick. "Oh, they always have a cold in the wintertime, coughing, and with running noses. But thank God, they still have never had anything serious yet. None of them has ever died, thank God."

"It's really hard here," adds Chaguito. "There are no doctors here in the campo. You have to go all the way to the *pueblo,* for anything at all. And doctors are really expensive here. Many of the people who are poorer here don't have any money to take their children to the doctor's and to buy medicine. Look at compadre Antonio. He's had three children die on him. The poor guy can't even afford to feed them, and when they get sick, he can't take them to a doctor."

"And when somebody gets sick here," I ask, "and he can't ride a horse, how do they get him out?"   .

"In a stretcher. Lots of times they'd make it from a bed, or from a blanket. And twenty or thirty men will get together and carry them out. The hardest part is when the river's swollen and you have to cross it. I can remember one night when Chelo got *colerín* (a gastrointestinal illness). About eight o'clock at night, he got an attack of diarrhea and he began vomiting. And by midnight, he was pale white. And I took him out to go to La Sierra. We left here at midnight. It was raining, and we were on horse. Me, Mélida, and compadre Colín. I had Chelo propped on top of the mule. The paths were slippery with so much rain. That was really dangerous!

"Thank God the river wasn't too swollen. We got to El Río about two in the morning. And I hired a jeep. When we got to the pueblo at three-thirty, Chelo was almost dead. But the doctor gave him some injections and saved him."

Colerín is one of the biggest killers of young children in Jaida Arriba. The simultaneous vomiting and diarrhea dehydrates a child in hours.

"Once," Chaguito continues, "Gilda had diphtheria—a really serious thing in her throat. She could hardly breathe. Now, with that disease, if you don't move quick, you're going to die. I got her out to a doctor who works for the government. He gave her some injections and she got better. He charged me three pesos and twenty cents."

"Haven't you ever gotten sick yourself?"

"I used to get these terrible colds."

"Where did they come from?"

"Well, sometimes they come from getting yourself wet when you're hot, and your blood goes bad. That would give me a headache, and my body didn't want to do anything. Like, it just didn't want to work. I didn't have strength, to work, or to take care of anything. I couldn't even put a machete on my shoulder—it was too much work. All the time I was plagued with this problem. I went through four years like that. I tried to go up to the conuco to work, and I couldn't go up. I was too weak. And here in my back, right here, the pain was so bad I couldn't stand it. And when I lay down, sometimes I'd feel something inside me, and I'd jump up—it was something inside me moving around. And my breath stopped—I couldn't breathe. And sometimes, when I was eating, I had to get up and run outside.

"I went to get medicines from local curers. But those people don't know anything—they give you a little herb tea and you get better, and everybody thinks they can cure you. They're witches."

"Why did you used to go to them then?"

"Well, I used to go to them because the doctors don't know about these colds. And some people used to tell me: 'so and so knows how to cure that.' And when you're that way, you don't really think straight. You go crazy, you lose your mind. I went to an old *curandero* in La Loma. He gave me a half a bottle with an old herb tea and he sent me away with that. He used to steal money from me. He charged me as much as two pesos. I went to him twice. Then I went to someone else. The other guy gave me some old thing— something bitter, a bitter twig in a bottle with something else. And a cream like Vicks Vapo Rub in a match box, to rub on my chest and back. It didn't work. He charged me three pesos for that."

"And did they use glasses of water and candles?"

"The first one did. He picked up a glass of water and he began looking at it, turning it around. And he looked in the water with the candle light and began telling me where my pain was. He'd say: 'you have a cold in your blood. And your head hurts you. And your body can hardly move because it hurts so much.' And he had a little bit of boiled water and a little powder. And he sprinkled that in the water and he gave me that for medicine. I used to believe in him. That's why I went back. But when the medicines didn't work, I said: 'Why in the world am I going to those scoundrels?' That was about ten years ago. Since that I haven't gone back. Mélida neither. I had that problem for four years. And finally I got better with something mamá sent me from Santiago—Menthol-Chino, it's a cream like Vapo Rub. You put a little bit on your tongue, and you drink a little bit of lukewarm water."

"Were there many people that went to those curanderos?"

"Oh . . . lots of people. Stupid people. That guy had more people than he knew what to do with. At that time we were blind. But now people aren't as blind. How's a horse's ass who's never gone to school going to know anything? A doctor's supposed to study all the parts of the body, for example. And that guy can't even write his name. If you haven't gone to school, you're nothing but a donkey."

I ask Mélida about giving birth in the campo. She says that nine of her ten children were born here in the house with the help of a midwife. Chaguito took Mélida to Santiago to have one child in the public hospital. The child was five days overdue, and Chaguito was worried. Medical attention at the public hospital was free, although Mélida had to bring a wash basin, cup, and spoon. And most medicines had to be paid for or bought at a nearby pharmacy. Chaguito needed about $35 to pay travel, food, and medical expenses, and he had no money at all at the time.

"I went to Don Pablo's house to see if he could lend me the money, but he told me he didn't have any. Then I went to Jose's house. Nothing! Those are people who've got two or three thousand pesos, but they want to keep it all for themselves. I was desperate. But then a cousin of mine called me over. He had heard that I was having problems and he told me: 'Look, if you need money, you'll find it here.' I told him I needed thirty-five pesos. He put his hand in his pocket and he said: 'Here's forty pesos.' And afterward when I paid him, he told me, 'You can always count on me anytime you need anything.'"

Gilda comes in from the bedroom cradling the eighteen-month-old. She tells her mother that the baby is coughing up everything she tries to give her. Mélida tells her to lay the baby down for now. She turns toward me: "His cough is so bad with that cold of his that he can hardly drink anything." She says that this second youngest child has never been well. I, too, had noticed that he had trouble holding his head upright. "It's as though he were weak in the bones. Right from the beginning he was weak in the neck. We took him to a doctor in the pueblo. He gave him an injection against vomiting and some vitamins too. That helped with the vomiting, but he was still weak in his neck and in his bones. He wants to stand up but he can't. Also, his eyes began to tremble. Chaguito says he's going to take him to another doctor, but he never actually does it."

Chaguito explains: "I haven't taken him to another doctor because I don't have any money yet. I'm hoping to take him this coming Saturday if I can find the money. I've got to find someone who would lend me the money. If I have to, I'll even sell my coffee *a la flor* (before the harvest). But up till now, thanks to the cooperative I haven't had to do that. But right now the cooperative doesn't have any money."

Before the cooperative, Chaguito had to "sell" some of his coffee before the harvest, obligating it to a comprador (buyer)—who was usually also a local comerciante (dry goods store owner)—to get cash for urgent needs: illnesses, baptisms, deaths, debts that had to be paid. But the price was always far less than the market value at harvest time.

"I always used to have plantains to sell. And when they began cutting down pine trees, there were always ways of earning some money. I got a pair of oxen, and I began to pull out trees for pay. I split the money with the owner of the oxen. I also used to saw. And I'd sell the wood. At that time, there wasn't a stable government [this was after Trujillo's death]; everybody was taking wood! Nobody was going hungry in those days. But when they forbid cutting wood again, I was in trouble. My coffee was producing about five or six *quintales,* and I had to sell almost all of it before the harvest. I also had to do day labor sometimes, weeding or husking."

"How much coffee did you have to sell before the harvest four years ago, the year before the cooperative was organized?"

"I began to sell coffee in June, July, and August to turn it over in March, April, and May of the following year. And I sold about four or five *fanegas* to Negro for $25 per fanega. At that time, other people were only receiving $20 or $22 the fanega. Maybe Negro paid me more since I was his brother. But, what kind of help is that?

"When harvest time came, I still had a fanega which I hadn't committed yet, and I was able to sell it for $40! That year, Negro ended up getting as much as $35 and $40 for the coffee he sold. Imagine: coffee for which he had had to pay only $20 or $25 buying it a la flor! And once during that same year I needed $10 about two months before the harvest, so I could bring a child of mine to the doctor. I had to sell Negro another fanega at $25. And harvest time was almost there already! Whenever you needed money you always had to sell coffee to some buyer at half price. If they couldn't earn double on it, they wouldn't buy it from you. And if you were hard up, you had no other choice."

"But weren't you grateful for this money that the buyers gave to you when you needed it so desperately?"

"I was grateful to them because, when things are tough, there's nothing else you can do. But I wasn't grateful for everything, no sir. I didn't want to sell it at that price. But when you're poor you have no choice. Some emergency comes along—like buying medicine, food, or solving some problem—and you have to go to those crooks.

The rain had let up and the slanting rays of the afternoon sun were breaking through the clouds. Chaguito and I leave to walk down to the cooperative general store. Mélida needs some oil and salt and a little kerosene. It is a forty-five-minute walk, but Chaguito enjoys the chance to get away from his conuco and to chat with others who may be at the store.

The trail drops steeply as it crosses the many streams, now fast and muddy. The red clay is oozing and slippery, and in many places the heavy mule and foot traffic has formed deep narrow ruts, cut even deeper by the rains. The small side trail soon intersects the main trail and we turn toward the comercio. To the left is a small shack set back from the trail. Its thatched roof sets it apart from the wood shingles of Chaguito's much larger house or the zinc sheets on those of other coffee growers. The packed dirt floor inside is bare of any furniture. The kitchen walls are made of cut poles bound together with pieces of vine. Its crude roof is of the dried, stiff stalks from the huge fallen palm leaves. In front, Beatrice has stopped her sweeping and is calling to us: "Come on in for a cup of coffee!" How old she is, this woman with her grey hair pulled back tight into a bun, her wrinkled, weathered skin drawn tightly over her fragile, thin frame. My seventy-year-old grandmother seems young in comparison; yet this woman still hikes half an hour to the store for food, rides by mule and jeep to see a doctor, washes clothes standing in the cold streams. Women age rapidly here, always pregnant or nursing, their anemic bodies providing little milk for their breasts. "No thanks, it's getting late," answers Chaguito with a wave.

Her tan, leathery face breaks into a broad smile revealing her shiny white false teeth and stretching the wrinkles around her eyes. "No, no! Come on in, come on in! It's still early."

"No, we're kind of in a hurry," I respond as we move on.

Beatrice has only one son living in Jaida Arriba. With no land to cultivate, he lives on what he can earn on odd jobs. When his wife died giving birth to her fifth child, her mother came to help tend the children, two of whom are crippled, still unable to walk at six and eight years of age. The community had collected money at Sunday chapel a few months before to help send them to the children's hospital in Santiago. The doctor there said the problem was lack of nourishment and a deficiency of calcium.

Continuing down, Chaguito talks of the poverty of Beatrice and her son and the problems they have surviving without any productive land. But he also adds that these people are among the many who often waste their money on *vicios* (vices): the local lottery, cockfighting, dice, and rum.

"What about you, haven't you ever had any vice?"

"All of us Dominicans have vices. But the only vice that's really got a hold of me is smoking."

"And what about before?"

"Well. There's an old man, Leonardo, who used to live near me when I was a young man. And he was always pulling my leg. He'd ask me: 'What is it you want to do most?' And I told him: 'Farming.' And he'd ask me: 'But aren't you interested in learning?' And I told him: 'Well, if I can learn something, I'll learn something.' He told me: 'Let me give you a piece of advice. A man has to learn everything, everything except stealing. He even has to learn how to gamble. Because the man who doesn't learn how to do that, won't have anything to live with in the future.' So, I decided to learn how to gamble. One Sunday, I left the house with twelve cents in my pocket to play dice. I earned three and a half pesos. When I had that money in my hand, I went home. Next week, I took twenty-five cents with me; I earned seven and a half pesos. But Leonardo told me: 'The day you have money, don't you gamble.' So after that every Saturday, I'd take only twenty-five or thirty cents, so I wouldn't gamble more than that. Then I had a losing streak of three weeks. After that I never gambled again."

"And what about the lottery, did you used to have a lot of luck with that?"

"I never played the lottery very much. I never figured that I was going to win anything in that. I used to spend a little bit of money just for the heck of it, but I never won a cent. As far as pool, I played once for a week or two. But I never did it as a vice. I used to play pool more than I played dice, but only for five or ten cents. Some guys used to lose as much as half a peso, and even a peso, but not me. I never played more than five or ten cents. It's a vice, when you want to be doing that all the time."

"And what about cockfights?"

"No, I never liked that. My compadre Pepé, he really likes that. He goes to the cockpit in La Loma every Sunday. He's a fanatic of that!"

We spot the tin-roofed, blue-painted chapel as we round a bend in the trail and enter the "commercial center" of Jaida Arriba. There is a small community hall, built by the peasants after they had finished the chapel; on either side of the trail are two small billiard halls (frequented most often on Sundays); three wood-framed kitchens whose hearths are fired on Sundays or fiestas by enterprising women to feed those who live too far to return to their homes for lunch; a butcher shop where the butcher blows his conch-shell horn once or twice a week to announce the slaughtering of a pig or, on Saturdays, a cow; two very small general stores that sell so little salt, sugar, rice, oil, and rum that their owners are constantly threatened with unpayable debts at the larger stores from which they buy; and in the center, facing each other, are Manuel's *comercio* (general store) and the cooperative store, their zinc roofs and blue paint emphasizing their size and prosperity amid the old, gray-colored structures around them.

We enter the cooperative. "Hallo! How you doing? Haven't seen you in a long time!" the administrator of the cooperative (a peasant chosen by the members) merrily greets us, giving each of us an *abrazo* (embrace). "What's new? How are they treating you?"

"Oh, I'm a little wet," I laugh. "How about yourself?"

"Pretty good, thank God."

I turn toward the four men concentrating on dominoes at the table near the door. Pepé triumphantly smacks his last domino on the table and the others display those they are left holding, totaling the penalty points. Amid the sound of the dominoes being reshuffled, they look up and yell greetings to Chaguito and me. I go over, clasping their arms above their wrists. But Pepé stands up smiling, head cocked, and gives me an embrace.

To be polite, I walk across the street to Manuel's comercio.

"Hallo! What's up?" I greet his wife.

"Where have you been hiding yourself? Haven't seen you for a long time! When are you going to drop in for another cup of coffee?"

"Any day now, any day now," I assure her, a bit embarrassed at not having returned after continual invitations. "Where is Manuel?"

"He's down in Santiago, buying some things. What can we do for you?"

I need nothing, but buy a pound of rice, a roll of toilet paper, and a handful of penny hard candies.

In the cooperative store, Chaguito and the administrator have gone into the back room to talk. Returning, I notice Victor, a poor peasant, sitting quietly in one corner. Had he been there when Chaguito and I came in and greeted everyone else? Barefooted, his shirt torn along the mends, he was among the many poor peasants who had not come forward to meet me when I arrived the year before. He had never invited me to his house. When I finally realized that so many of these poor peasants lived in Jaida Arriba, I made a special effort to overcome their embarrassment at having little to offer me if I came to their homes. But I had never become acquainted with Victor, except in passing.

I inquire about his family. His little girl is seriously ill, but Victor rubs his thumb against his fingers, indicating lack of cash for a doctor. I am almost sorry I asked. Continually facing people with acute needs for money, I am always torn by guilt for not making individual offers despite my rational resolve that I cannot give to one without giving to all, unless, as often occurs, there is a community collection.

Chaguito calls me into the back room of the store, a room that doubles as a bar and dance floor on Sundays. The administrator is treating his compadre Chaguito to a glass of pear nectar. There is a third glass on the table for me.

Chaguito had called his compadre aside to discuss the money he owes the cooperative store and his shortage of cash. Chaguito's problem is a constant one for all the peasants in Jaida Arriba: the coffee-growing peasants need money until the harvest; the poorer peasants, until they can find the work to earn it. Historically, the comerciantes have met these money shortages, providing the capital in the form of cash advances or credit on food and implements. The ability of a peasant to clear, fence, plant, weed, and harvest often depends on a comerciante being willing to advance the production costs and enough credit for food so the peasant can work his own land and not be forced to sell his labor to feed his family. Before the cooperative all the peasants in Jaida Arriba spent most or all of the year in debt, continually worried about where they would get credit and how they would repay it.

"I used to have to take stuff on credit almost all year long," explained Chaguito, "June, July, August, September, October, those were the worst months because there was no way of making money in those months. Those months are always like that. I really have a hard time. When the coffee harvest has passed, there's nothing you can grab onto. So you're buying all your food on credit. And when you're buying on credit, you've always got a big worry in your mind. You're always afraid that nobody's going to want to give you anything on credit. And there's another thing. Let's suppose that I go into a general store and I see that they're taking a long time to wait on me. So you begin to think, it's because you're buying on credit. That makes you feel kind of ashamed. And even when the harvest came, it didn't leave you enough money to pay off food you had taken on credit. So you always ended up still in debt, and you had to wait for the following harvest. All the time you're worrying about where you're going to get the money, because you want to pay off your debt, and get that money. And all the time you're worried about where you're going to be able to find food on credit."

The comerciantes charged higher prices when selling on credit. And in return for credit, the peasant usually was obligated to pay his debt with his coffee or other crops. The comerciantes made most of their profits here, offering less for the crops than the *campesino* (peasant) could get elsewhere. Furthermore, with the purchase of coffee, there were often great differences (unknown to the peasant) between the price paid the peasant (for example, $28 a quintal) and the price the comerciante received (for example, $35 a quintal).

The cooperatives organized in Jaida Arriba aimed at solving the problems of preharvest money shortages by loaning members money accumulated from savings during the harvest or derived from funds lent by government cooperative agencies.

This month, however, the Cooperativa Agropecuaria (the Coffee Marketing Cooperative) has no money to lend. The Cooperativa de Consumo (the Consumer Cooperative, or the cooperative general store) discourages its members from buying on credit. But Chaguito has called the administrator aside to see if he might be advanced a little more until the promised, but long overdue, government loans arrive. The administrator agrees before I am called in. Now the conversation turns to the amazing effects that the new fertilizer for the coffee seems to be having. We sip our pear nectar and chat. But night is falling and soon it is time to leave.

The rocks and ruts in the trail are barely visible by the time we see the warm firelight glowing through the cracks in Chaguito's kitchen. We hear the clanking of spoons on plates and the eternal radio, and step into the light.

"Blessings, father! Blessings, Ken!" shout the children.

"God bless you," we respond.

Chaguito gives Mélida the special treat he has brought her: malt beer and condensed milk to help her regain her strength. She also takes the peanut oil she has been waiting for to make the *tostones* (flattened plantain slices fried in oil). We sit down at the table and the children, some still munching their boiled banana dinner, gather around us. Excitedly, they tell Chaguito of the mice they have seen running around the wood pile. He assures them that he will get a mousetrap the next day.

Dinner is spaghetti, tostones, and a vegetable soup prepared with a Maggi bouillon cube, oil, garlic, onions, spaghettilike noodles, and squash. Mélida places a small makeshift kerosene light near us. The priest talking over the radio laments the death of another university student at the hands of La Banda (the band) and criticizes both the police for supporting these right-wing terrorists and the president for taking no action. Chaguito looks up from his food.

"This republic doesn't want the campesinos to learn how to defend themselves. But the priests, they keep on speaking the truth. And even though those priests are telling the truth, the government even calls them communists, and other names that aren't true."

"And what do you think about all that?"

"Me . . . as far as I'm concerned, it's the government. It's O.K. But, there's just one thing. I don't know if it's because the president's afraid, but he lets a lot of people get killed."

"Who's responsible for killing so many people?"

"Balaguer [the president] is responsible. He's supporting them—because he's not doing anything. And those people in La Banda don't do anything except kill people."

"Have you ever changed your ideas about the government?"

"Yes. Since the year before the last election."

"What caused you to change your ideas?"

"Because so many people were getting killed and he didn't do a thing."

"What about the people here, are they afraid of the government?"

"Well, that depends. Some people are afraid. I ran into somebody who didn't know you and he told me: 'Maybe it's the government who sent this guy Ken. Maybe he's a detective gathering information for the government. He sure acts like a detective, he's always asking questions!' "

"Let me ask you another question. What do you think of the idea of writing letters to the president when you have some kind of personal problem—let's say a bad house, or you need money, or some of your children are sick?"

"No, not me. We campesinos are wasting our time writing to the government. Because the government offers a lot during elections, but afterward, it forgets you. Officials don't keep the promises they make. In my opinion, if we unite, we can do more for ourselves than anything the government is going to do for us."

"Why is that?"

"If all of us campesinos would unite, in cooperatives, once the cooperative has two or three thousand pesos—or a million pesos, or more, we can set up all sorts of businesses which will help us so that we'll have at least a little income every day. That seems to me to be a much better idea than to be asking the government for help."

A week earlier, a poor day laborer approached me to help him write a letter to El Presidente asking for a job and a new house. To what extent had Chaguito picked up this "we can do it ourselves" ethic through his experiences in the cooperative, or was it also part of a pioneer ethic of these families who had first cleared and settled Jaida Arriba? Did it also make some difference that his coffee crop and the cooperative gave Chaguito some opportunity to pick himself up by his bootstraps with the cooperative's help, while the day laborer, with no money to save and no crop to sell, had neither bootstraps nor help? On the radio, the priest continues attacking the crimes of La Banda. Chaguito piles more spaghetti on his plate and turns to me.

"I think that the laws of the United States are better than the laws here. Because if there's one thing I like it's order. Because there, in New York, according to what they've told me, there's law and order. And what does the government here do? If they don't let us chop down pine trees, where are we going to farm? In the United States, even though they may not let you chop down trees, at least they have a way of putting everybody to work. Here, most people still wouldn't want this to be a state of the U.S. But that's because the guys up top spend most of their time scratching their belly buttons—that means, they're there sitting on their rear ends giving you orders, and maybe paying you a peso. And they don't want this to be a state of the U.S. because then they'd have to work hard too. That's the way it is. We Dominicans are such schemers that we're not looking after the welfare of others. If you can screw somebody else, you screw them.

"We campesinos spend all our time down and out, breaking our backs but never getting anywhere. Let's imagine that the Americans came here, look what they could do. If the Americans were here, there would be better places for us to live in. Here we can't produce enough to buy shoes or clothing. We can only produce enough for our food, and even that's hard work. Down in the plains, any little plot that's irrigated produces well. That's what hurts. There are two or three people who have all that land, and several thousands of people without anything. And still, there are many people who say: we don't want the Americans here. But then, they want to go live in the States."

Supper over, Gilda takes some of the younger children into the house to bed. Mélida stokes the fires with dry wood and places an old cast-iron pan over the fire. Pouring in dried coffee beans to roast, she begins to stir them slowly with a flat wooden stick. Chaguito gets up and takes the stick from her hands. She fills a baby bottle with warm spice tea, puts a towel over her hair, and goes out into the house. Chepe and his sister stand near the fire and warm themselves against the chill night air as they watch their father. The beans begin to ping as they roast; a thick, hot smoke pours from the pot and fills the kitchen. Chaguito's wrist flicks back and forth, skillfully moving the stick through the beans. He does not want Mélida to roast the coffee because the heat and smoke "are just not good for a woman."

Chaguito's concern and affection for his wife are rare in Jaida Arriba. Before Gilda was ten and could get up to start the morning fires and the water boiling for coffee, Chaguito would do it rather than send his wife as most men do.

The coffee roasted and laid on a flat wooden board to cool, Chaguito and I sit down to sip some hot tea before going to bed. I question him about his starting the morning fires and his roasting the coffee.

"You won't find many men who do that. A lot of men would say that that's why they took a wife, so she would take care of them. But a man and a woman have to share the work. The woman has to take care of the man, but the man also has to take care of the woman. You have to share the woman's suffering, half and half. You have to balance things off. I used to cook for Mélida when she was sick so she wouldn't have to work so hard. And I've even carried water, when the children were too young. You have to realize that your wife is a human being. And she is weaker than us men. We can take more. But there are men hoping that their wives will die so that they can go out again and get another one."

"Did you used to think this way before?"

"I've always thought this way. I remember how my father used to treat my mother like a slave. I used to notice that my mother would cry—though afterward my father straightened out, maybe through some advice that others gave him. A lot of men used to tell him that he shouldn't treat her that way. It used to hurt me to see my mother cry. Maybe that's why I began to think, when I'd see my mother that way. Because those are the people you love. And you have to share with your wife."

"Are there a lot of men here who have other women?"

"There used to be. But, during the last few years, you don't see much of that anymore. As for me, ever since I've been married, I've never had another woman. The other women are like pieces of candy—they're just for the moment. But not your wife. She's forever. My head's not turned by pretty women. I wouldn't trade this woman for the prettiest woman in the world. And I won't get a crush on another woman just because she strikes me as pretty. Next October will be my thirteenth wedding anniversary, and I've never had another woman. Never. I've never chased after another skirt."

We are alone in the kitchen now. The embers in the hearth barely glow. Chaguito takes some warm water from a pot, empties it into a wash basin on the floor and cleans the day's dust and mud from his feet. Then we go out to the house. I climb, exhausted, into bed. Chaguito goes into the bedroom, but immediately appears again, goes back out to the kitchen and reappears with the malt beer, condensed milk, and a glass.

Mélida laughs to me through the open door: "I don't have much milk in me, and if I'm going to feed this child, I have to feed myself too!"

The small kerosene light flickers in the bedroom. Gilda's voice comes out of the shadows: "He doesn't want to drink his tea tonight, Mama."

"O.K. Don't force him," replies Mélida quietly.

Chaguito blows out the flame. From the dark the children call: "Mama! Papa!"

"God bless you," they respond.

CHAPTER 2

CONTROL IN THE
COFFEE-MARKETING SYSTEM

A MEETING IN THE CAPITAL

It is 24 April, 1972. The International Coffee Organization (ICO) has just increased the Dominican coffee export quota. The unexpected authorization increases the original quota of 351,000 bags by 9,000 bags (1 bag weighs 75 kilograms). This means that the Dominican Republic can export an extra 9,000 bags of coffee during the April-May-June trimester, but also that a decision must be made as to which exporter or coffee grower will be allowed to receive the profit. In a back corner of the quality control room of the Department of Agriculture's Institute of Coffee and Cacao a small group meets to make that decision.

On this permanent Commission for the Assignment of Coffee Quotas are representatives of six of the major Dominican coffee-exporting houses and six coffee growers, all but one among the largest in the country. He represents an association of peasant coffee growers. Presiding is the highly respected undersecretary for agriculture, Juan Pablo Duarte, himself a large coffee grower. At his side is the executive secretary of the commission, a leading Dominican authority on the international politics of coffee. Assistants sit against the wall close by the members, some whispering, others waiting. The air is rich with the aroma of coffee being roasted, ground, and brewed for testing by machines and techniques as foreign to Chaguito as the meeting about to be held.

The sensitive task of dividing up the extra quota is not tackled immediately. The executive secretary opens by informing the group of a crisis within the International Coffee Organization that might threaten the international quota system and thus the export of their coffee. He has just received a London *Times* article of 12 April from the Dominican consulate in England, which he reads aloud. In early April eleven coffee-producing countries met in Geneva and signed a document aimed at depriving consuming nations of a voice in regulating prices. Brazil, Columbia, and the other signatories (who together account for 90 percent of world coffee exports) were upset by the December devaluation of the dollar, which sharply reduced the purchasing power of the foreign exchange reserves of these developing countries. The Geneva document challenged the 1962 International Coffee Agreement between producing and consuming nations by threatening to put control of coffee supplies and prices in the hands of the coffee-producing countries.

The discussion that follows is short. Should the Dominican Republic take a position? What should it be? The consensus is to wait and see what happens.

The executive secretary presents a second problem: there will be a coffee surplus this year, perhaps as much as 120,000 bags beyond national consumption needs and the assigned export quota. Unsalable abroad, this surplus will force exporters to tie up capital in storing the excess and will force prices down for the growers. A number of suggestions are made amid expressions of dismay, but discussion is postponed for another meeting. The members are anxious to turn to the more immediate problem: dividing up the new 9,000-bag quota.

One of the largest exporters in the country opens the discussion by asking to "borrow" the entire excess to use this third trimester. He explains that next month he must meet a contract he made to sell coffee in Puerto Rico and will not be able to do so without more quota. He mistakenly had estimated a much smaller national harvest this year and had assumed he would be able to get sufficient quota when the contract was due. In return he offers to "give back" an equal amount of quota to the commission from that already assigned to him in the fourth quarter.

A debate ensues. Great politeness and respect pervade the tense atmosphere as men defend their personal interests with compelling arguments as to what is best for the general good. One commission member (a large grower and personal friend of the exporter) supports the request. He argues that the high price in the Puerto Rican contract will help the Dominican foreign exchange position, and further, that this exporter "is a good friend of the government, a good citizen and a good colleague." Others on the commission argue that they too have needs.

After much discussion, the one representative of the peasant growers speaks up: "I represent hundreds of small producers, people who depend on their coffee to eat, people who need the money from this coffee for sick wives and children, poor campesinos who can't afford to hold their coffee for another trimester. If anyone should borrow this quota it should be us." Heads nod politely while he talks, but it is clear that such peasant needs will not affect the final decision. That decision is postponed a week while the large exporter flies to Puerto Rico with another commission member (an exporter who also has a contract in Puerto Rico but more than enough quota to cover it) to see if a special arrangement can be made.

WHO CONTROLS WHAT

THE COFFEE-MARKETING SYSTEM. Like most unorganized, small agricultural producers, the coffee-growing peasant in Jaida Arriba has no control over the price of his crop. It is determined by economic and political forces outside his control and comprehension. His coffee moves through a system of marketing and processing extending to the world coffee market; at a number of strategic points exporting houses, government institutions, international organizations, and individual buyers exercise the power that determines the price he will receive.

Coffee export is controlled largely by twelve export houses: Bordas & Cía., Curacao Trading Company Dom., Font Gamundi & Cía., Induban, Felipe Isa, Mecca, A. Melo, Munné y Cía., Antonio Olivar Cía. Exportadora, J. Paiewonky e hijos., Juan Francisco Pérez Velázquez., and Toral Hermanos. Over 50 percent is exported by four of these: Induban, Melo, Munné, and Paiewonsky. These firms have access to the capital needed to purchase the expensive but requisite processing equipment and to buy, warehouse, and prepare coffee for export. Further, they have the necessary contacts in the United States and Europe. Such control over exporting is the economic basis of the country's powerful commercial bourgeoisie, giving it a crucial position in the export-based national economy (sugar, coffee, cacao, and tobacco are the major sources of foreign exchange).

The price these exporters receive for their coffee is partly determined by world supply and demand and partly regulated by the International Coffee Organization. The exporters, in turn, buy most of their coffee (except that produced by the few very large growers) through independent compradores in the *campo* (countryside) to whom they advance capital. The price paid these compradores depends on such factors as the price exporters receive in the international market, the supply of coffee in the country relative to combined national demand and assigned Dominican export quota, and the distribution of the quota among exporters. The compradores then buy either directly from the peasants or, more often, employ smaller compradores on a commission basis to do the buying. These smaller compradores may, in turn, also employ others as their buyers (see Chart 2.1). The price offered a peasant by a comprador will depend on the price this buyer is receiving from the comprador (or exporter) above him in the marketing chain, the number of other compradores buying in the area, price-fixing agreements among these compradores, the knowledge the peasants have of prices, and the peasants'

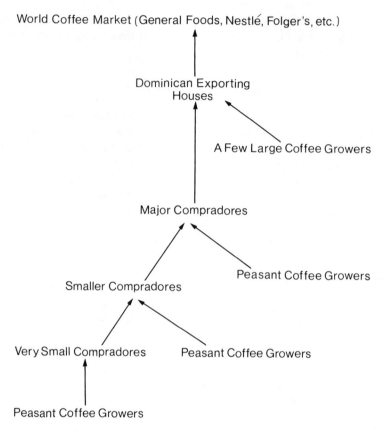

CHART 2.1
Buying Coffee: From the Peasant to the International Market

moral and economic indebtedness to a particular comprador. Who exercises what kind of control at each strategic point in the marketing system is the subject of the following sections.

INTERNATIONAL CONTROL. The Dominican Republic, as a signer of the International Coffee Agreement (ICA) and member of the International Coffee Organization (ICO), each year is assigned a percentage of the total world export quota agreed upon in London by the ICO. This total is decided after hard negotiations between forty-one producer countries and twenty-four consumer countries whose relative voting power is determined by the size of their coffee production relative to world totals (Brazil and Columbia together control almost 50 percent of the producer votes; the U.S. has 40 percent of the consumer votes). At stake is the supply and thus the price of coffee on the international market.[1] Although the international coffee prices and the quota assigned to the Dominican Republic critically affect these exporters, compradores, and peasant coffee growers, the Dominican Republic, with its relatively small production (it has about 1 percent of the producer votes), has little influence over the prices or its quota. But how that quota is divided up—which Dominicans get access to the profits to be made on the international market—is a decision made within the national political economy.

CONTROL OVER THE DOMINICAN COFFEE QUOTA: EXPORTERS VERSUS GROWERS. The exporting houses and coffee growers all have a fundamental economic interest in maximizing their share of the quota. Quotas assigned directly to coffee growers guarantee that their coffee may be exported. If they do not export themselves (few do), they can use these quotas to get higher prices from the exporting houses—one to ten dollars more per hundred pounds (depending on the world coffee market price, the national supply and demand, and the amount of quota a particular exporter has relative to national supply). Concomitantly, grower access to quotas often means loss of profit to the exporter. (See Table 2.1.)

Before 1965, the exporting houses had complete control of the quotas. The conflict between the large growers and the exporters led to small distributions of quotas to some growers during the 1965–66 harvest and to the appointment of the evenly divided Commission for the Assignment of Quotas by presidential decree on 27 August 1968.[2] Since then, quotas to growers have increased gradually, but little benefit has filtered down to the peasants, who produce the bulk of Dominican coffee.[3] How coffee-growing peasants like Chaguito are largely excluded from access to quota demands an understanding of the mechanics and politics of quota distribution.

The ICO-assigned quota to the Dominican Republic is divided up into four trimesters beginning in October. Roughly 30 percent of the total comes in each of the first two trimesters and 20 percent in each of the second two trimesters. The amounts in each trimester are subject to modification by the ICO as it releases more quota or retracts part of the initially assigned quota in an effort to control prices by controlling world supply.

TABLE 2.1
Approximate Price Paid by Exporter for Coffee "without" Quota and "with" Quota, October 1971 through May 1972 (Price per 50 kilograms)

	Oct.–Jan.	Jan.–March	March–May
Price for coffee "without" quota	$28	$40	$31
Price for coffee "with" quota	$35	$41	$41

SOURCE: An exporting house representative.

To divide up this quota the commission each year makes rules for distribution. In 1972 three mechanisms were used. Each one was applied to a portion of the quota, and each one favored either the exporters or the growers. The first mechanism long favored the exporters: the division of a portion of the quota among applicants according to their percentage of the previous year's total exports. Before 1965–66, this mechanism was applied to the entire quota of the first and second trimesters. During this harvest the second mechanism was introduced to provide a share for the growers: a portion of the quota was set aside to be divided according to each grower's percentage of the total production of the applicants. In 1965–66 this portion of the quota was 10 percent of the first and second trimester quotas (6 percent of the total yearly quota), leaving 90 percent still to be apportioned among exporters through the first mechanism. By 1970–71 the share for the growers had reached 40 percent of the first and second trimester quotas (24 percent of the total yearly quota). In 1971–72 the growers were given 20 percent of the first trimester quota, 30 percent of the second, and 60 percent of the third and fourth trimester quotas, or a total of 39 percent of the total yearly quota (see Table 2.2).

The third mechanism, usually applied to the quota of the third and fourth trimesters, is based on the exportable stocks of coffee possessed by each applicant. Each applicant's share depends upon the percentage he has of the total exportable stock claimed by all those applying. In the years when quota exceeds stock, an applicant has little trouble getting a quota for all the coffee he has. But in the harvests of 1970–71 and 1971–72 the previous pattern of a coffee deficit relative to the total needs (quota plus national consumption) was reversed, and a surplus in stock surpassed the quota available. In 1971–72

TABLE 2.2

Approximate Percentages of Initial Uncorrected First and Second Trimester
Quotas Distributed Specifically by Previous Year's Export or by Production;
and the Percentage of the Total Yearly Quota Constituted by this Portion
Distributed by Production

	First and Second Trimester Quota		
	Percent by Previous Year's Export	Percent by Production	Percent of Total Quota Distributed by Production
1964–65	100	0	0
1965–66	90	10	6
1966–67	85	15	9
1967–68	80	20	12
1968–69	66.6	33.3	20
1969–70	60	40	24
1970–71	60	40	24
1971–72	0	15	39[a]

SOURCE: Instituto de Café y Cacao.

each applicant was awarded quotas for only 9.71 percent of his exportable stock. The various portions of the quota divided up by each mechanism since 1968 can be summarized by Table 2.3.

We now need to know the political-economic meaning of these three quota mechanisms for the exporting houses, the large coffee growers, the peasant producers, and the middlemen (the buyers or compradores). Under the first criterion, the quota is divided among the applicants according to the percentage each exported the year before. With a few exceptions among the largest growers, only exporting houses actually export coffee, effectively leaving them in control of coffee so assigned. In 1970–71 only forty groups or individuals exported (exporting houses, large growers, large middlemen, and eight small-grower organizations); and the vast bulk was controlled by the major exporting houses. The timing of this mechanism greatly favors the exporters. Most of the Dominican coffee is harvested during these first two trimesters, and all but the largest growers must sell to the exporters immediately. They need the money to pay accumulated debts and to meet pressing household needs. Even peasant associations or cooperatives have difficulty borrowing the money needed to hold their coffee until the third and fourth trimesters, or, if they can get loans, they must pay high interest rates. These smaller growers thus have no exportable stock with which to gain quotas in the third and fourth trimesters.

I will leave for a moment the second mechanism of quota distribution and turn to the third: division of a share of the quota according to the percentage an applicant has of the total exportable stock claimed by those applying. This mechanism does not exclude growers but, as indicated above, greatly favors the exporting houses. Only 175 applicants in 1971–72 claimed to have exportable coffee in stock, and about 80 percent of this exportable coffee was in the hands of the exporting houses. Thus only about 20 percent of the quota allotted by this procedure went to the growers and compradores; with the exception of eight small producer organizations, all the growers and compradores were large-sized ones.

The exporting houses have another advantage here: many of them can

TABLE 2.3
Shares of the (Uncorrected-Initial) Total Yearly Quota Divided According
to Each of the Three Mechanisms (*in Percentages*)

	By Previous Year's Exports	By Production	By Exportable Stock
1968–69	40	20	40
1969–70	36	24	40
1970–71	36	24	40
1971–72	0[5]	39	61

SOURCE: Instituto de Café y Cacao.

artificially inflate the amount they claim to have in stock, and thus get an even larger percentage of the total. When the inspector comes to verify the amount of exportable coffee they have in stock, they may use many ploys. One export house presented an inspector with a warehouse filled from floor to ceiling and front to back with sacks of coffee, but the sacks in the center—difficult to see or get to—were actually filled with unexportable (poor grade) coffee. A common variation of this ploy is to fill the center sacks with beans, corn, corn husks, or rice. One exporting house drove a large truck into the center of its warehouse, covered it with a tarp, and piled coffee around and on top of it, giving the appearance of a solid mass of stacked coffee. Other exporters have built false rooms or platforms, hollow inside, around and above which coffee sacks are stacked. Once, after verifying the amount of exportable coffee in stock in an exporter's Barahona warehouse, the inspector appeared the next day at this exporter's warehouses in Santo Domingo only to find trucks arriving from Barahona with the same coffee to be stacked in the Santo Domingo warehouse. These and other tricks are difficult to discover, the more so because inspectors sometimes are willing to accept bribes for "closing their eyes" or simply inflating figures. Those who are most able to gain access to higher quotas through such artificial inflation of their stock are the exporting houses or the very large growers or compradores with money available to "grease the palms of the inspectors."

The remaining mechanism for distributing quotas is based on production and clearly favors coffee growers. Each grower applying is given a proportionate percentage of the total production of all the applicants. This share of the total quota has been increasing steadily since 1965 (see Table 2.2). But few peasant coffee growers have benefited from the increased percentages. Out of over ninety thousand farms or plots[6] that cultivate coffee, only two thousand applications were made in 1971–72 for this share of the quota, and most of the quota share went to large growers or to middlemen posing as growers or grower organizations. Before the cooperative was organized, none of the coffee growers in Jaida Arriba ever applied for a quota. Few even knew the possibility existed. But had they known, they would have faced other difficulties: making an application to an unknown agency in the faraway capital is difficult and awesome for a peasant who can barely read or write.

Yet another obstacle to peasant access to this quota reserved for producers is the control exercised by the compradores over the peasant's coffee. Long before their harvests, most peasants have presold their coffee to these middlemen in order to get money for food and production needs. Many of these middlemen are even able to acquire the peasant quotas for themselves. At least one major comprador in the Jaida Arriba region, for example, collected the signatures of the unknowing peasants who sold coffee to him, claimed a grower's quota in their name, and then used the quota himself. Even if the peasants knew of such manipulations, they would be hesitant to "go over the heads" of the compradores. (This attitude will be discussed in chapter 7.)

The shift in control over access to the quota is thus largely a shift from control by the exporting houses to a sharing between the exporters on the one hand and the large producers and compradores on the other, even though technically any coffee grower has access to the "production" portion of the quota. This institutional access, however, is potentially important to the small producer if he can organize a group (such as a cooperative) and if he can make use of the access he legally has. These two problematic "ifs" will be discussed at greater length in Chapter 9.

CONTROL IN THE MARKETING SYSTEM: FROM EXPORTER TO MIDDLEMAN. The price peasants receive for their coffee is, in part, affected by the price the exporters offer to the major compradores. A number of factors determine this price.

The "demand" for coffee in the Dominican Republic is roughly the national consumption plus the national quota. The supply of coffee fluctuates yearly depending on weather, the age and health of the coffee trees (quality of pruning and control of shade), the soil, and the use of fertilizers. Little data are available to predict production. Yet for the exporting houses, such knowledge is crucial. The national supply will affect the distribution of quotas, particularly in the third and fourth trimesters. Underestimating the supply will mean overbuying and then paying to warehouse coffee for which they have no quota. Exporter estimates, often wrong, greatly affect the price of coffee. At the beginning of the first trimester of the 1971–72 coffee harvest, for example, there was an estimated over stock of about 150,000 75-kilogram sacks from the previous year. The exporting houses had little immediate need to buy coffee during this first trimester and were concerned about another surplus. Such calculations created a low-demand/high-supply situation. Prices in October, November, and December offered by the exporting houses to the major compradores ranged from $25 to $28 per quintal for coffee "without" quota, and up to about $32 per quintal for coffee "with" quota (coffee sold by producers or compradores who had been assigned quotas). The prices the exporting houses were receiving abroad (F.O.B. Puerto Plata) ranged from $37 up to $40 per quintal. As the October to December harvests came in, the exporting houses discovered that the coffee crop had been smaller than expected. Because the coffee harvested during this period usually constitutes the bulk (about 80 percent) of the yearly total, they estimated that coffee production would fall short of the quota and national consumption needs. Estimates of a shortage became a key factor in creating a much higher demand and an increase in the price offered by exporting houses. Beginning in January, the price rose to $32 and then in

February up to $36 per quintal for coffee "without" quota. Coffee "with" quota went up to $38 per quintal. The world market price (F.O.B. Puerto Plata) remained roughly steady at $41.50 per quintal. But in March, when the harvest from the higher mountain areas began to come in, many exporters realized that they had underestimated the size of the later harvests, and the price began to drop. At this time, one of the largest exporting houses estimated that instead of a deficit there would be a surplus of from 60,000 to 100,000 75-kilogram sacks of coffee. By April and May the price of coffee "without" quota had plummeted back down to $28 per quintal. But the price of coffee "with" quota stayed about the same, $38 per quintal. The price fluctuations for the first three trimesters of the 1971–1972 coffee year are summarized in Table 2.4.

The actions of one or two large exporting houses also can have a great impact on coffee prices. Indeed another factor important in explaining the dramatic price rise from $25 to $36 per quintal was an unusually large contract made by one of the large exporters to sell 25,000 75-kilogram sacks of coffee (semiroasted) to Puerto Rico at a preferential price. Assuming little problem obtaining the necessary quota and willing to offer a higher price (because of the preferential price in Puerto Rico), he bought coffee "without" quota for over $36 per quintal. To assure the 25,000 sacks he needed, he even bought coffee (with and without quota) from another one of the large exporting houses. The shortage created by his demand at one point drove prices so high that a better price could be obtained selling the coffee to him in the Dominican Republic than abroad. Although this exporter later discovered his miscalculation and found that a coffee surplus rather than a deficit made it impossible to obtain the quota he needed to export all the coffee he had bought, his actions greatly affected the rise of prices in early 1972.

Exporting houses and large growers often try to use political influence to get preferential treatment in the assignment of quotas. Some appeal to the

TABLE 2.4
Fluctuations in Price Paid to Exporters and Compradores for Coffee,
October 1971 through May 1972 (Price per Quintal)

Price Paid	Oct.–Jan.	Jan.–March	March–May
To Exporter (FOB Puerto Plata)	$37–$40	$41.50	$42
To Comprador ("without" quota)	$25–$28	$32–$36	$28–$31
To Comprador ("with" quota)	$32	$38	$38

SOURCE: Interviews with exporters and compradores.

president of the Dominican Republic to intercede on their behalf. Others approach high-ranking officials in the Instituto de Café y Cacao—personal friends, politically important people in the ruling Partido Reformista—with requests for special treatment; but according to one official, "this is one agency in the country where politics or friendship just does not hold water." Such politicking can, however, affect prices. One very large exporter, unhappy with his share of the quota, started a press campaign demanding that the president intervene in the "unfair" procedures used by the commission. Although the commission's decision was not reversed, the public criticism and ensuing threats of resignation by some commission members created such uncertainty that, as one exporter explained, "nobody was willing to buy coffee because they were afraid they might lose their quotas." As a result, the price offered by the exporting houses plummeted, and the peasant growers absorbed the losses.

CONTROL IN THE MARKETING SYSTEM: FROM MIDDLEMAN TO PEASANT. The Dominican coffee exporters do not buy their coffee directly from the peasants because of the great risk involved: buying a peasant's coffee demands financing his preharvest production costs and household needs, and such capital advances easily can be lost. As one exporter explained: "The peasant might even have the best intentions, but his situation is such that if a child gets sick, he's just not going to have the money to pay back what I advanced him." The exporters prefer to advance capital to independent middlemen—usually local commerciantes with the economic position to guarantee such advances—and let these compradores absorb the risk. These local middlemen have direct knowledge of their clientele (who can be trusted, who has the production to guarantee and advance) and can control much of the regional coffee market through advances of credit and cash.

In the region of Jaida Arriba there were three major compradores before 1968 when the cooperative was formed. The three, Arturo, Francisco, and Isidro, were all comerciantes with large general stores and good access to credit in the Santiago warehouses that supplied them with food and other consumer goods. Each had a small factory for hulling coffee: large cement drying floors, a motor-driven huller, and a large warehouse for storing the coffee in hundred-pound sacks before trucking it to exporters in Santiago or Puerto Plata. Many peasants gave at least part of their coffee to these compradores to pay back credit advances on food before the harvest. But these compradores also paid cash for coffee not already owed. This money was advanced to them interest-free by the exporting houses with which they signed fixed-price contracts to deliver the coffee, usually within a month of the advance.

The prices these compradores could offer the peasants (see Table 2.5) were

TABLE 2.5
Prices Received for Coffee by Peasants, Compradores (without Quotas),
and Exporters, October 1971 through May 1972

Price Paid	Oct.–Dec.	Dec.–March	March–May
To Exporter			
(FOB Puerto Plata)	$37–$40/qq	$41.50/qq	$42/qq
To Comprador			
(without quota)	$25–$28/qq	$32–$36/qq	$28–$31/qq
To Peasant	$21–$24/fanega	$25–$29/fanega	$24–$27/fanega

SOURCE: Interviews with exporters, compradores, and peasants.

limited both by the price set in the above-mentioned contract and by their
own costs of preparing and transporting the coffee to the exporter. If we
look for illustration at a region near Jaida Arriba unaffected by the cooperative movement, we can see the price changes of coffee (1971–72) as it moves
from the peasants to the exporting houses through the compradores.

At the height of the harvest season, in mid-February, there were compradores who made contracts with the large exporting houses to sell them
coffee for $36 per quintal, who then bought coffee from the peasants at $29
per *fanega* (a local unit of volume). Shifts from fanegas of coffee (which
normally weighed less than a quintal) to quintales meant gross profits that
exceeded this $7.00 difference by $1.80 or more;[7] and the net profit was
usually at least $7.30. If a comprador had a quota he could earn even higher
profits.

These major compradores often bought much of their coffee through small
compradores, thus lowering peasant earnings by about another $2 (see Table
2.6). The coffee-growing peasants would often sell to a smaller comprador because of ties of personal friendship or trust, or to repay this smaller comprador—often a commerciante himself—for credit advanced before the harvest. In
some cases these smaller compradores contract out yet another buyer to buy
for them, lowering the price received by the peasant still further. The price is

TABLE 2.6
Prices Received for Coffee by Peasants, Small Compradores, Compradores
(without Quotas), and Exporters, October 1971 through May 1972

Price Paid	Oct.–Dec.	Dec.–March	March–May
To Exporter			
(FOB Puerto Plata)	$37–$40/qq	$41.50/qq	$42/qq
To Comprador			
(without quota)	$25–$28/qq	$32–$36/qq	$28–$31/qq
To Small Comprador	$22–$25/qq	$26–$30/qq	$25–$28/qq
To Peasant	$20–$23/fanega	$24–$28/fanega	$23–$26/fanega

SOURCE: Interviews with exporters, compradores, small compradores, and peasants.

often lowered even further in situations where the coffee grower is forced to "sell" his coffee at a great loss before the actual harvest (a la flor) in order to quickly raise cash he needs to meet crises such as illness or death in his family.

The coffee-growing peasants have little choice but to deal with these compradores at the prices they set. Not only will the exporters not deal with him because of his small production, but long before the harvest he is already "bound" to the middlemen: he is in debt to them for credit advances to help him sustain his family and meet production costs, and in return he obligates much of his coffee to them. It is the middleman's control over credit urgently needed by the peasant that most directly gives him control over the price of the peasant's coffee. To understand this control we must know more about the basic needs of various classes of peasants for money prior to harvest time and the part played by the commerciantes (who are also the compradores) in meeting these needs of everyday existence. This demands a careful understanding of the pressures confronting Chaguito and his neighbors, pressures deriving from the forms of production, family size, and inheritance patterns. To these pressures we now turn.

CHAPTER 3

THE PEASANTS' DILEMMAS

A peasant's existence depends on his ability adequately to meet certain basic needs. At a minimum, he must provide the food, clothing, and shelter that sustain his family. Such minima are in part physiological and in part climatic and cultural (Wolf 1966b:4–6). Beyond such a subsistence level, the norms of any particular culture usually define a "decent" standard of living in terms of both physical well-being and social obligations (Wolf 1956b:206). Chaguito's family normally maintains what would be considered in Jaida Arriba a minimally "decent" standard of living. He usually can provide three meals a day; rice and beans for the lunch, the big meal of the day; foods such as plantains, sweet potatoes, and *yuca* at each meal; coffee after meals and for hospitality; chickens for eggs and for meat on holidays; a few pounds of meat at least once a week; salt, cooking oil, tomato paste, onions, garlic, and other spices such as clove, cinnamon, anise, and nutmeg; milk for the youngest children; one bed with wire mesh springs for each two to four children and for Chaguito and his wife; a store-bought pair of pants, shirt, shoes, and dresses (sometimes homemade) for going to town or Sunday church; a solidly built house of pine with a pine-shingle roof that does not leak and a wood-plank floor; a mule or burrow for travel and hauling; a few cows and some pigs for emergency cash needs; three grades of education for his children at the local school; enough money for the expenses of baptisms and weddings; and some money for medicine and visits to doctors in the pueblo in cases of serious illness. Chaguito also is able to buy the implements he needs for his coffee production and for maintaining his farm. For these and many other needs, Chaguito and the peasants of Jaida Arriba must depend on money to supplement what they can make or produce themselves. These peasants face at least two difficulties common to peasants in most parts of the world: a scarcity of cultivable land and a continual money shortage between harvests, both of which affect their ability to meet immediate and future family needs. These difficulties stem from pressures impinging on and often challenging their very existence: pressures that derive from their forms of production, from the social system of the peasantry, and from the larger society of which the peasants form a part.[1]

In this chapter I will focus on the pressures that derive from the forms of production and the social system in Jaida Arriba and then look at the different kinds of hardships they impose on different classes of peasants. In Chapter 4, I will add to this analysis one pressure that emanates from the wider society: the control exercised by the middlemen.

FORMS OF PRODUCTION

The peasants in Jaida Arriba depend on three basic forms of agricultural production: slash-and-burn cultivation, coffee production, and to a lesser degree, livestock.[2]

In slash-and-burn cultivation, the peasants are limited by decreasing fertility of the soil and lack of new lands to clear (Wolf 1966b:20). Heavy seasonal rains erode the rich but thin layer of mountain topsoil exposed after initial clearing. The roots of most crops scarcely hold the soil and are removed at harvest time. The plantains and banana trees that are left standing are too wide apart to act as effective barriers against erosion. Weeding with a broad machete blade scrapes away at the thin layer of topsoil. The cultivation of the same subsistence crops on the same piece of land further tires what soil remains. Within one to three years, most peasants with slash-and-burn plots must look for more land to clear.[3] Yet little new land is available. When Chaguito was growing up, the amount of forest land seemed unlimited. Chaguito's parents and the other original settlers often cleared new plots of virgin forest each year. But extensive clearing, increased settlement, and growing families have all but eliminated land for new conucos. And the lack of capital and know-how for more intensive cultivation has not opened this possibility. The clearing of remaining land is hampered by the foresters and rural police who now enforce the forestry law. Settling the forest lands in the National Park, in the highlands above Jaida Arriba, similarly is prohibited.[4] The lack of good land is felt as an urgent problem for most of the peasants:

If you clear a new piece of forest land, you get something. But planting on this used-up land—it's useless. . . . All the vitamins in the soil have gone with the rains down the main trail. Just look at that conuco that I made last year! I still have debts from it! I plowed it by hand, with a pick. I planted fifteen bags of peanuts and all I made was a lousy $32—and that was over 30 tareas that we plowed and planted! We also planted yuca, but there was barely enough to eat. We planted beans, but they didn't even flower. We planted sweet potatoes, but some little bug got in and finished them off. The land here is so tired that it doesn't give you anything.

The result of this situation is an increasing scarcity of subsistence crops compounded with fewer cash crops to provide the money with which to buy the food that no longer can be produced.

Coffee growing alleviates one of the major problems of slash-and-burn cultivation. The roots of this perennial hold the soil and check erosion. After maturity in four or five years, the coffee will continue to bear fruit for many years if properly weeded. Once the plot is planted with coffee, the peasant does not face the same immediate land pressure of slash-and-burn cultivation; but in the absence of money and techniques for more intensive cultivating, he does need more forest land to expand production to meet the needs of a growing family.[5] Further, the majority of the peasants have no land under coffee cultivation and would need fresh forest lands to plant coffee. Even for coffee cultivation, then, the unavailability of lands for clearing poses a difficult situation.

Raising cattle and pigs for food and market was an important activity when Chaguito was a boy. His father had more than seventy cows and hundreds of pigs, all branded but roaming free in the unsettled forest lands. But increasing colonization, enclosure, and planting of these open lands have limited most grazing to enclosed pastures (most often former conucos put to grass after the first good harvests). In any case, few people can support more than two or three cows. The three largest herds in Jaida Arriba have about fifty, forty, and thirty-five cows, but these are exceptions. Lack of available grazing land has been intensified by government restrictions against the ranging of pigs.

Each form of production thus imposes a need on the peasant for more land. But each also imposes on him an urgent, immediate need for capital: the peasants have little or no savings, yet there is always a lapse between the time when production costs must be paid and the harvest (or maturation) of the crop (or animal). In the interim, the peasant needs money to sustain his family. The amount of money depends on the type and extent of production, family size, and other basic needs.

Production costs for slash-and-burn cultivation are based upon the amount of land cleared, the need for fencing, and the crops planted. Taking as an example Chaguito's new one-acre conuco we find the following costs for clearing, planting, and harvesting (see Table 3.1).

Hired labor may add cash costs to nonlabor costs. Pay for day labor becomes particularly important in clearing and planting larger conucos. In Chaguito's case, his children are still too young to work, so he had to hire others to help for two days in early August and four days at harvest time. These six days cost him (including food plus wages) $8.75. His total preharvest costs (labor and nonlabor) were thus $37.85. But most of these costs had to be met at least three months before he had his first cash crop, the beans. More seriously, Chaguito had to feed and care for his family during these months. In this sense, his days of labor on his own land are not "free" but are labor

TABLE 3.1
Typical Costs for Clearing, Planting, and Harvesting a
One-Acre Cultivated Plot

Task	Days of Labor	Nonlabor Costs	Month
Cutting underbrush and felling trees	4		late June
Burning the brush and trees	2		early August
Clearing and cleaning off after burning	4		early August
Placing a fence with a 2-foot high base of horizontally laid rails and 3 strands of barbed wire (about 3 rolls of wire at $6/roll)	12	$18	mid-August
Planting (bean seeds cost $9.60 and corn $1.50 at this time; plantain bulbs, sweet potatoes, yucca, and small coffee plants are all readily available from his own conuco or that of a neighbor without cost; days of labor include labor of digging up and transporting these plantain bulbs, etc.)	8	$11.10	early September
Weeding	4		mid-October
Harvesting (calculation for bean harvest; other crops are not harvested as such, except coffee after 4 years, in a conuco this size but rather picked daily to meet family's food needs)	6		early December
Total days of labor	40		
Total nonlabor costs		$29.10	

SOURCE: Personal interview.

costs for him: they are days when he could be working for someone else to earn money to feed his family. Among the poorer peasants in Jaida Arriba, this presents a serious dilemma: compelled to work for pay, they are prevented from working what little land they do have.

Coffee-production costs are similar to those of slash-and-burn agriculture during the first few years since coffee is initially planted along with the other subsistence crops in the conuco. As the coffee begins to mature, other crops are not replanted and the conuco slowly becomes a coffee grove, thus posing a different set of weeding and harvesting expenses.[6] Because weeding takes a day or two per tarea and must be done during the dry days from July through August,[7] most coffee growers are forced to pay others to help them. The cost to weed a tarea is approximately $1.50 (depending on the growth) plus breakfast and the noonday meal. One peasant, Santiago, with 85 tareas of coffee, weeded 15 tareas himself, but had to pay $145 for the other 70 tareas ($110 labor costs, plus about $35 in food).

The other major expense for the coffee producer is his harvesting. Although costs vary from year to year, in 1971, Santiago paid his coffee pickers $8.50 per fanega with no breakfast and lunch. He and his family picked 10 fanegas themselves, but he had to pay $170 to have the remaining 20 picked.[8] The two other common costs of coffee production are removing the bean from the berry (with a small, hand-powered mill) and transporting the coffee beans by mule to the comprador, $1.50 and approximately 70 cents per fanega, respectively. But Santiago saved these costs by milling the coffee himself and using his own animals for transport.

Financing the coffee harvest poses an important complication. Usually a delay of three to four weeks comes between the time the coffee is picked and the time it is removed from the berry, dried, and finally sold. Yet the pickers must be paid immediately. The difficulty in coffee production is, then, similar to, but far more serious than, that in slash-and-burn cultivation: money is needed to finance production long before the harvest is in. Santiago thus needed $145 in August for weeding, six months before his first sizable harvest in March, and another large sum to pay the pickers more than a month before the harvest was marketable. Furthermore, during this period of waiting for the harvest, the coffee producer must meet the money expenses of caring for his family.

Cattle raising presents similar presale money needs. Pastures must be fenced and small trees and grass-killing weeds cut or removed. Once a sizable herd has been developed, a cow can be sold whenever there is a severe need for money without seriously affecting the future growth of the herd. But to develop such a herd is difficult. It takes a few years before a calf can be marketed profitably, and a peasant living on the edge of subsistence often must sell his few cows (or pigs) to raise cash in times of illness or great debt. Further, livestock production provides no immediate way to meet daily family subsistence needs.

Many peasants in Jaida Arriba (over 65 percent of the households) cannot meet their basic needs employing any or all of these forms of production and are forced to sell their labor. We shall look more closely at the difficulties they face after a brief examination of social system pressures.

SOCIAL SYSTEM PRESSURES:
GROWING FAMILIES AND INHERITANCE PATTERNS

Growing families and inheritance patterns exert still more pressures on the peasants. A large family may cut cash production costs by using family labor, but more children mean more mouths to feed. Family size thus intensifies the pressures deriving from the forms of production and environment.

With rudimentary knowledge of birth control only just being introduced into Jaida Arriba (and with little abstinence), families commonly add a new member at least every two years. Table 3.2 indicates that 61 percent of the families in Jaida Arriba have more than six children, and 40 percent have six to eight children. Families with fewer children are frequently those more recently wed who have only begun to procreate. With continually increasing family size added to the problems of soil erosion and lack of new

TABLE 3.2
Number of Children, Presently
Living, Born to Women Presently
Residing in Jaida Arriba
(January 1972)

Percent of Families	Number of Children
4	0
15	1 to 3
20	4 to 5
40	6 to 8
12	9 to 10
6	11 to 12
3	more than 12
100	

(Note: Since few women are not living with
their original husbands, by legal, religious,
or consensual unions, and since there are
few widows, these figures are approximately
those of nuclear family size, excluding the
man and woman.)
SOURCE: Personal interviews.

lands or methods for intensive cultivation, provision for family needs becomes increasingly difficult.

The "partible inheritance" system presents yet another problem.[9] The custom in Jaida Arriba is to divide all land and other property equally among all the children, male and female, upon the death of the parents. Before then, the father usually will give plots to his sons upon marriage so that they can start their own households. The difficulties posed by this system of inheritance are clearly illustrated in the case of Chaguito. When the 1,600 tareas of his father's land is officially divided up among Chaguito and his nine brothers and sisters, each will receive 160 tareas. When Chaguito divides this land among his present children, each child will obtain about 16 tareas, or a little more than two acres, of which only one acre will be suitable for coffee production. A basic dynamic in Jaida Arriba, then, is this: scarce and often unproductive land is being divided into ever-smaller units which must support new and growing families.

SOCIOECONOMIC STRUCTURE

The difficulties of land scarcity and continual money shortage in the face of growing families with both immediate and long-term needs confront all the peasants, though not always equally. Because of the different circumstances among each economic class—forms of production, resources, access to land—these difficulties have a different impact on each class. I will briefly examine four different economic classes and look at the meaning of class for a "typical" peasant family in each.[10]

AGRICULTURAL DAY LABORERS. Peasants who must work as agricultural day laborers depend entirely on selling their labor (or that of their families) to meet their money needs. This group is small, about 10 percent of the households. If a day laborer has any land, it produces neither enough basic family foodstuffs nor cash crops for sale. At least three forces have shaped their lives: the decreasing fertility of existing land, the lack of new forest lands to clear, and the large size of families. Some are recent migrants who arrived too late to claim fertile forest land; others are the children of settlers whose slash-and-burn agriculture left them with poor land to divide among their many offspring. The pressures of land scarcity are immediate and severe for the day laborer.

Working "for pay" takes three major forms. The day laborer can sell his labor for a daily wage of about $1.00 plus breakfast and the noonday meal. Work may be planting or clearing, repairing fences, digging latrines, or driving a mule team. He can work "per area," often weeding or clearing underbrush, and earn $1.00 to $1.50 a day plus breakfast and noonday meal depending on the deal he strikes. Coffee picking is the most profitable form of paid labor: paid by the quantity picked, a skilled coffee picker can earn $2.00 to $3.00 per day at the peak harvest seasons. A household's earnings can be increased by the labor of the wife, children (six and older), and sometimes the grandparents. Unfortunately, peak harvest times last for but a few weeks.

Some day laborers supplement their own meager produce by sharecropping the land of others. But such opportunities are rare: few peasants have extra land to let, and when they do, it is rarely very productive. Although the sharecropper must provide all the labor, and often the costs of seed, wire, and other supplies, the gross production and not the net profits are split. The arrangement is usually *a medias,* 50 percent for the owner and 50 percent for the sharecropper.

Most day laborers have neither the land to support cows or pigs nor the capital to buy them. More seriously, day laborers rarely can hold animals long enough to fatten them: with their continual money shortage, serious illnesses are always forcing quick sales for the cash needed to pay doctors and buy medicine.

We can understand better the everyday meaning of being a day laborer by looking at the basic subsistence needs and life chances of Ramón, a peasant who owns only the half-acre plot on which his family lives. Ramón's father, one of the original settlers in Jaida Arriba, had sold off all his land to meet medical expenses of a severe, prolonged illness. Ramón himself grows plantains and bananas on the small plot and tries to nurture a few young coffee trees. He has no animals, save a few chickens and a pig he is raising in co-ownership with a neighboring large holder. Ramón must buy all the food that comprises his family's poor diet. The children have little or no milk, and the baby's bottle is most often filled with sweetened tea made from the leaves of the bitter orange tree. There are often two or four days in the week when Ramón does not have enough money to buy rice and beans for the noonday meal, and the family must get by on boiled plantains, spaghetti, and broth. Their weekly consumption of spices such as onions and garlic (a quarter of a pound), cooking oil (a little over a pint), and tomato paste (eight ounces) is extremely small, and these items are considered luxuries. Meals lack greens and contain little protein: Ramón rarely brings home more than a pound of meat per week, and only on occasion does the family enjoy one or two eggs. Malnutrition has weakened his children's resistance to sickness; and lack of quick cash thrice has prevented him from rushing three of his children, sick with colerín, to a doctor in time to save their lives. He has tried to keep his twelve-year-old son in school, but learning seems a problem. Ramón reckons that his brain has not developed for lack of food. But further, Ramón often needs his son's labor and must take him away from school.

Ramón, like other day laborers, continually asks himself where he is going to get the money to feed his family the following day. With no harvest to hope for, no cash crop to sell, he continually searches for someone who will "pay him a day's work." His monthly expenditure for food averages $29.14 (see Table 3.3); yet there were five months (March, April, May, June, and July) when he was unable to earn even that much. During such hard times, Ramón sometimes is able to get credit on food from a local comerciante. But the amount is always small: the comerciante knows that Ramón's low and intermittent daily wages limit his ability to repay credit advanced.

In March, Ramón was unable to find work; and beyond food expenses, he needed $7.00 for medicine when his pregnant wife took ill. To get cash, he sold a pig he had been raising in co-ownership for $51.50; but his share was only $25.80. The other half was paid to the neighbor who had given him $7.00 of the $14.00 he originally had needed to buy the pig the year before. But even with this sale, he hardly had enough money to sustain his family in March. Another crisis came in May when his wife, who had to be taken to a Santiago hospital, suffered a miscarriage. Despite free medical care, Ramón had to pay for medicine, food, and transportation expenses, a total of about $16.00. He was able to get a neighbor to advance him $15.00 for clearing his pasture, which he completed in the following weeks. But while he was working to repay the advanced money, he was not actually earning the money he needed to feed his family.

Again in July, over half of the $27 he earned clearing ground went for medicine when his two youngest children had to see a doctor; the visits and the medicine cost him $14. They, like most children in Jaida Arriba, had parasites; but so severe was their case that they could barely eat and were growing dangerously anemic. In January, Ramón himself fell ill with severe pains in his groin and spent $16 on doctors and medicine; and in September, three injections for an infected foot cost him another $12.

TABLE 3.3
Monthly Cash Flow Chart #1[11]
RAMÓN (Day Laborer)
Size of Household: 7

Total Year's Cash Income	$488.80	Expenses Greater than Income (DEFICIT):	9 months
Total Year's Cash Expenses	479.88		
Total Year's Surplus	$ 8.92	Income Greater than Expenses (SURPLUS):	3 months

January

Income:
Weeding
Picking Coffee $29.00
Total 15.00
$44.00

Expenses:
Food $29.14
Medicine 16.00
Total $45.14

DEFICIT: $ 1.14

February

Income:
Picking Coffee $90.00
Total $90.00

Expenses:
Food $29.14
Clothing 10.00
Blankets 7.00
Shoes 7.00
Total $53.14

SURPLUS: $36.86

March

Income:
Selling a pig $25.80
Total $25.80

Expenses:
Food $29.14
Medicine 7.00
Total $36.14

DEFICIT: $10.34

April

Income:
Clearing ground $20.00
Total $20.00

Expenses:
Food $29.14
Total $29.14

May

Income:
Clearing ground $15.00
Total $15.00

Expenses:
Food $29.14
Doctor/Medicine 16.00
Total $45.14

June

Income:
Clearing ground $25.00
Total $25.00

Expenses:
Food $29.14
Total $29.14

July

DEFICIT: $ 9.14

Income:
Clearing Ground	$27.00
Total	$27.00

Expenses:
Food	$29.14
Medicine	14.00
Total	$43.14

DEFICIT: $16.14

August

DEFICIT: $30.14

Income:
Clearing Ground	$ 8.00
Weeding	22.00
Total	$30.00

Expenses:
Food	$29.14
Cooking Pot	3.00
Total	$32.14

DEFICIT: $ 2.14

September

DEFICIT: $ 4.14

Income:
Planting Coffee	$35.00
Total	$35.00

Expenses:
Food	$29.14
Medicine	12.00
Total	$41.14

DEFICIT: $ 6.14

October

Income:
Weeding	$40.00
Total	$40.00

Expenses:
Food	$29.14
Total	$29.14

SURPLUS: $10.86

November

Income:
Picking Coffee	$62.00
Clearing Ground	40.00
Total	$102.00

Expenses:
Food	$29.14
Clothing	4.00
Shoes	3.00
Machete	1.20
Total	$37.34

SURPLUS: $64.66

December

Income:
Weeding	$35.00
Total	$35.00

Expenses:
Food	$29.14
Clothing	15.00
Shoes	8.00
Christmas	7.00
Total	$59.14

DEFICIT: $24.14

SOURCE: Personal interviews.

Ramón's best earning months were September through January when he found such work as planting coffee and weeding more plentiful. During the coffee harvest, he, his wife, and son were able to earn $62 in November, $15 in January, and $90 in February. He then was able to buy some of the nonfood supplies he and his family needed: dress material for his wife and daughters, plastic shoes or sandals for each member of the family to wear to Sunday church, a new shirt and pair of pants for himself, two new blankets, and a machete.

Ramón's yearly cash income was about $9 more than his cash expenses. These albeit rough figures illustrate Ramón's inability to save money. Day laborers, like Ramón, live a marginal existence in which all they earn is spent instantly on pressing needs or repaying debts. Much more important than this yearly account, however, are the daily crises of money shortages that Ramón and other day laborers face: they are not struggling to "make it" until their harvest is in, but to survive until tomorrow when again they must look for work.

SMALL HOLDERS. The small holders, the largest group in Jaida Arriba, make up 55 percent of the households. A small holder has sufficient land to meet some of his family's food needs. Occasionally he even sells a small part of his crop. But he also must sell his labor to sustain his family. Unlike the day laborer, however, he is not totally dependent on working for pay. Few small holders have any of the fertile forest lands that their fathers had cleared ten or fifteen years ago; some do reclear land left fallow for five or more years. The reused land yields two or three harvests at most; but even the best of these harvests is considered poor. The small holder's most common cash crops are beans and peanuts. With these, he often plants subsistence crops such as plantains, sweet potatoes, sweet manioc, and bananas. Coffee trees around their houses (fertilized by the organic wastes from the kitchen) often provide enough for home use, but lack of suitable land prohibits production for the market. Some small holders may have a few pigs and a cow or two. But the constant need of money makes it hard to accumulate such livestock.

What little money a small holder earns comes largely from two sources: the seasonal work in coffee groves (weeding and harvesting) and his own meager cash crops. The difficulties faced by most small holders are typical of those of Colín and his family.

Colín has 116 tareas (about nineteen acres) of land, two cows, a calf, and some chickens. In 1946 he was ten when his family settled in Jaida Arriba on 50 tareas of land bought for $18. When Colín married in 1955, this land lay tired and fallow. Indeed his father had nothing to give him or his six brothers to start their own households. But his father-in-law gave him 10 tareas for a conuco, and over the years, he gave Colín another 24 tareas. Colín was able to buy 42 tareas more of used land for about $2.50 a tarea. He cleared and farmed another 30 tareas of state land in the early 1960s when the forestry law was relaxed after Trujillo's death. But he has not yet been able to afford the barbed wire to enclose the land (such enclosure would enable him to claim it, at least unofficially, and use it for pasture). Only a small part of Colín's land is cultivable: 76 tareas are so depleted they scarcely serve as pasture for his two cows and calf; 25 tareas lie fallow; and only 15 tareas are planted with subsistence crops for his wife and nine children.

Despite Colín's ability to produce more basic foodstuffs, his family hardly eats better than Ramóns because Colín's family is twice as large. But Colín's house is better built, with wood floors, a partitioned space where the older boys sleep, a wood-shingled roof that does not leak, and fairly solid wood plank construction.

Colín struggles to keep his second oldest son, aged eleven, and his daughter, ten, in school to finish the third grade, but they miss many days when he needs them in the fields. He manages to find the 80 cents a month for his oldest son, fourteen, to study fourth grade at night on the church-run radio school on Radio Santa María. But his children's life chances are severely limited: the little land he has is barely able to support his family now, let alone enough to provide them with any start in life. He has no money to send them outside Jaida Arriba for the eighth-grade education they need to enter a profession such as elementary school teacher.

Despite his much larger family size, Colín's monthly food expenses are not much more than Ramón's because his conuco produces many of the basic staples Ramón is forced to buy. Colín depends heavily for his cash needs on the pay he and his sons get for picking coffee, but unlike Ramón, he has minor sources of cash in addition to the sale of his labor. His wife, who has a small sewing machine, often earns a few pesos a month sewing clothes. In past years Colín has been able to sell small harvests of beans and peanuts; but this year he had another unexpected source of income. An unusually good harvest from coffee surrounding his house allowed him both to meet his household needs and sell enough to earn $42.19.

Colín hopes to be able to earn a little more cash when he can plant beans and peanuts on his other 25 tareas. But his continual need to work for hire to meet his family's basic needs has hindered such efforts. Part of the reason is seen in Table 3.4. Only by continually working picking coffee and weeding is he able to meet even the food needs of his family. Eight months of the year his expenses exceed his income. He also fears that if he did plant, the harvests would not yield enough to pay debts incurred (such as credit at the comercio) while he was working his own land instead of working for hire.

Urgent cash demands pose severe crises for Colín. When his wife gave birth in August, Colín paid over $30 in expenses (for medicine, the midwife, and extra foods such as milk, meat, malt beer, and juices bought to give strength to his wife). To meet these expenses and pay accumulating debts (medical

TABLE 3.4
Monthly Cash Flow Chart #2
COLIN (Small Holder)
Size of Household: 11

Total Year's Cash Income	$489.97	Expenses Greater than Income (DEFICIT):	8 months
Total Year's Cash Expenses	504.02		
		Income Greater than Expenses (SURPLUS):	4 months
Total Year's Deficit	$ 14.05		

January

Income:
Picking Coffee $40.00
Selling Coffee 15.50
Sewing 5.00
Total $60.50
Expenses:
Food $30.76
Hoe 2.00
Total $32.76
SURPLUS: $27.74

February

Income:
Picking Coffee $17.00
Clearing Ground 14.00
Sewing 4.00
Total $35.00
Expenses:
Food $30.76
Medicine $5/Travel $5 10.00
Radio $10/Cooking pot,
wash basin, mugs $7 17.00
Clothing 5.00
Total $62.76
DEFICIT: $27.76

March

Income:
Picking Coffee $22.00
Clearing Ground 12.00
Sewing 4.00
Total $38.00
Expenses:
Food $30.76
Machete 1.20
Total $31.96
SURPLUS: $ 6.04

April

Income:
Picking Coffee $27.00
Clearing Ground 5.00
Sewing 4.00
Total $36.00

May

Income:
Picking Coffee $15.00
Clearing Ground 11.00
Sewing 4.00
Total $30.00

June

Income:
Clearing Ground $17.00
Weeding 12.00
Total $29.00

Expenses:
Food $30.76
Clothing 8.35
Total $39.11

DEFICIT: $ 3.11

Expenses:
Food $30.76
Clothing 3.30
Total $34.06

DEFICIT: $ 4.06

Expenses:
Food $30.76
Medicine 9.00
Total $39.76

DEFICIT: $10.76

July

Income:
Selling Calf $45.00
Clearing Ground 12.00
Weeding 14.00
Total $71.00

Expenses:
Food $30.76
Bed 7.60
Clothing 8.50
Total $46.86

SURPLUS: $24.14

August

Income:
Selling pig $11.50
Weeding 35.00
Total $46.50

Expenses:
Food $30.76
Medicine (childbirth
 expenses including
 extra food for wife) 31.50
Total $62.26

DEFICIT: $15.76

September

Income:
Picking Coffee
 (advance payment) $ 5.00
Weeding 26.00
Total $31.00

Expenses:
Food $30.76
Medicine 4.50
Travel 3.00
Total $38.26

DEFICIT: $ 7.26

October

Income:
Selling Coffee $13.50
Picking Coffee-advance 13.50
Sinking Fence Posts 5.00
Total $32.00

Expenses:
Food $30.76
Travel 3.00
Total $33.76

DEFICIT: $ 1.76

November

Income:
Selling Coffee $ 7.59
Picking Coffee-advance 17.00
Weeding-advance payment 7.00
Sewing 3.78
Total $35.37

Expenses:
Food $30.76
Clothing 3.15
Medicine 6.50
Total $40.31

DEFICIT: $ 4.94

December

Income:
Selling Coffee $ 5.60
Picking Coffee 35.00
Sewing 5.00
Total $45.60

Expenses:
Food $30.76
Machete 1.40
Christmas 10.00
Total $42.16

SURPLUS: $ 3.44

SOURCE: Personal interviews.

expenses in June, a new bed and clothing in July), he was forced to sell a young pig and a calf which he had been painstakingly raising to build his stock. For cash needs in September (for medicine), October (a trip to the pueblo to declare his child), in November (medicine and a trip to a doctor), he obtained advances on coffee picking and weeding.

Colín's yearly cash income and expenses shows a deficit of $14.05. Although many approximations are used in the calculations, this figure clearly indicates his inability to generate savings and the immediate absorption of all earnings on basic needs. The daily problems imposed by land scarcity and the need to sell labor are seen even more dramatically by examining his situation month by month. In spite of his production of basic foodstuffs and meager cash earnings from coffee, he was almost continually in debt. He had to depend heavily on finding someone to buy his labor in order to meet these expenses and on a comerciante to advance food in the meantime.

MIDDLE HOLDERS. The middle holders constitute about 21 percent of the households in Jaida Arriba. Unlike the small holders, they have access to land suitable for either coffee production or grazing, and, in some rare cases, new forest lands for slash-and-burn cultivation. They can produce not only subsistence crops and the occasional cash harvest of beans or peanuts, but unlike the small holders, can meet most of their cash needs with coffee or, in a few cases, with cattle. They need not depend on the sale of their personal or family labor. Indeed, they sometimes even hire two or three men to help them in planting, weeding, and harvesting. Yet their position is not so secure that the need to work for hire is nonexistent. They continually walk the line between being independent, self-sustaining producers, and laborers forced to work for pay.

The small cash crop and subsistence production of the middle holders often enable them to eat slightly better than do the small holders. Chaguito's family of eleven, for example, is the same size as Colín's, and the children are about the same ages. Yet Chaguito was able to spend about $525 to feed his family and Colín only $326. It is rare that Chaguito's family does not have rice and beans every day for lunch; tomato paste, onions, garlic, cooking oil, clove, and cinnamon are all more plentiful at his house. With three cows, he has more milk. When there is no fresh milk, Chaguito can buy powdered milk in the general store so that his two youngest children can always have at least a pint a day. Occasionally there is even chocolate in the milk at breakfast.

Unlike small holders such as Colín, Chaguito easily can get credit for food or the cash he needs in times of crisis. His production of coffee guarantees him a means to repay any credit or cash advanced. He does not have to depend on selling his labor at $1 a day to repay a loan.

Chaguito's work load is made easier than Colín's because he has a mule to help him carry wood, crops, and supplies, all of which Colín must carry on his back. When Chaguito goes to El Río or to the pueblo, he can go on his mule; Colín must make the two-hour trip on foot. Chaguito is also more fortunate because his eleven-year-old son is not yet needed in the fields but can go to school regularly. Chaguito hopes to send a few of his children to live with relatives in the pueblo where they can continue their education beyond the third grade.

Although the middle holders have larger yearly cash earnings than the small holders and day laborers, their seasonal money needs are often greater. Since they rarely work for hire, they must have money to sustain their families during the preharvest times when they are working their land. Further, they must pay for extra help in weeding and harvesting coffee because family labor alone is inadequate. As can be seen in Table 3.5, Chaguito needed about $44 each month to feed his family. Yet for seven months he earned less than this; for three months he had no income. Here his access to credit from the comerciantes (before the cooperative was organized) was particularly important. October, following four particularly difficult months, would have been extremely hard on his family if they had not received $100 from his fifty-eight-year-old mother (now working as a part-time seamstress in New York) and his seventy-year-old father (who washes dishes there). Beyond his food expenses, Chaguito also had to meet production expenses that Ramón and Colín did not face.

In January, for instance, as the peak harvest season began, he had to pay $44 to laborers to pick about 5.5 quintales of coffee; he himself picked about 1.5. These seven quintales, however, were not ready for sale until February. The only income he had that month was from a quintal he himself had gathered in December. In January, with food expenses and pay for the hired help, he was short almost $58.

Chaguito grossed about $665 in coffee production (not including what he kept for household use). After paying his coffee-production expenses ($123), he still netted $542. Adding the $110 sent from his parents and the $16 from the little tobacco he grew, his year's net cash income, after production expenses of $668, was about $178 more than Colín was able to make. Yet because of the seasonal nature of the coffee harvest and high production costs, Chaguito faced seven months of money shortage. For Chaguito, however, unlike Ramón or Colín, his harvest gave him hope and a greater access to food credit and money advances.

LARGE HOLDERS. The large holders, about 14 percent of the households in Jaida Arriba, have access to land suitable for producing coffee, raising cattle, and sometimes for slash-and-burn cultivation. Unlike most other peasants, they produce enough cash crops or cattle to avoid selling their own labor, although they all work themselves. They are, in fact, most often buyers

TABLE 3.5
Monthly Cash Flow Chart #3
CHAGUITO (Middle Holder)
Size of Household: 12

Total Year's Cash Income	$791.00	Expenses Greater than Income (DEFICIT): 7 months
Total Year's Cash Expenses	730.39	
Total Year's Surplus	$ 60.61	Income Greater than Expenses (SURPLUS): 5 months

January

Income:
Selling coffee (1 fanega) $30.00
Total $30.00

Expenses:
Food $43.88
Paying coffee pickers   44.00
Total $87.88

DEFICIT: $57.88

February

Income:
Selling coffee (7 fanegas) $210.00
Total $210.00

Expenses:
Food $ 43.88
Paying coffee pickers   40.00
Clothing   16.00
Total $ 99.88

SURPLUS: $110.12

March

Income:
Selling coffee (6 fanegas) $180.00
Total $180.00

Expenses:
Food $ 43.88
Paying coffee pickers   16.00
Clothing   15.00
Total $ 74.88

SURPLUS: $105.12

April

Income:
Selling coffee (4 fanegas) $120.00
Total $120.00

Expenses:
Food $43.88
Paying coffee pickers   16.00
Clothing   12.05
Medicine   11.00
Total $82.93

May

Income:
Selling coffee (3 fanegas) $ 90.00
Total $ 90.00

Expenses:
Food $ 43.88
Cooking Pot   3.00
Total $ 46.88

June

Income:
Selling tobacco $ 16.00
Total $ 16.00

Expenses:
Food $ 43.88
Paying labor (clearing)   5.00
Paying *junta* food costs   7.00
Travel   2.70
Total $ 58.58

	July		August		September	
		SURPLUS: $37.07		SURPLUS: $43.12		DEFICIT: $42.58

July

Income:
No Income	$00.00
Total	$00.00

Expenses:
Food	$43.88
Total	$43.88

DEFICIT: $43.88

August

Income:
No Income	$00.00
Total	$00.00

Expenses:
Food	$43.88
Paying labor (burning and clearning)	1.50
Total	$45.38

DEFICIT; $45.38

September

Income:
No Income	$00.00
Total	$00.00

Expenses:
Food	$43.88
Paying labor (planting)	2.25
Travel	2.53
Total	$48.66

DEFICIT: $48.66

October

Income:
Selling Coffee	$ 5.00
Money sent from family in New York City	100.00
Total	$105.00

Expenses:
Food	$ 45.88
Cups and plates	1.80
Total	$ 47.68

SURPLUS: $ 57.32

November

Income:
Money sent from family in New York City	$10.00
Total	$10.00

Expenses:
Food	$43.88
Total	$43.88

DEFICIT: $33.88

December

Income:
Selling coffee (1 fanega)	$30.00
Total	$30.00

Expenses:
Food	$43.88
Christmas	8.00
Total	$51.88

DEFICIT: $21.88

SOURCE: Personal interviews.

of labor, especially at weeding and harvesting time. Most day laborers and small holders must depend upon the coffee production of these large holders.

The largest coffee producer in Jaida Arriba has 600 tareas (100 acres), only some of which have high coffee yields. In a good year, this land might produce up to 200 quintales of coffee. The next largest coffee producer has about 200 tareas (34 acres), which might yield 70 quintales in a year. Most of the large holders, however, produce somewhere between 25 and 60 quintales of coffee a year. A few also depend on cattle grazing, the six largest herds ranging from fifty to twenty-five head. As a result of their larger cash crop productions and some supplementary livestock, the large holders can sustain their families better than the middle holders.

Mamón has fifteen children. He spends almost $1,050 a year to feed his family, almost twice as much as Chaguito, and brings home more than five pounds of meat a week. His children all have been able to drink milk until they were four or five years old. Breakfasts of spaghetti and plantains often include milk mixed with chocolate or oats and occasionally dried cod. Rice and beans are staples at the noonday meal. Frequently, they can afford a can or two of sardines and a salad of beets, cabbage, eggs, and potatoes.

At fifty-two, Mamón has never had to work for hire. When Mamón was married, his father gave him fertile land to clear for his first conuco and money for production and family expenses until the first harvest. The more than 100 tareas Mamón now has in coffee, the 20 tareas in conucos and young coffee, the 60 tareas in pasture land, and the 10 tareas of forest land for future clearing all were given to him as forest land by his father.

Mamón's major source of cash income is coffee. His 41 quintales of coffee yielded about $1,230. This he supplemented with $205 earned from nine quintales of tobacco. With his greater cash crop production, he enjoys certain benefits denied to Chaguito. He can take his wife for an examination in Santiago each time she is pregnant. If a difficult childbirth is anticipated, he can afford to pay the medical costs in the pueblo. He and his wife have their own bedroom. In September, he could give his daughter a proper wedding and celebration—four roast pigs, rum, wine, cake from Santiago, a white dress, and a wedding crown. He owns three mules so he and his family can ride instead of walk and carry loads he might otherwise have to bear.

The life chances Mamón can give to his sons will be limited. His land, though adequate to support his family, will provide no more than a few acres for each child. Yet his cash crop income has given Mamón the possibility of educating at least some of his children. He has a son starting high school in the pueblo and another daughter finishing eighth grade in a convent school. He hopes that someday they will have a profession—perhaps as elementary school teachers—and be able to help him and his family.

Unlike the other peasants of Jaida Arriba, the kind of land pressure that Mamón and the other large holders face is less severe and immediate. Besides having sufficient land and incomes, they have possibilities for capital accumulation: reinvestment in production (buying more land, planting more coffee, buying more cows), investment in a small comercio, the lending of capital for interest, or the use of such capital to buy the products of others and resell them (as small-scale compradores) for higher prices. Despite larger yearly incomes, however, the seasonal money shortages of the large holders often are greater than those of the middle holders. In part, this is because of higher standards of living; in part because of higher production costs.

In July and August, for example, Mamón and his sons were able to weed about 30 tareas of coffee land (in addition to weeding their 20 tareas of conuco); but Mamón had to pay $135 for the weeding of the other 70 tareas. (See Table 3.6.) He had some cash from the previous harvest, but needed another $40 from the compradores. To get this, he "sold" two fanegas of coffee "before the harvest." In February, he harvested five fanegas of coffee, three with family labor and two with day laborers. Although he had to pay $16 to the pickers immediately, the coffee was not ready for sale until March. From March through July, despite a steady income from coffee and tobacco, he already owed much of this coffee to pay past debts and needed much of the remaining income for family expenses. Thus the money to pay for harvesting in March and April ($32) and some of the money in May had to be borrowed from the compradores. His daughter's wedding in September, a large expense, was financed by selling one of his cows for $90. In November he had to pay over $100 for his two children in school, but this was money that he had carefully laid aside during the harvest.

Despite his production of a cash crop, then, Mamón, like many large holders, still faces the pressures of a cash shortage. For seven months of the year his expenses were greater than his income. This particular year with expenses for the marriage, school, and medicine, Mamón actually ended up $150 short. Debts and cash shortages are thus as common to the large holders in Jaida Arriba as they are to other groups of peasants. Yet large holders like Mamón have relatively easy access to credit and cash advances because their next harvests will bring the money to pay.

CONCLUSION

Although the peasants in Jaida Arriba do not "see class" in terms of the four categories outlined above,[12] these analytic divisions show differences in how groups are related to the forms of production that will prove important in explaining why only certain classes can create power through cooperative organization. Further, these divisions highlight the different effects of pressures deriving from the forms of production and social system on the daily existence and life chances of different peasants. All of the peasants in Jaida Arriba face pressures from land scarcity and dwindling resources, but for the

TABLE 3.6.
Monthly Cash Flow Chart #4
MAMÓN (Large Holder)
Size of Household: 17

Total Year's Cash Income	$1530.00	Expenses Greater than Income (DEFICIT): 7 months
Total Year's Cash Expenses	1681.00	
		Income Greater than Expenses (SURPLUS): 5 months
Total Year's Deficit	$ 151.00	

January

Income:
Selling coffee (3 fanegas) $ 90.00
Total $ 90.00

Expenses:
Food $ 87.00
Clothing   15.00
Travel   3.00
Total $105.00

DEFICIT: $ 15.00

February

Income:
No income $ 00.00
Total $ 00.00

Expenses:
Food $ 87.00
Paying coffee pickers   16.00
Travel   5.00
Total $108.00

DEFICIT: $108.00

March

Income:
Selling coffee (5 fanegas) $150.00
Selling tobacco (1 quintal)   18.00
Total $168.00

Expenses:
Food $ 87.00
Paying coffee pickers   32.00
Clothing $10/Travel $2   12.00
Total $131.00

SURPLUS: $ 37.00

April

Income:
Selling coffee (7 fanegas) $210.00
Selling tobacco (2 quintales)   44.00
Total $254.00

Expenses:
Food $ 87.00
Paying coffee pickers   32.00
Medicine $10/Clothing
  $15/Travel $6   31.00
Total $150.00

May

Income:
Selling coffee
  (8 fanegas) $240.00
Total $240.00

Expenses:
Food $ 87.00
Paying coffee pickers   48.00
Clothing   15.00
Total $150.00

June

Income:
Selling coffee (10 fanegas) $300.00
Selling Tobacco (3 quintales)   80.00
Total $380.00

Expenses:
Food $ 87.00
Paying coffee pickers   20.00
Clothing $10/Travel $5   15.00
Total $122.00

July

Income:
Selling coffee (6 fanegas)	$180.00
Selling tobacco (2 quintales)	50.00
Total	$230.00

Expenses:
Food	$ 87.00
Travel	5.00
Total	$ 92.00

SURPLUS: $138.00

August

Income:
Selling tobacco (1 quintal)	$ 18.00
Total	$ 18.00

Expenses:
Food	$ 87.00
Paying labor (weeding)	135.00
Total	$222.00

DEFICIT: $204.00

September

Income:
Selling cow	$ 90.00
Total	$ 90.00

Expenses:
Food	$ 87.00
Buying bean seeds	4.00
Daughter's wedding	105.00
Total	$196.00

DEFICIT: $106.00

October

Income:
No income	$ 00.00
Total	$ 00.00

Expenses:
Food	$ 87.00
Medicine	25.00
Total	$112.00

DEFICIT: $112.00

November

Income:
No income	$ 00.00
Total	$ 00.00

Expenses:
Food	$ 87.00
School books $40/ School Clothing $50 (2 children)	90.00
Travel	10.00
Total	$187.00

DEFICIT: $187.00

December

Income:
Selling coffee (2 fanegas)	$ 60.00
Total	$ 60.00

Expenses:
Food	$ 87.00
Clothing	5.00
Travel	2.00
Christmas	12.00
Total	$106.00

DEFICIT: $ 46.00

SOURCE: Personal interviews.

small holders and day laborers, the pressure is severe and immediate, affecting their chances of feeding their families tomorrow. The continual money shortage also has a different impact on each class: those with greater cash crop production can command better access to existing sources of credit because they can produce the cash crops with which to repay loans. But there is an important commonality here, too. For seven or eight months of the year almost all of the peasants in Jaida Arriba need more money than they can earn to sustain their families and meet production expenses. It is this continual money shortage, and their lack of access to such low-interest sources of credit as banks, that creates the possibility of control by another group over the peasants of Jaida Arriba: the middlemen from whom they must obtain the cash and credit they desperately need.

CHAPTER 4

THE CONTROL OF THE MIDDLEMEN

The major comerciantes in Jaida Arriba (all of whom were major or small coffee compradores) exercised their economic control through the prices they charged for consumer goods and the prices they offered for coffee. Their power rested on their accumulated capital, their access to credit, and the peasants' urgent needs for food and cash which only they could supply.

CONTROL OVER CONSUMER GOODS

Before the Cooperativa de Consumo was organized in 1969, the peasants depended on local comercios for their basic staples (sugar, rice, salt, beans, cooking oil, tomato paste, spaghetti), common medicines (aspirin, boric acid, baking soda, vitamin tonics, penicillin, laxatives), implements (machetes, colines, nails, barbed wire), rum, and a variety of other items including baby bottles, pencils, notebooks, cups, and saucers. The comerciantes were able to provide these goods because they had both the capital needed at the outset to build and stock their stores ($400 to $600 would be needed to get started) and then continual access to credit at the big food warehouses in Santiago that advanced them most of the goods they sold to the peasants.

Some indication of the meaning of control over consumer goods is provided by a comparison of comerciantes' prices charged in the months before the cooperative was first organized and the prices then charged by the cooperative. (National market prices were relatively constant during this period.) In its first year, the cooperative's net earnings were about $1,000, yet the prices it offered (and often forced the other stores to offer) were lower on certain basic items (see Table 4.1).

There was little price competition among the comerciantes, and peasant credit needs made it difficult to take advantage of what competition existed. Their continual money shortage forced the peasants to buy from those who would extend them credit, and, often desperate to feed their families, they

TABLE 4.1
Comparison of Consumer Goods Prices Precooperative and Postcooperative

Items	Precooperative	Postcooperative	Price Differences	
			Absolute	Percent
Spaghetti	$.19/lb.	$.17/lb.	$.02/lb.	10
Rice	$.16/lb.	$.14/lb.	$.02/lb.	12
Sugar	$.08/lb.	$.075/lb.	$.005/lb.	6
Peanut Oil	$.80/bottle	$.60/bottle	$.20/bottle	25
Pacifier	$.10 each	$.05 each	$.05 each	50
Penicillin	$.25/injection	$.15/injection	$.10/injection	40

SOURCE: Interviews with comerciantes and peasants.

were in no position to go looking for the best prices. "When you're hungry, you're even willing to shell out a peso for a pound of sweet potatoes."

The credit prices were even higher than the cash prices. How much higher is difficult to estimate accurately because credit prices varied among comerciantes and purposely were kept somewhat vague. A former comerciante, however, specified price increases for credit purchases (see Table 4.2).

If these price differences are calculated as interest charged for credit, there is a great variation in the interest earned by the comerciantes according to the length of time credit was extended. If a comerciante charged a day laborer 21 cents a pound for spaghetti, and the day laborer had to pay his bill at the end of the week, the comerciante earned 10 percent interest that week (or an annual interest of 520 percent). If the same credit were extended to a large holder who paid back the loan in six months, the comerciante earned the equivalent of only 20 percent annual interest. The comerciante did, however, have to pay interest (12 percent to 24 percent annual rate) if his bill was not paid at the Santiago warehouse within a month. Further, he continually

TABLE 4.2
Difference between Credit and Cash Prices

Item	Cash Price (precooperative)	Credit Price (precooperative)	Price Differences	
			Absolute	Percent
Spaghetti	$.19/lb.	$.20–.21/lb.	$.01–.02/lb.	5–10
Rice	$.16/lb.	$.17–.18/lb.	$.01–.02/lb.	6–12
Sugar	$.08/lb.	$.09/lb.	$.01/lb.	13
Peanut Oil	$.80/bottle	$.85/bottle	$.05/bottle	6
Pacifier	$.10 each	$.12 each	$.02 each	20

SOURCE: A former comerciante.

risked losing the money he advanced as credit, particularly to the day laborers and small holders, if they were unable to pay. The risk was much less among the middle- and large-holding peasants, who guaranteed their loans with their coffee crop. Such preharvest obligations not only ensured credit but were the foundation of the major form of control exercised by the comerciantes: control over the price of peasant crops.

CONTROL OVER THE COFFEE CROP

The comerciantes in the region of Jaida Arriba all were compradores too. In buying the peasants' crops and reselling them in the campo or directly in the pueblo, they served as the middlemen between the peasants and the wider markets outside the community.[1] Their control over the price of peasant crops came in part from the difficulties the peasant had in marketing his goods directly. His small harvests and inability (for lack of capital) to store and accumulate produce made direct marketing uneconomical: his lack of contacts with buyers in the city and his suspicion and fear of such *gente del pueblo* posed further obstacles. But beyond these difficulties, few peasants even had the choice of marketing their crops, often having obligated them long before the harvest to a comerciante to obtain the cash or credit for family needs and production costs.

Such preharvest obligations took two forms. One was based on credit. "In debt" and "grateful" to the comerciante for advancing him credit, a peasant was obligated to sell his crops to him at whatever price was set. Although legally the peasant could pay his debt in cash and sell his crop to another, such "ingratitude" would be remembered if the peasant came back for credit. The other form of obligation was more severe: the peasant would "sell" his crops before the actual harvest. Such "selling" was a cash advance against his promise to sell a fixed quantity of his produce at a set price, likely far lower than the crop's market value at harvest time.

While such price control affected all peasant crops, coffee, the major cash crop of Jaida Arriba, provided the comerciantes with their greatest profits and the peasants with their greatest losses. In the coffee trade, the comerciante as comprador formed the link between the peasant coffee grower and the national and international coffee-marketing system. Cash and credit needed by the peasant was channeled into the campo through this middleman, and the obligations incurred by such advances forced the peasant to enter the coffee market via the middleman.

The compradores' profit possibilities were limited by the cost they paid for the money needed to make advances to the peasants (they could obtain interest-free advances for a month from large exporters or Santiago warehouses; longer-term loans cost 2 percent to 5 percent a month)[2] and by the prices paid them by the large exporters. The standard prices for coffee sold at harvest time in a campo near Jaida Arriba in 1971–72 (a campo as yet unaffected by any cooperative effort) are given in Table 2.5. These prices indicate that the gross profits of the major compradores ranged from $4 to $7 (in 1969–70 they were $14 to $18). But such figures actually underestimate gross profits. An example would prove useful. The prices in mid-February 1972 (the peak harvest time that year) indicate an apparent gross profit of $7. But the margin was even greater. The compradores bought coffee from the peasants by the fanega, a volume measure "more or less" a quintal (100 pounds). (The exact weight cannot be known until the comprador has given the coffee a final drying, removed the hull, and weighed the beans.) But because of the excellent growing conditions in Jaida Arriba, most fanegas of coffee weigh from 105 to 110 pounds. Buying by the fanega and selling by the quintal, the comprador thus made five to ten pounds extra on each quintal, or, at the prices above (he was getting 36 cents per pound) $1.80 to $3.60. The gross profit of the major comprador was thus $8.80 to $10.60 per quintal.

The costs to the comprador were about $1.50 per quintal for processing and transporting the coffee to the exporting houses.[3] His net profit was thus $7.30 to $9.10 (25 percent to 31 percent) per quintal. What did such middleman profits mean to the peasant coffee grower?

For Chaguito, a middle holder able to use his own labor for many production tasks, cash production costs were about $6 per fanega. His net profit on coffee sold for $29 per fanega was about $23. The $7.30 he would have lost selling his coffee through the comprador (before the cooperative) would have been about 33 percent. To lose $7.30 on each fanega of coffee would have meant a total loss to Chaguito of $153 on his 21-fanega harvest. With this amount, Chaguito could have weeded the eight tareas of coffee that he had neither the time nor the money to prepare ($20), could have added four more pounds of meat a week to the 1.75 pounds his family of eleven lived on ($48), could have given all of his children at least a glass of milk each day instead of having milk only for the youngest two ($67), and with the $18 left could have afforded two visits to a doctor in the pueblo (including medicine) or perhaps a childbirth in a hospital in the pueblo if such needs had arisen. Alternatively, this $153 would have been enough to educate two or three children in the pueblo for one year (if he could have found relatives or friends to take them in). Relative losses are even greater for coffee-growing peasants whose production costs are higher. Miguel, a large holder with an 85-tarea coffee grove producing about 30 fanegas, had production costs of $14 per fanega because his children were yet too young to help with the production. Had he sold through these middlemen, his net profit would have been only $15 on each fanega and the loss of $7.30 on each fanega relatively more serious for him (a loss of about 49 percent of his net profit).

To the losses incurred by the peasant by having to enter the marketing system through the middlemen, we can also add the losses of having to enter the international market through the exporting houses. In February 1972, an exporter sold the quintal of coffee bought from the comprador at $36 per quintal for $41.50 per quintal, a gross profit of $5.50 per quintal. With costs of about $4 per quintal to process the coffee and get it ready for embarkation, the exporter netted about $1.50 for each quintal of this coffee. But a few months later (March through May) the price of coffee received by the exporter was $42 per quintal, and the price paid to the comprador had dropped to $28–$31 per quintal (because of the surplus of coffee relative to quota). In this situation the exporter was netting from $7 to $10 per quintal.[4]

The most common way the peasant committed his coffee to the compradores was through the credit mechanism discussed above. But a much more severe form of price control was preharvest selling, which took two forms. One was selling a la flor. Although the term literally means "at the flowering" it referred to any coffee sold to a comerciante from the time of flowering until a few months before harvest time. Selling coffee a la flor was a way to meet urgent cash needs, even to the extent of selling the entire harvest a la flor. A la flor prices might vary a peso or two among compradores; but the peasant, in desperate need of cash, was in little position to bargain. A peasant with a February harvest who sold a la flor in September might lose $9 to $12 per fanega, or about one-third to two-fifths the value of his coffee (see Table 4.3). A peasant like Chaguito with production costs of $6 per fanega who sold his coffee a la flor at $20 netted only $14 per fanega. The comprador, selling this coffee at $36 per quintal would have netted $13.90 per quintal even if he paid 2 percent a month interest to borrow the $20 he used to buy the coffee.[5] Selling coffee a la flor at these prices, Chaguito thus would have lost to the comprador as much as he himself earned. In everyday terms the $27 thus lost would have been enough to pay the major part of a monthly food bill. The relative loss of such a la flor selling to his neighbor Miguel, with production expenses of $14 per fanega, would have been even more severe: for each fanega Miguel had to sell at $20, he would have earned only

TABLE 4.3
Price Differences for a la Flor Sale of Coffee

Form of Sale	Price	Absolute Difference	Percent of Income Lost
At harvest time (Feb.–March)	$29/fanega		31–41[6]
		$9–$12	
A la Flor (July–Sept.)	$17–$20/fanega		

SOURCE: Interviews with compradores and peasants.

$6—leaving the comprador earning almost two and a half times what Miguel himself was earning.

The second variant of preharvest selling usually occurred two to six weeks before harvest time when the coffee growers needed cash to pay their pickers or, in some cases, to meet other serious cash needs. In January, for example, Chaguito needed $44 to pay for the picking of 5.5 fanegas of coffee, which was not actually sold until February. He thus needed a one-month advance to pay the pickers. To get such cash, peasants again had to promise a part of their coffee to the comprador. The price might have been fixed at that time, or a fixed amount to be deducted from the going harvest price agreed upon. The loss to the peasant for such preharvest selling frequently ranged from $2 to $4, as the table for the 1971–72 season indicates. The absolute losses to the peasant as a result of such immediate preharvest selling were much less than the losses selling a la flor. But the amount of coffee obligated a few weeks before the harvest frequently exceeded the amount obligated a la flor. Moreover, the actual interest rate the peasant was paying on these advances was often greater than when he sold a la flor (see Table 4.4).

The above data are only rough estimates. Each comprador had slightly different terms; individual peasants often were treated slightly differently depending on the amount of their coffee, their business "savvy," their timidity, and their personal relations with the comprador. But the data do give a good idea of the magnitude of control over the prices of coffee exercised by the compradores in the region of Jaida Arriba before the cooperative was established.

If the basis for this middleman control was the peasant's need for cash or credit, why did the peasant not try to avoid this control by saving his money during the harvest season and using it to live on until the next harvest? For one thing, these peasants were hardly in the habit of saving cash, no local institutions (except "under the mattress") allowed or encouraged such cash savings. The little cash people did accumulate beyond the cost of living and production needs often was invested in cows or pigs or land. Thus, cash was not readily available when needed to buy food, pay for weeding, or meet medical expenses. Traditionally the way to get such capital was via the comerciantes. And once people began to buy on credit, or to sell coffee

TABLE 4.4
Price Differences for Preharvest Sale of Coffee (1971–72)

Form of Sale	Price	Absolute Difference	Percent of Income Lost
At harvest time	$29/fanega		
1 to 2 months preharvest	$25–$27/fanega	$2–$4	7–14

SOURCE: Interviews with compradores and peasants.

before the harvest, they found themselves in a cycle of continual debt to these middlemen. They were fortunate if the money they could earn was enough to repay the debts, let alone have anything left. And because so little money was left after debts were paid, most peasants soon were forced back upon the comerciantes because of new money shortages.

The peasant might have been able to break out of this debt cycle and avoid some of his dependency on the middleman if other sources of credit were available to him—but none were. Commercial banks considered peasants too great a risk. Limited and insufficient loans (at 8 percent a year) from the government-supported Banco Agrícola were available to only a few large holders. These constraints on sources of capital forced the peasants to turn to the middlemen.

THE MIDDLEMEN: WHO CONTROLLED WHAT IN JAIDA ARRIBA?

When Chaguito was growing up the only major comerciante in the region was Arturo. Born and reared in the pueblo, Arturo had come to El Río as a young man in the early 1920s. He started a small *pulpería* selling sugar, rice, salt, oil, and rum. With family and friends in the pueblo, he was able to get the credit to underwrite the rapid expansion of his small store, which soon became the largest comercio in the region. Chaguito's father and his father's friends, neighbors, and kin in El Río grew to depend on Arturo for their cash and credit needs between harvests. In return, they sold him the abundant harvests of plantains, sweet potatoes, corn, tobacco, and yuca.

When Chaguito and his generation married and settled in Jaida Arriba, they continued to buy from and sell to Arturo. Arturo helped them finance their first harvest and advanced them cash a la flor when their wives or children fell gravely ill and needed medical attention. In addition, Arturo wielded political clout because his economic position gave him the respect of the local, government-appointed, political officials (such as the *alcalde*) and the few rural police who patrolled the area. His influence was strengthened by his kinship and friendship connections with political officials in the pueblo, his "home town."[7] It was natural for the peasants to turn to Arturo when they needed help in interceding with political or military authorities.

Arturo's political advice exercised great sway in the campo, particularly after the fall of Trujillo when competition for votes became important at election times. He was thought wise to the ways of the world outside the campo and was respected as a *sabio* (one who knew). One of the original settlers in Jaida Arriba explained:

> Back then, during political campaigns, we didn't even know who the town's politicians were. The only person we knew was Arturo; he was the biggest politician here. He had a lot of influence. For example, when we went into his store he'd tell us: "Now, I hope you people use

your heads . . . I hope that you realize that the person that you should elect for president is so and so. He's a good man, not a selfish man, he's not after money for himself. He's a man I know well. I know him inside out." Most of the time the party he supported was the one that would win. He had the entire region in his pocket because everyone used to go to his store. And we were kind of blind—because when Trujillo was alive, we went through thirty years of dictatorship, and we never saw any other candidates.

The peasants respected his opinions in nonpolitical matters, too, turning to him for advice because "everyone sort of figured that Arturo was a really smart fellow—that he knew a lot more than they did. Arturo was the guy who knew most. And everyone was willing to ask him for all sorts of advice." People would ask him where to clear a conuco, or the price to pay for a piece of land, or how to settle a conflict with a neighbor whose animal had broken into a conuco and destroyed the crops.

Arturo's social position further reinforced his prestige. By marriage he was brother-in-law to three of the major coffee growers in Jaida Arriba and to two more of the large coffee growers in Jaida Arriba through his wife's sisters. Such kinship ties gave these peasants privileged access to Arturo's assistance for credit, advances, or help with the authorities. In turn, these peasants felt a special obligation to deal with him rather than with other comerciantes. Such ties of kinship were extended even further through fictive kinship: as godfather, he became the compadre of more than seventy peasants. Although formally a religious tie, such bonds of ritual coparenthood had other social meanings. Between compadres (parents and godparents) there were special relations of trust, confidence, and respect. One would not argue or haggle with the other or doubt his word or honesty.

Many peasants sought Arturo as a godfather not merely out of affection or friendship, but because they truly felt that this tie would give them special access to help (credit or money). As a godparent, Arturo would have a hard time turning them down. But Arturo, in turn, encouraged this practice because it obligated them to him: a peasant came under moral pressure to buy from and sell to Arturo. "There's a greater respect and a deeper trust among compadres. Some people used to think: 'My compadre Arturo knows more than I do.' That's where the trust came from. And afterward, people felt ashamed to turn away from him." Having such clients assured "good relations," but for the peasant such "good relations" might mean accepting wrongdoings or injustices without question or complaint. One peasant who thought himself overcharged for credit by his compadre did not want to argue the matter: "It's like this. He is my compadre and this is a very delicate thing. One doesn't want him to think that you're talking behind his back. I just can't go up to him and say: 'Compadre, you're wrong,' because if he disagrees with me, then what am I supposed to say? You can't say anything; you have to avoid bad feelings. We have to suffer but keep our mouths shut all the time."[8]

When the peasants began to plant coffee in Jaida Arriba in the mid- and late-1930s, they sold their beans to Arturo. By the mid-1940s he had established relations with a large exporter in Puerto Plata who gave him advances to buy as much coffee as he could. He then began to commission other smaller compradores to buy coffee for him in some of the more remote campos. One such small comprador was Paulo, a large-holding coffee grower in Jaida Arriba and an uncle of Arturo's wife. Paulo, however, also had some contacts in the pueblo and soon was able to make contracts and get advances directly from an exporting house. In the early 1950s, Paulo bought a general store in Jaida Arriba for his son Pedro. The store, which barely had eked out an existence for its previous owners, grew rapidly under Pedro. Through his father, Pedro gained access to credit in the Santiago warehouses and was able to advance credit in return for peasant crops. Using his father's contacts with exporting houses, he got advances with which to buy coffee. His growing economic power was strengthened by social ties: he was a cousin, nephew, or compadre to most of the large holders in Jaida Arriba. Further, many of the new settlers coming to Jaida Arriba had no previous relations with Arturo and dealt with Pedro from the day they arrived. Pedro could offer the peasants all the credit they needed, and Pedro's store brought salt, sugar, rice, and oil two hours closer to the kitchens of Jaida Arriba than Arturo's.

By the mid-1950s, Pedro's comercio had grown to rival that of Arturo's among the peasants of Jaida Arriba. Some of the older peasants with kinship, compadre, or close friendship ties to Arturo continued to buy at his comercio, but the dominant economic power in Jaida Arriba was Pedro.

In the late 1950s, Pedro expanded his economic power still further by opening a small coffee-processing factory in El Río. Arturo, facing a threat to both his competitive position and prestige, soon built an even larger factory. In the early 1960s, however, Pedro fell upon hard times. He incurred high losses gambling. Furthermore, he had borrowed too much and overextended credit to peasants who had trouble paying him when his own bills in Santiago came due. He decided to leave Jaida Arriba for New York City. He rented his factory to Francisco, the brother of a major comprador in a neighboring region with whom Pedro often had worked closely. He left the store in charge of his assistant, Manuel, agreeing to "split earnings" with him.[9]

With Pedro's departure, the dominance of a single comerciante in Jaida Arriba ended. Manuel not only lacked the prestige and social relations of Pedro and the political connections of Arturo, but initially was looked upon as a mere hired hand. The son of a small holder in El Río, Manuel had spent much of his youth as a hired laborer, sometimes weeding coffee groves in Jaida Arriba. The large holders considered him a poor peasant "in pretty bad straits." Manual had no close kinship relations in Jaida Arriba and no compadres. He eventually married the daughter of a small holder and, after he took over management of Pedro's comercio, some of the poorer peasants asked him to serve as a godparent at baptisms. His only compadres among the middle and large holders were those he asked to be godparents at the baptisms of his children.

Manuel's prestige suffered not only from his low economic position and lack of social relations, but from his tougher policy on credit and debts to offset the store's own debts to the Santiago warehouses. Manuel was more careful than Pedro in advancing money and judged peasants in terms of economic risks. Those who owed, though never forced to pay up, were reminded of their debts, and Manuel placed limits on their credit. Manuel was respected as a hard worker, and people were grateful to him for credit and advances. But following Pedro's liberal credit policy, and living in a culture where "those who have" are considered morally obligated to help "those in need," Manuel was not beloved: "Pedro was a *projimista* (good neighbor), he was always helping his fellow men. He never used to squeeze the poor men like that guy Manuel. Pedro was a person who cared. Manuel was just out for himself: he'd rather take from the poor, rather than give anything of his own away." To worsen matters, Manuel did not have the same friendly, kindly, paternalistic style that Pedro and Arturo shared.

> Pedro and Arturo were involved in more things, and people liked them more. They knew how to talk to a guy. They talked softly, gently, explaining themselves. If somebody happened to owe them money, they'd call him aside; they'd try to see how they could settle matters. They'd say: "Let's see if we can straighten this thing out." Sometimes they'd even offer a poor guy some sort of job, to help him pay off his debts. But Manuel was different. He was a lot harder.

Manuel not only lacked the social prestige of Pedro and Arturo but, perhaps most significantly, he lacked their economic power. He had neither the capital nor the access to credit that Pedro and Arturo had. His only income was half of the earnings of the comercio, and the store was in debt when he took it over. Most seriously, Manuel lacked direct access to advances from exporters with which to buy coffee. Without these connections, Manuel turned to Arturo for advances, working for him as a comprador on a commission basis. To buy coffee, Manuel thus had to depend on advances from Arturo and on some small loans obtained from individuals in Santiago (at 2 percent to 5 percent a month) for preharvest buying. Because of his limited access to cash advances and credit, and his lack of prestige and social relations, Manuel lost some of the large-holding coffee growers to Arturo and Francisco in El Río. (It was only in 1968, after the cooperative was organized, that Pedro, visiting from New York, took Manuel to an exporting house and vouched for his reliability, thus giving Manuel access to advances from exporters and a way to market coffee directly.)

Francisco, like Arturo and Manuel, had a large comercio that advanced credit and bought coffee. When Pedro rented him his coffee-processing factory, Francisco quickly became a major comprador with access to cash advances from the exporting houses. Although he never gained great influence in Jaida Arriba, his factory and the readily available cash advances he offered provided attractive alternatives to some coffee growers in Jaida Arriba. Nine peasants—all large holders—eventually left Manuel for the better price (50 cents to $1.50 per fanega) offered by Francisco. Indeed a few even began to bargain with Arturo and Francisco to see who could offer the best prices. Most important, what Francisco and Arturo could provide them that Manuel could not was the cash they needed before the harvest to meet family and production needs.

Manuel's power was further weakened by another event that occurred soon after Pedro's departure: the growth of a new comercio in Jaida Arriba. This new store was higher into the mountains (in an area of Jaida Arriba known as Las Barrancas), much closer to the homes of many coffee growers than was Manuel's store. Most significantly, its proprietor gave credit to the large holders without obligating them to pay with their crops. Thus, a coffee grower could still obtain credit for food (albeit more limited credit than that offered by Manuel) but free himself from having to pay with his coffee. The proprietor of this new comercio was Puro.

Puro had come with his family to Jaida Arriba in the mid-1950s. Buying a large tract of uncleared forest land, they had, with the help of neighbors, planted subsistence crops and coffee and soon had become large holders. His family was liked and respected in the community. Puro was considered intelligent, honest, and friendly. In the early 1960s he took over a tiny general store that had been started in Las Barrancas four years earlier but had been doing badly. Puro was quick to learn the ways of business. His simple, honest, and friendly manner gained him the confidence not only of the peasants but of such comerciantes as Arturo and, soon, the owners of warehouses in Santiago. He rapidly developed close ties of friendship with neighboring coffee growers and was asked by many to serve as godfather. Puro's store grew rapidly and by 1968 was doing about half the volume of Manuel's comercio. But he, like Manuel, was handicapped by lack of access to cash advances from exporting houses; both were small compradores dependent on major compradores. He first started working on a commission basis for Arturo, but after a few years began dealing with Isidro, a major comprador in a neighboring campo who not only could offer him greater cash advances than Arturo, but who had a warehouse in Santiago from which Puro could stock his store. Isidro was himself a powerful and influential figure in the neighboring campo: he had a large comercio, a coffee-hulling factory and warehouse, access to advances from the large exporting houses, and much political influence and prestige. But he had few direct economic dealings with the peasants in Jaida Arriba. Most of the coffee he bought there came through Puro.

In Jaida Arriba in late 1967 and early 1968 no one man totally dominated either the selling of basic foodstuffs or the buying of coffee. The almost unchallenged dominance of Arturo long since had given way to a sharing of economic power among a number of comerciantes. The comercio that did the largest volume of business was the one managed by Manuel. Of the approximately 150 small holders and day laborers in Jaida Arriba, about 100 bought their basic staples from Manuel and sold to him what few beans, plantains, sweet manioc, and sweet potatoes their tired conucos produced. From him they could get the credit they needed to tide them over for a week or two while they sought work with which to pay him back, or perhaps even for a month or two if their small harvests looked promising. Among the middle-holding coffee growers (see Table 4.5) about two-thirds bought from Manuel. But among the large-holding coffee growers only about one-third bought from Manuel. Puro's comercio picked up almost all the other middle- and large-holding coffee growers (as well as many of the day laborers who did not deal with Manuel). Only three large holders and one middle holder bought supplies from Arturo.[10]

TABLE 4.5
From Whom the Peasants Bought Their Consumer Goods and to Whom They Sold Their Coffee (Before the Cooperative Was Organized)

	The Middle Holders (Total: 27)					
	Manuel	Puro	Arturo	Francisco	Isidro	Other small comerciantes
Bought consumer goods from	18	7	1	0	0	1
Sold coffee to	17	7	1	0	1	1
	The Large Holders (Total: 26)					
	Manuel	Puro	Arturo	Francisco	Isidro	Other small comerciantes
Bought consumer goods from	9	11	3	0	0	3
Sold coffee to	7	4	5	9	1	0

SOURCE: Interviews with comerciantes and peasants.

As compradores of middle holders' coffee, Manuel and Puro exercised the same relative control they did over the sale of consumer goods. Manuel was still the dominant figure, buying coffee from about two-thirds of the middle holders. Most of the remaining middle holders sold to Puro. The role of credit in "capturing" the coffee of these middle holders is interesting to note here: seventeen of the eighteen middle-holding coffee growers who bought their staples from Manuel also sold him their coffee; all seven of the middle-holding coffee growers who bought from Puro sold him their coffee.

Manuel and Puro had to share their control over the large-holding coffee growers with Arturo and Francisco. Only a little more than one-fourth of the large holders sold their coffee to Manuel. Over half of the large holders brought their coffee to El Río to sell to Arturo and Francisco. Only four sold their coffee to Puro—his father and brothers. The control exercised over the large-holding coffee growers through the use of credit at the comercios was less than for the middle-holding coffee growers because of Puro's casualness about obligating his large-holding neighbors to sell to him: six of the eleven who bought from him sold their coffee to Arturo or Francisco and one to Isidro. For Manuel, however, credit was still an important mechanism for controlling the coffee of large holders: only two of the nine large holders who bought from him sold their coffee elsewhere.[11]

The lack of a monopoly of economic power in Jaida Arriba was an important factor in the later success of the cooperative's early organizing attempts. Furthermore, although Manuel was the major comerciante, he lacked the social status and prestige of Arturo, Francisco, and Puro. That at least some of the large holders felt free to leave the comercios that supplied them with credit and seek better coffee prices with Arturo or Francisco, was to prove important when the cooperative promised even better prices. An important obstacle to the cooperative was the fact that many of the large holders and almost all the middle and small holders felt obligated to sell their crops to the comercio that gave them credit.

Although there was no monopoly over economic power in Jaida Arriba, there was little competition among the comerciantes of any benefit to the peasants. Few peasants could look for better prices because, as continual debtors, they usually felt obligated to the comercio willing to advance them credit and were hesitant to bite the hand that fed them. The few exceptions occurred among some large-holding coffee growers who were able and willing to use the bargaining power their coffee production gave them (and the opportunities provided by Puro's more relaxed credit policy) to seek better prices. They could turn to Arturo or Francisco, major compradores who could offer them a better price than small compradores such as Manuel and Puro. The competition between Arturo and Francisco was, however, limited. They, together with the major compradores (such as Isidro) in neighboring campos, would fix the prices they would offer the peasants for their coffee.

CHAPTER 5

THE COOPERATIVE ORGANIZES

A PEASANT MEETING

On the last Sunday in November 1967, some thirty peasants gathered in the simple wood-frame chapel they had helped build four years before. They wore their Sunday clothes: dark wool trousers from the pueblo and neatly ironed store-bought shirts, some with a few careful stitches. They sat quietly, respectfully, in the roughhewn pews; their often sockless feet rested uncomfortably in their vinyl shoes. Their weathered but clean-shaven faces were turned attentively toward the speaker. Two women sat among these men. One had been in charge of the family, house, and coffee groves since her husband had left to try to find a temporary job in New York. Teresa, the young schoolmistress, was the other.

This day in church it was not El Padre[1] who spoke. He had made his monthly visit three weeks before. This Sunday, the speaker was a peasant like themselves, a neighbor, a brother, a compadre, a friend. He stood somewhat awkwardly, shifting his weight from one foot to the other, unaccustomed to speaking in front of a large group, uneasy standing there in the chapel. But he spoke clearly, his young eyes alive with an excitement that only occasionally burst through his slow, calm, reasoned tones. He was the one who had passed the word to gather in the chapel. Now he explained why. He told of the meeting that he, Teresa, and two others attended two days earlier in the neighboring campo of La Loma, where they and others had listened for many hours to two men from the pueblo, one an agronomist and the other a government agency official. They had asked these gente del pueblo many questions. The men had come to explain how a cooperative could be organized and the benefits it would bring. They had been brought to the campo by El Padre, the priest of the local parish. Now the peasant repeated what the men had said.

He related the story they had told of the formation of the first cooperative:

They told us that the first cooperative was founded in England with only twenty-seven men and one woman. Their bosses made them work for sixteen hours a day and they did not know how to free themselves from this slavery. They decided to save four cents each week so that they would be able to leave this slavery. After many weeks, they had a fund of $60 and with this they started a comercio. But they did not dare open the doors of the comercio, so much fear did they have of the big merchants. But the woman said: "You cannot be afraid. We must open the doors even if they throw stones at us." So they opened the doors. And today these people have millions!

He went on to explain how they, the peasants in Jaida Arriba, were exploited by the chain of merchants. They all sold their coffee to the comerciantes who then sold it to others who sold it to still others, each one making three or four pesos per quintal. And they, the peasants, could earn this money if they could unite in a cooperative and sell their crops together, directly. The men in La Loma had told of peasants who had once been paid $27 or $28 for their coffee but now received $40 and more.

Those in the chapel nodded their heads and murmured to one another. The speaker leaned over toward Teresa, and she spoke a few words to him. "The important thing we must do," he continued after a moment, "is to start saving money, just as the people who formed the first cooperative did. We've got to save the little money we have in order to make a fund. And with that fund, we won't have to go to the comerciantes and sell a la flor. And we can store our harvest and sell it all together at a better price." He stopped again and turned to talk to the teacher.

Some people began to speak now all at once, asking questions, declaring their agreement, repeating what they had heard at the meeting. The young speaker did his best to restore order, and each was given his turn to comment individually. Those few who now spoke did so hesitantly, nervously, embarrassed by their poor speech.

He did his best to respond to questions, elaborating with what he remembered from the La Loma meeting. He told them that the agronomist had spoken of getting loans and fertilizers through the cooperative once one was formed. He repeated the warnings these men had given: the comerciantes in other campos often had tried to destroy cooperatives. But he stressed over and over the strength they would have if they all united together.

At the end of the meeting, he explained how the agronomist had said a cooperative could be started. Each person who wanted to join would have to pledge some money, as much or as little as he could afford. The amount would be written down by their names in a notebook.

When the meeting broke up, twelve people came forward, and Teresa carefully recorded their names and first pledges. They totaled a little over $4. The first name on the list was that of the young speaker who had led the meeting: Puro. Within a few months, Puro was to sell his comercio, give up the buying and selling of coffee, and become an important leader of the cooperative in Jaida Arriba. How it was that this up-and-coming comerciante and the long-passive Catholic church came together to try to organize a peasant movement in Jaida Arriba is the subject of this chapter.

FROM THE "SPIRITUAL" TO THE "MATERIAL": THE CATHOLIC CHURCH TAKES SOCIAL ACTION

A bishop and a priest were the first ones to encourage the peasants of Jaida Arriba to form a cooperative and struggle collectively to change their situation. The notion that such collective struggle was one's Christian duty brought to the campo an interpretation of Catholicism drastically different from what the peasants were accustomed to. The church's promotion of such a cooperative effort reflected a basic change in diocesan policy.

MYSTERY AND *TEMOR*: RELIGION IN JAIDA ARRIBA. Religious rituals and symbols traditionally had very different meanings for the peasants and the priests, and this gap was sustained by the peasant's limited contact with institutional Catholicism. The first priest actually to visit Jaida Arriba did not come until 1961 and few peasants attended mass regularly: the three-hour mule or foot trip to El Río (where a priest came once a month to hold mass) was warranted only on special occasions (baptisms, marriages, deaths). Those who did go to mass understood little. The rituals seemed holy and sacred, but mysterious; the Latin a foreign tongue. Only the priests had Bibles, and it was said that reading one was dangerous because "it would make you crazy." A few peasants had had formal religious education in catechism classes when they had lived as young children in El Río. But learning by rote memorization, they understood little and remembered less. "Who could learn all this. It was impossible for kids—even for adults! And nobody ever explained anything. We just repeated from memory!" The children were left with little except a certain sense of awe, of mystery, and of *temor* (fear).
   Such fear was often inspired by the priests.

> The priests used to scare the hell out of us. They never made salvation look easy. We used to think it was much too difficult, because you had to stick to it, bit by bit, in order to be saved. People used to think that, if anything, they would be going to purgatory. The priests used to speak real harshly. They talked about God as someone who was really going to get at you. And we all tried to stick to those commandments, not out of love, but out of fear.

Such fear also was embodied in many rituals. On Holy Thursday, for instance, the adults solemnly maintained absolute silence and menaced the children with threats to do the same. During the nine days after death, the mourners stayed inside with doors and windows closed, while others came to say rosaries whose passages not only were difficult to read and understand, but which contained images of the flames of hell and desperate pleas for mercy.

Facing crises of illness and death, threatened by forces of drought or deluge, and worried about problems of hunger and debt, the peasants often turned to help from above. But few prayed directly to God: their brokers were the priests, the bishop, and, above all, the saints. "The priests themselves told us to pray to the saints—since this saint could speak to God in the proper way and could help us. . . . Of course, no one is going to say: 'I have a saint that gives me whatever I want.' No. One prays to his Saint, and asks a favor. And perhaps the miracle comes." The peasants would offer promises in return for help. They would ask for a sick child to be cured, a harvest to be successful, or a lost wallet to be found, and promise to pass a whole mass on their knees or to give an offering of $5.

The priests also urged the peasants to form prayer groups of thirty families. Each group was given a holy picture of the Sacred Heart of Jesus to pass from house to house throughout the month. At each house the family and neighbors would do a devotion. This was a series of passages, one set for each month, read from a small book that accompanied the image. During pauses between the readings, people would sing or recite ten Ave Marias. Once each month there would be a devotion for the entire community. Here talks were given by respected members of the prayer groups who could read and were thought "to know." Their presentations were often fire-and-brimstone sermons, posing against man's many sins the threat of hell and eternal damnation.

Unknown or ignored by the priests until the early 1950s, beliefs in the power of saints were important elements in the healing power attributed to local curanderos, many of whom sold medicines of herbs, roots, and leaves as well as ointments such as Vapo-Rub. But they often discovered what cures to apply by appealing—through mysterious ceremonies—to the advice of certain saints. Certain curers, the *brujos* (witches, sorcerers) were believed to be healers not merely of sickness but of problems caused by the evil eye or the spirit of a dead one. An "attack of screams," for instance, often was explained as the spirit of a dead person mounted on a living person. Someone who wanted to do evil to another could go to a brujo and have him put the spirit on someone else. In such cases, the brujos sometimes cured with such drastic means as beating the patient with a stout switch to drive out the spirit.

The extraordinary powers attributed to the saints beyond those sanctioned by the priests were only a part of the religious folk beliefs with which the peasants made sense of certain life crises within a world that often seemed shrouded in mystery and ruled by a fear-inspiring God. New powers given to religious objects held out possibilities of cures for unknown ailments. People often saved the holy water from the Saturday midnight Easter service. Guarding it in small bottles, many people would drink it to cure themselves of gas or menstrual pain. When women were afflicted with an "attack of screams," they would drink this water or throw it on their heads. Religious objects also were thought to have the power to protect one from the frequent threats of uncontrollable forces. Holy water, for example, might be thrown in the air to protect a house from gale winds. People often saved the palm branches, blessed by the priest on Palm Sunday, "to burn in times of thunder and windstorms to protect the house."[2]

Religion in Jaida Arriba before 1966 was thus a mixture of church and folk beliefs based on mystery and fear. No priest came to preach activism or collective struggle: if anything, the priests encouraged patient resignation or appeal to help from above. But such teachings changed drastically in 1966.

FROM *TEMOR* TO *AMOR*: THE DUTY TO STRUGGLE TOGETHER. In March 1966, Padre Roque Adames became bishop of the Diocese of Santiago. He brought to the bishopric an active concern for the peasantry, not merely for their spiritual well-being, but for their this-worldly, material sufferings. Born in a peasant village himself, he grew more sensitive to their plight through his studies and teaching of philosophy, which exposed him to the social doctrines not only of the church, but of social theorists critical of the effect that present society had on human dignity and possibility. "Our society permits only a few to develop themselves. The goods of production, of culture, reach the hands of only a small nucleus." His views were supported and influenced by papal encyclicals (Rerum Novarum, Quadregesino Anno, Mater et Megistra) and Vatican II. He rejected the capitalist, socialist, and communist models he studied ("because they all created a situation of slavery and dependency"), but the outlines of a new model were still unclear. He felt it should be one in which the elimination of the economic injustices and inequalities of capitalism would not cost the loss of dignity or human rights at the hands of a new set of rulers:

> What we are looking for is a way to help our population find its way to a political and social organization with a socialist-communitarian base—which respects the community dimension and which gives importance to respect and to the value of human dignity, the rights of the individual; which gives to everyone a genuine possibility of participating in the riches and in the poverty of the country, because this latter is a heritage of us all, and not only of a group.

The bishop's first goal was to create an *espíritu comunitario* (communal spirit); then to find ways in which this communal spirit could be put into practice so that men would not live at the expense of others. Rather they would believe that they fulfilled themselves by helping others fulfill themselves. But the bishop saw a major obstacle to the development of such an espíritu comunitario: the egoism that existed in society; the self-interest and its correlates of mistrust and suspicion.

He sought to overcome this obstacle through religion: its basis would be the principle of love of fellow man enunciated by Christ. But this meant some basic changes in religious beliefs of both priests and peasants. The emphasis shifted from prohibitions based on fear and punishment to proscriptions based on love and responsibility; it demanded expanding the spiritual relations of man to God to include an emphasis on the material relations of man to man. Inspired by Vatican II, the bishop sought to move religion outside the spheres of church and ritual and make it an active, lived part of everyday life. He urged a demystification of much of the ritual in the mass: Spanish completely replaced Latin; priests began to appear in street clothes, putting on their robes only before mass (and in full public view). He encouraged the priests to put aside many old customs (like the requirement of fasting and confession before communion) and to explain the meaning of those rituals retained. Devotions to images of saints were discouraged, though not prohibited; and the images themselves gradually were removed from the churches. The reorientation the bishop sought, however, demanded a fundamental resocialization. He saw a revamped catechism (aimed at adults as well as children) as his central instrument.

Instituting such a catechism necessitated first educating the educators. The bishop sent six priests and nuns to Colombia to be trained in the new social-oriented, humanistic catechism. In July 1966 the Instituto de Catequésis (Catechism Institute) was opened formally in the diocese.

In early 1967, El Padre, the parish priest, chose the first two lay people from Jaida Arriba (Teresa and a twenty-one-year-old youth) to take the week-long training program in the new catechism. They returned and immediately began to give classes. As others went to the institute to be trained as catechists, weekly groups for men, women, and children were set up in each district of Jaida Arriba. Each month two experienced catechists would go to a regional meeting given by a priest or a nun to learn that month's catechism lessons. Returning, they would explain the lessons to the other catechists in Jaida Arriba, who then would lead their small classes.

At first, many adults shied away from these classes, remembering the unpleasant hours of memorization as children. But as respected adults in the community became catechists and as classes moved from the chapel into their own kitchens, more and more people attended. The new catechism began to counter the fear and superstition that were so much a part of religion. For the common images of God as fearsome, mystical, and distant, the catechism substituted the notion of a more loving, human God with whom man could talk and communicate. It taught that God demands love from man; and this love is to be expressed, as Christ explained, by love of one's fellow man. It urged the peasants to discuss actively in class particular aspects of the "human condition" (envy, joy, passive conformity, lack of communication, possession) instead of the old rote memorization.

The importance of religion in everyday life and the espíritu comunitario which the catechism tried to teach in words began to take on a real, felt meaning through the meetings of neighbors, sitting around the kitchen fires, drinking coffee, joking, chatting, and breaking up the hard and often lonely everyday work routine. Important, too, was the *alegría* (joy) the catechists brought to their classes in the campo.

The catechists taught that such alegría was Christian, an expression of *amor* (love). It was the spirit that Christ himself wished to spread among his fellow man. Dancing, previously frowned upon or forbidden as sinful, especially for unmarried youth, was encouraged for all as a way to live the "joy of Christ." Perhaps most important in creating this joy were the new songs drawn everywhere from happy, lively traditional merengues to moving black spirituals. They became an integral part of catechism group meetings. Choruses were formed, and these new religious folk songs were incorporated into the mass. The communion procession might be accompanied by a song, for example, sung to the tune of "The Saints Go Marching In."

In addition to the catechism classes, another important part of the church's efforts were its Cursillos de Cristiandad (Christianity courses). These courses sought to take actual or potential community leaders and infuse them with a sense of Christian dedication: their mission here in this world to live as true Christians by setting high moral standards and by struggling for their fellow man, not merely for themselves. Intensive discussion and often dramatic presentations, accompanied individual meditation. Each participant was required to reflect upon his life up until then and to make certain vows about changes for the future. Small attendance, highly selective standards, the maintenance of secrecy about the content of a course, and special attendance certificates imbued an elitist spirit among the members. Small groups of these "graduates" were then set up in many communities, and each year a conference for them was held. Many left the course feeling transformed, inspired with a mystic sacredness, and anxious to put into practice the new Christianity they had learned.

The bishop saw the development of an espíritu comunitario as only a first step. Such changes in values had to be put into practice through collective action by communities. "The plan was first to create a consciousness: through the catechism the peasants are able to discover a sense of community. And then, when an organization is formed it will have a mystique, something that is very important. We wanted the cooperative to appear as a way through which they could live their Christianity authentically." To carry out his plan, the bishop needed the help of the parish priests. Such support for the new catechism and social action could not be commanded. The bishop, despite the formal hierarchical organization of the church, had little actual power over the priests below him. They had to be convinced.[3]

To gain support, the bishop began writing papers on the mission of the church among the peasants and circulating them to the parish priests. In his pastoral letter of June 1966, he wrote movingly of the "hardships and desperation" of the peasantry: "the large mass of peasants, which include 72% of the population, without land, without fertilizers, without technical preparation, lacking in health, moving about in an atmosphere that is unfavorable to the development of moral virtues, and overwhelmed, in a pathetic manner by the dramatic demographic explosion which fills their houses with children whom they can neither feed nor educate." He wrote of the "obligation of the believer" to put his efforts, and even his life, into struggling so that his "neighbor—the image of God on earth—can enjoy a life that is worthy of a human being, free from basic necessities, redeemed from the injustices of the unscrupulous. . . . The Christian, more than anyone else, and from time immemorial, shares the sorrow of those whom forture has mistreated, repudiates and condemns the iniquities of the evil, demands bread, shelter, clothing, education, health, and opportunity for all, thus establishing a firm and right balance among rights and their corresponding duties" (Adames 1966a:5–6, n.).

In late February 1967, the bishop organized a conference for parish priests and activist Jesuits. Papers and discussions focused on such topics as "The Priest and His Relation to the Solution of the Peasant Socio-Economic Problems." Fatalism and paternalism in the peasant culture were identified as the major obstacles to action; they were the forces that blocked the initiative of the pueblo and made the peasants totally apathetic toward change. The major problem thus was defined as cultural, not political: peasants lacked consciousness. They lacked an espíritu comunitario, they were unaware of being exploited, they did not see that only by uniting in collective action could they live their lives as true Christians and bring about a change in material situations. These religious leaders had some notions of what the collective forms of action would look like (agrarian leagues, cooperatives), but paid scant attention to the connection between concientización and successful action: they ignored the social structural obstacles to the creation of power.[4]

Among the few parish priests who initially were inspired to take action was El Padre. He urged the bishop to talk to the parishioners, and when the bishop came in November 1967, Jaida Arriba was one of the campos he visited. The chapel was packed and overflowing; this was the first time a bishop had ever visited the community. The bishop encouraged the peasants to continue attending the new catechism classes to learn to live as true Christians; Christianity meant more than masses and confession: they had to live like Christians each day of their lives. They could do this only by organizing together in cooperatives and struggling to help the whole community improve its lot. He reminded them of the great benefits of working together in their traditional exchange labor teams (*juntas*) and stressed that in a cooperative they could help each other even more: there would be better prices for their crops, money for their children's future, and a fund of capital to provide money in times of need.

One peasant who remembered his words vividly was Puro: "The bishop told us that a cooperative was the only way to do anything for the peasants." Later that afternoon, Puro went to talk with the bishop and El Padre. He told them that he himself had been thinking for many months about how important a cooperative could be in Jaida Arriba, and he expressed interest in doing something. The bishop told him that he and El Padre were going to try to find somebody who could help them organize a cooperative. A meeting would be called, and he would be notified.

How Puro came to step forward after hearing the bishop talk, and how he came to take upon himself the responsibility for the initial organization of the cooperative in Jaida Arriba, may in part be understood in terms of the effect of the church's new orientation upon him, but it must also be understood in terms of Puro's character and personality. A brief look at his life as he sees it may give us at least a glimpse into the personal history of a peasant who acted to do something about the social world he lived in when an institution, the church, provided the possibility.

A PEASANT LEADER

As we grew to be friends, I learned much about Puro. I discovered in Puro certain qualities rare among most in Jaida Arriba. He possessed a thirst for knowledge that led him to teach himself to read and write, an inquisitiveness that was not crushed by parental demands for strict obedience nor drained by rote work in school or catechism. Puro also believed that human action and struggle mattered. He believed he could change himself and also that world which most of those around him regarded as immutable. A touch of invention resided in Puro: what others saw as impossible seemed only difficult for him. But rarest of all was Puro's willingness to sacrifice for others. Other peasants with Puro's drive and entrepreneurial abilities had become successes in the campo. Other comerciantes had helped organize "cooperatives" which they then used for their own private interests. Puro, however, gave up his fast-growing comercio and fell back on his coffee grove and conuco to dedicate himself to the cooperative. His dedication was hardly apostolic or saintly, but human. He was keenly aware of the costs to himself, his wife, and children. Torn between their well-being and the good of the community, he suffered. I cannot "explain" Puro, but some understanding of the man is captured by what he told me of himself.[5]

EARLY LIFE AND EDUCATION. Puro was born in a campo near Santiago in 1938, the first son of a large holder who grew tobacco and subsistence crops. When he was eight, the area was hit by a severe drought that ruined his father's crops. The family moved to the rainy, wooded slopes of the distant mountains. Puro and his father worked together to clear the virgin forest and to plant beans, plantains, and tobacco. As a boy he often was sent on mule with crops to sell in El Río, four hours away along treacherous mountain paths and across raging mountain streams. To earn a few pennies for himself, he would plant crops along the unplanted edges of the family conucos while the others rested from work at the noonday meal.

By the time he reached his adolescence, Puro became acutely conscious of his illiteracy. "I was kind of desperate to learn. I was fourteen years old and I still couldn't even read a little piece of paper. If someone would send me to the pulpería with a piece of paper, I couldn't read it to find out what I was supposed to buy. I was ashamed of myself." Puro decided to teach himself. His self-education moved along so quickly that when Trujillo set up a literacy school in his area Puro found that he knew more than those who had been appointed as teachers. Puro wanted to continue his education formally, but he ran up against his father's opposition. His father had decided that his brother Manolito was the family scholar. He told Puro to farm the hillsides instead. This was poor advice, as Puro must have known: "After I had begun to study I realized that studying is something which teaches you how to think, how to do something. And without studies you can't solve any problem, your mind is kind of closed. When you study, there are a lot of exercises that help you to come up with different types of solutions which don't have any practical use—they only help you to train your mind so that in the future you can tackle real problems. Your schooling has to be so good that your mind learns how to work hard so that you can come up with new ideas, know how to make a decision, get rid of the mental blocks that you have." Although Puro never received any formal education, he continued to teach himself, enlisting the aid of a young schoolteacher with whom he would work at nights or after lunch.

BECOMING INDEPENDENT. At the time that Puro began to court his wife, his father preferred that Puro continue to live and work with him. When Puro pointed out that he and his future wife would have difficulty confiding in each other if they stayed within the father's household, Puro's father said he understood and he would give him land. But he refused to give him money to get started. Although Puro fiercely wanted to become his own man, he just as fiercely resented his father's refusal to give him money. "Back then, parents were like dictators. I really felt bitter about that." Puro secured a loan from a friend and cleared his land, although his father thought that he had cleared too much land and would end up losing money. Puro paid off his debt in five months at 24 percent interest, and after acquiring some expertise in the intricacies of the Santiago tobacco market, he managed to clear $600 profit by the year's end. "I cleared another conuco—more beans and 50 quintales more tobacco! I was a real farmer! I knew how to work: if I had to weed, I weeded; when planting time came, I planted on time. I got married with my own funds." But, he needed more of his father's land, and the fact was that the land had to be split up between Puro and his brothers. Puro's share could not support his family. He bought a store from the man who had given him his first loan. Although the store's profits were small, Puro only closed it when he became interested in the cooperative. Still, Puro's proprietorship of this store provided him with a sturdy knowledge of the commercial world in Santiago.

RELIGIOUS TRANSFORMATION. When Puro was a young boy in the back mountain country, there was no church, only the Holy Hour, a devotion held once a month in a local house. "I can remember that there used to be some people who would speak very harshly in their comments. They spoke more about damnation than about the salvation of man—sort of trying to prove that if people didn't do what they said, they'd go to hell. For me, religion at that time was filled with temor. I thought that a human being had to subject himself to many laws, had to deprive himself of many things which were forbidden by creation. But matters of serving the rest, of struggling for the problems of the community, nobody spoke about those things."

As well as the Holy Hour, the holy picture of the Sacred Heart of Jesus played an important part in the religion of his youth. "At that time, when the Sacred Heart would come to your house, it was something very big. There was a lot of respect. I thought that it was as if God himself were in my house. But at the same time, the notion of acting as a Christian, the notion of charity, those things were kind of forgotten. And what's the good of getting down on your knees in front of a picture, if you don't lead a Christian life, if you don't help your neighbors? Well, after the Cursillo de Cristiandad, I was able to understand that the picture is nothing but an image, a reminder; but God still demands something from us. And we have to fulfill the word that he sends us: to love. Love God. Love your neighbor as yourself."

Puro began to realize that he was looking at religion much differently than those around him, particularly when it came to human capacity for causing change. "In times past people used to say: '*Si Dios quiere*' (If God wills it). But for God to help man, man also has to make an effort. Because God always wills. When a man works, it's just like sending a message to God that he's asking for something. That man who works, always receives.

"They used to say: 'we have to be resigned.' We can't be resigned. Because God's always waiting for man to make some kind of effort, so he can help him out.

"There used to be a habit among the older folks here. They had such a deep faith that it was as though everything came from heaven, that God would perform miracles without them making any effort. That came from their very poverty. People used to say that 'the person who was destined to be poor, will always be poor. And the person who was destined to get money, God will see that he gets money easily.'

"We even went so far as to believe that God loved some but not others. It's this bad habit that has given leeway to exploitation by more intelligent individuals who use their heads to save money and exploit others.

"The only kind of an instruction we used to get came from the priests. They'd tell us that we had to be resigned to God's will. And since they really didn't have any dialogue with us, the priests didn't learn about our problems and our suffering. They said mass and went back to the rectory, and nobody dared talk to them. As far as I am concerned, that was one of the reasons why we were slaves to people who were sharper than us."

From the marriage of his everyday concerns and his evolving view of the possibilities for love and freedom within religion, Puro came to interpret his experiences in a new way.

"At that time, we didn't think that those smarter people were exploiters; we thought that they were our intimate friends. The comerciante was a friend because he gave us stuff on credit. But after we opened our eyes, we realized what he was: we realized how the intelligent man went about things, and how he didn't care about anyone else. We realized that the man who was resigned ended up exploited. We used to be blind before: because we didn't know how we were being exploited. God turned over the world to man, so that man would dominate the world, not for the world to dominate man. And those of us who were sitting on the side, we were foolish and let other people grab all that right for themselves.

"I began to change my own sense of resignation around 1964. I was doing business, and I had contact with people who knew more than I did. And I learned how they were tricking us.

"But there are still a lot of people here who haven't changed, as far as knowing what the rights of man are—they're still living the same way we used to live before 1966. The reason is that many of those individuals have always lived a very routine life; they may do a day's work, but even on the days they work they don't know how to take advantage. They gamble away the sweat of their brow in the lottery. And also, there are still men who believe that the sacrifice a man makes to live disunited is better than the sacrifice he makes to live united. They're still thinking in terms of the past, in the way their fathers used to live. And they think they're going to live that way too. A person who doesn't try to read books doesn't learn. I myself didn't know anything. But after reading books, I realized how it is that we should live. We still have quite a way to go before we'll see the day that our people free themselves from this ignorance, this slavery.

"As long as a man just works in the day so he can have something to eat at night, he's completely trapped. What's sad is when you see that a man like that really has no aspirations to get out of such a life. He still seems to be resigned, waiting for someone else to solve his problems for him, because he can't do it alone.

"That's why this country is such a long way from being developed, as long as most people still think that way. Because the intelligent men who have all the economic power in their hands, and the social power too, are still trying to keep us down, making it hard for the poor man to free himself. They've managed to make money on us, and they can use that money to cut off our own freedom, the freedom for the poor man to get out of his slavery. Now that they've put together a big bank account from the poor people, they've gotten rich on the poor man. With those savings of theirs, they can wage war against the impoverished masses, putting up all kinds of obstacles in the way of progress.

"The man from the campo doesn't have any way to study, whereas the rich man continues educating himself. That's why the generations of the poor are getting more ignorant all the time. For the poor people in the campo, there's no such thing as school. But for the rich, there are universities. And that's why it's hard to see how the poor man could ever be independent. For us to reach that goal, we'd have to win the right to get educated so that men who are now ignorant can one day break that chain, which has got us all bound, hand and foot."

The turning point for Puro came with the Cursillo de Cristiandad. In this course Puro seems to have integrated his own concerns with the lessons he drew from religion. "The Cursillo de Cristiandad was in October of 1966. That's what inspired me to start the cooperative. Since we were blind, it was hard for us to make any progress. In that cursillo I came to understand who Christ was, and how Christ demands love from a man. I was able to meditate a little on how that love consists of a struggle for the common good of man, without selfishness. And since I was working all by myself in my business, I thought that there were many people around me who were blind. I thought that I could help them out a lot with the knowledge that I had. Since I already knew how to break out of the slavery of the intermediaries to be able to control our own products and since I wasn't doing anything about it, I thought that that was a sin on my part. So I stepped forward and began to fight.

"In the Cursillo de Cristiandad, I felt such a tremendous change in my ideas that I myself was surprised. The message that's given, the words that are spoken, they're things you've already heard. But maybe it was the way they explained what the life of a united Christian is. And they demand of each person an answer: how he has lived his life up to now, and what he should do to change it. Then there was a private meditation, calm, without one word being spoken, so we could analyze what we had done with our lives and what we should do in the future and how. And at that moment I began meditating about the life that I had lived. I realized that I myself hadn't done anything. And I used to think that it was only by having a lot of money that you would have the power to do something for others. But then I realized that it was foolishness. What's important is the desire to do something, because, even without money, a person who wants to can do a lot to help others.

"When each and every man is involved in the struggle—as though it were one of the commandments—then we can move ahead. And even though the big guys have ways of trying to crush the movement—even if they tried to dominate it—they wouldn't be able to, if we constituted the majority of the citizens. Even the government would respect us. If the poor people were all united, even the government would be afraid. But it's not afraid because it sees the masses are ignorant and not united."

BECOMING A PEASANT LEADER. Puro had discussed forming a cooperative with some friends, one of whom was familiar with a cooperative in San Juan de la Sierra. "Before Monseñor visited us here about 1966, Pucho and I had already talked about starting a cooperative here. We spoke about it in my store. Juanito and Rodolfo were also there. Juanito knew a little bit about cooperatives because he was in the one they started in town, and he was one of the very few that had benefited from this cooperative." Although this cooperative was still functioning in San Juan, it had collapsed in the surrounding countryside and had left many peasants suspicious. But Puro and his friends thought that a wholly peasant cooperative, right in Jaida Arriba, could succeed where the other had failed.

"The first idea that we had here was to save some money with the intention of first starting a consumer cooperative. I already knew a little bit about business. I realized that in a place where there were two or three stores, instead of buying from them, if there were one of our own, it would benefit the entire community. There wouldn't be any selfishness. It wouldn't be one person that's earning money, but rather, the whole community would be earning. I was also always thinking about the idea of selling our crops together—tobacco, corn, beans, coffee. I realized that it was a chain, and that every *negociante* (dealer, businessman) ended up with some profit in his pocket. And that's why the producer ended up selling cheaply. But if we would all get together, we could sell for a better price—not from hand to hand but directly to the consumer."

There were some difficulties, however, in starting the cooperative. "There just wasn't that interest in having a dialogue, in speaking. It was the sort of thing that made you kind of discouraged. And since we weren't too clear about the idea, we didn't want to go out on a limb. At that time I was always talking about the problems, but I still hadn't made up my mind to face them head-on. I was too afraid. I knew that I was completely ignorant about the movement and I was afraid I'd fail. And since I was a businessman, I always figured that others were going to say that I was gathering that money to use it for myself. And I looked at the community and saw that it was a bit individualistic, each to his own. But since Monseñor had spoken to us about the importance of having a cooperative for all of us, and since he spoke to the entire community, I felt somewhat more confident about joining. Since he was the one that had brought up the idea, I could go right away and speak to Monseñor and ask him: 'how could we begin that?' And he told me: 'Don't worry, I'm going to send you a *promotor* (promoter, organizer).' "

Puro suffered from a lack of confidence as well. "I knew that I was getting involved in something that I didn't understand too well. I had the right kind of organizational spirit, but I still hadn't had any experience at that time." And although Puro decided to go ahead with the cooperative, he discovered that there were tremendous personal costs to be paid. "If a trip had to be made to Santiago or to the capital, I was the one that had to go. And for the most part, if I didn't take the lead, it wasn't very likely that the others would do anything. And I used to leave my family alone, without anyone to cut wood for them! When we formed the headquarters in El Río, I was hardly ever home. And I had to break my neck working, till late at night, working with the books, keeping records so as not to lose money. And I thought about my children back home, thinking how they would have to go without the affection of their father. But I know I had no way out; there was no excuse for me not going to such and such a meeting. Not me. I was the one that always had to keep things moving."

This realization caused him to notice certain crucial differences between himself and others in the cooperative. "Most people are like Thomas: 'They have to see to believe.' But they don't have enough faith to throw themselves into working for the good of others. You still see a lot of that individualism, that self-interest: 'If I don't see anything in it for me, I can't have anything to do with it.' What a sad world! All I ask from God is that he give me the strength to keep going. You struggle so much—and you see that others are still treating this as though it were a business. I want to see one of those doubters get transformed so that he can take my place. Because I don't want to be in this position. I'm sacrificing my own future and the lives of my children. All the needs that a human being has—all the obligations which a father has toward his children—teaching them the human qualities that they need to be a worthy person; a person who would be at the service of others; a person who knows how to resolve his problems for himself. I see my children there, and it makes me sad. I get home and they're sleeping. They need to speak with me now. You feel like a prisoner in that cooperative. You don't feel free. If I'm in the cooperative today, it's because I don't want to see the thing fail. But I know that in the long run, I'm doing harm to myself. I want to take my children to Santiago, teach them how to take care of themselves, wake them up. But I also feel a responsibility for the other people here, this feeling that I must try to help the community."

But Puro's painful awareness of personal cost and of his own dedication came well after the cooperative was established. The actual genesis of the cooperative came when Puro's life intersected with the new orientation of the church and the person of the Monseñor. As the Monseñor had promised, a promotor was sent.

"After Monseñor's visit, we went to La Loma, to listen to a promotor he had sent. When we got to Jaida Arriba, everyone was waiting: 'What did they say in the meeting?' That was on Saturday. On Sunday, we invited everybody that was interested to hear what we had to say, and to sit around and talk for a while. The meeting was at the chapel. We hardly knew anything at that time, but we started off tentatively. Teresa—she was a young schoolteacher with a lot of enthusiasm—she was very smart and she asked a lot of questions in La Loma, and the promoters were able to explain a little bit to us. They told us that we had to get together and begin saving, saving, little by little, it didn't matter how much. So, twelve of us decided to begin saving."

THE COOPERATIVE ORGANIZES

After the first meeting in the chapel, Puro organized weekly meetings. This cooperative caused a great stir in Jaida Arriba. Around the hearths at night, families and neighbors voiced great skepticism: "Yes, perhaps one could save a little. And it would be good to borrow money so easily and cheaply to buy a mule or take a child to a doctor, and not have to sell coffee a la flor. But look at the cooperative that those people from the city once tried to start here. Back then, everybody lost their money. We're stupid people. What do we know about those things? No, no. You shouldn't get mixed up with something like that. Wait and see what happens."

Those who came into Manuel's comercio were given no cause to think differently. He did not openly attack the cooperative, but he encouraged and reinforced their many doubts. But in Puro's store, people heard a different story. Quietly, convincingly, without pressure, he would argue the case for the cooperative: the fund they could create, the help they could give each other, their Christian responsibility, the defense of their products before the harvest.

At the weekly meetings, Puro repeated his explanations. He encouraged questions and discussion, trying to calm the fears and remove the doubts of those who came. Thirty or forty might gather at the meetings; but the group of those who actually committed their money grew slowly. After six weeks there were still less than twenty.

While Puro spoke and organized in Jaida Arriba, El Padre and the bishop were active. To help organize cooperatives in the region, they recruited Fidel.

A young Catholic, formerly active in opposition politics, he understood the peasants and loved the campo as few city folk did. The bishop and El Padre received promises of support from two cooperative agencies. One was Idecoop, the Instituto de Desarrollo y Crédito Cooperativo (Institute of Cooperative Development and Credit), a government agency initially encouraged by the Alliance for Progress and largely supported by funds from the United States Agency for International Development (AID). The other was Fenacoop, the Federación Nacional de Cooperativas Agropecuarias (National Federation of Agropecuarion Cooperatives). More a centralized organization than a true federation, Fenacoop was in the process of organizing and running a few cooperatives, maintaining centralized control of loans, marketing, and part of the capital of the "member" cooperatives.[6] One of the agronomists brought by El Padre to the original meeting in La Loma worked for Idecoop. Soon after, both Idecoop and Fenacoop agreed to send organizers for a second, larger meeting.

About one hundred people came from all over the surrounding mountains, but the largest group (about fifteen) came from Jaida Arriba. Present, too, were Arturo, Francisco, and Isidor. It was the first public confrontation between the cooperative and the compradores.

The meeting was held in the old wooden church set back on a knoll just above Arturo's comercio, warehouse, and coffee-processing factory. It started calmly. Fidel explained the purpose of the meeting. He and the others had been asked to come by El Padre and the bishop. It was time the peasants stopped being passive and broke the "bad habit in us of staying still, with our arms folded"; it was their Christian duty to love their neighbors by organizing and struggling with them to help one another help themselves. Clearly this was a man of the pueblo who spoke to the peasants. He wore leather shoes and trousers that did not bag, and his pronunciation was clear. But he spoke to them simply, plainly. What he said made sense. And some there knew him to be "of good stock," one who always had dealt fairly with the people of the campo.

Fidel introduced the promotores from Idecoop and Fenacoop. But such acronyms meant little to those sitting or standing in their ill-fitting Sunday best. The peasants saw men from another world, *la Capital,* who worked for the president and were agronomists. Awe, respect, deference, and hopeful anticipation mingled with suspicion and mistrust in the peasants' eyes that saw the ten-gallon hats, the fancy pleated shirts, the polished leather cowboy boots, the shiny belt buckles, and the gleaming watches.

The promotores spoke of the great advantages a cooperative could bring: money when they needed it without having to sell their crops prematurely, better prices for their coffee. Fenacoop, they said, would buy their coffee directly, and they could earn $5 or $10 more on each quintal they sold. "Even now while you are selling your coffee at $30 and $31, Fenacoop is buying from other cooperatives at $40 a quintal."

Such prices seemed incredible. The peasants had suspected the compradores were earning much money, but that much? Could it be possible? Yet these were government agronomists from the capital, sent by El Padre.

The compradores sat amid the peasants. They had come somewhat concerned, but hopeful too: perhaps the cooperative might be useful to them, a way to get loans from the government and better prices. But as the promotores spoke, their concern grew. A cooperative, the promotores warned, must exclude any compradores. Arturo spoke for the compradores, assuming the role of a defender of the peasants. Few peasants dared to speak, let alone disagree. "There was like a wave of terror. Many of us owed money to them. And we couldn't find the right words to speak. Thank God that the promotores had a sharp tongue."

Arturo stood, speaking with calm reassurance. Such prices, he said, were exaggerated. Everybody knew that the prices for coffee were fixed. Nobody could pay the prices Fenacoop was promising.

"No," the promotores told the peasants. "You're being hurt because of the chain of compradores that there is in the market. There are so many hands earning a profit that the peasants lose thousands and thousands of pesos. And that money ends up in the pockets of the compradores. But if you put all your coffee together, and if you sell it directly, those thousands and thousands of pesos will end up in your own pockets."

These words against the compradores were strong. The peasants had never heard officials of the government attacking such *gente grande* (powerful people).

Arturo was soon on his feet again. "Most of these people owe us money. These people can't turn their coffee over to Fenacoop, because they may default with us. And we're the ones who give them credit when they need it. When their coffee is growing and their children get sick, we are the ones that give them money. And when their coffee is ripe, and they need money to pick it, we are the ones who give them the money. We're the first ones that should enter the cooperative. Without our help, a cooperative here would turn out to be a failure."

The promotores argued back.

As the discussion continued, Arturo's ire grew: "How can we trust these unknown city folk? Where will they be when you need money for your harvests?"

"These middlemen would be happy if you saved them and condemned yourselves to poverty," responded one agronomist. "And it's not going to be us that run the cooperative, but you, the peasants will be in charge."

The meeting broke up with little settled. But as the peasants from Jaida Arriba rode their mules up the winding trails to their homes, they talked of nothing else. Again and again they ran through the interchanges between Arturo and the promotores, incredulous but pleased to hear agronomists' words of challenge and defiance repeated on their own lips.

Jaida Arriba buzzed with stories of the meeting. At the next two weekly cooperative meetings, this was the only topic of conversation. Many new faces appeared to listen, to hear the tale of El Río repeated. On the third week, Fidel returned with the promotores, but this time to Jaida Arriba itself. Manuel stayed in his store as about eighty people assembled in the chapel to hear these men. The promotores ended the meeting by helping the people formally appoint a directorate to continue organization efforts in Jaida Arriba. Names were suggested from those assembled. A quiet, somewhat timid, but much respected large holder, Salvador, was chosen as president, Teresa as secretary, and Puro as treasurer. When the promotores departed, they left behind a spirit that had not existed before: to the sacred aura given by the church, they had added the stamp of official government approval.

Within a few weeks, a series of *cursillos* (short courses) began. First El Padre arranged with a progressive Jesuit, Padre Rodolfo, to bring his four-day Cursillo de Promoción Social (Social Promotion Course) to the region. Scores of peasants came from the surrounding mountains to attend. To presentations and films on organic fertilizers, proper planting, and plant diseases were added talks about the natural rights of man, the equality of human beings, the economic injustices suffered by the peasants, and the call to community action as part of one's Christian duty. If the peasants joined together and struggled united, they could have better lives for themselves and their children. Many still remember how the priest set a rope upon the ground and assigned two peasants to be the middlemen and six to be peasants. He first had the two middlemen pull together against the six who all pulled in different directions, the few overpowering the many. But then, amid the cheers of those assembled, he had the six pull together, dragging the "compradores" behind them.

Soon after the course in social action, Puro attended a month-long course in San Cristobal, near the capital, sponsored by Idecoop. Puro was accompanied by another peasant, Pucho, a large holder who had just returned from New York.[7]

The month-long course taught the basics of organizing a cooperative: elections, simple accounting, how to make loans. Puro and Pucho learned that there were various kinds of cooperatives, and they had formed a Cooperativa de Ahorros y Crédito (a savings and loan cooperative). If they wanted to market their coffee, they needed a Cooperativa Agropecuaria. And if they wanted to buy and sell their own staples and supplies, a Cooperativa de Consumo.

Soon after their return, other shorter courses were organized in Santiago and San Juan de La Sierra for larger groups of peasants. Most were directed, not by officials from Idecoop or Fenacoop, but by another Jesuit, Padre Miguel, a skilled teacher who understood well the difficulties of setting up a cooperative. Fidel worked closely with Padre Miguel, learning as he assisted. Padre Miguel patiently gave classes on cooperative administration. He taught them how to keep notes on meetings and maintain records and how to calculate savings, loans, guarantees, interest, and depreciation. Everything he taught was practiced by the peasants; they held elections, ran mock meetings, kept records. Important too were Padre Miguel's efforts to teach the peasants how to talk in public. During the classes, all who attended had to take turns standing in front of those assembled and speaking extemporaneously on topics the Padre presented: a newspaper article attacking certain priests as communist agitators who stirred up trouble among the peasants; the problems the peasants had with the compradores. When those attending the meetings and courses returned to Jaida Arriba, they were met with great interest and excitement to hear what knowledge had been bestowed by the professors and agronomists, the people "who knew." Everyone who had been to the course wanted to tell about it. "We came back so excited that the others caught our enthusiasm."

Once or twice a month meetings were held at Fidel's house in the pueblo. Leaders from Jaida Arriba and three other cooperatives in the region would meet to discuss the problems and ask questions, to share experiences, to get to know one another. Often they discussed a future constituting assembly, where the cooperatives would be officially constituted and could apply to Idecoop for legal incorporation by the president.

In late winter of 1968 another event occurred that drew many more people down to the chapel on Sundays, the days when the weekly cooperative meetings were held. Pablo, a small-holding peasant (the chief organizer of the earlier chapel-building efforts) was chosen by El Padre to be Presidente de la Asamblea (president of the assembly). This was a lay post created by the bishop so that church services could be held in the campo in the absence of a priest. After a course of instruction, Pablo was consecrated by the bishop to give communion (though not to consecrate the host) and taught to lead a special Sunday service, La Palabra de Dios (The Word of God).

Services soon began every Sunday in the chapel. When Pablo gave his sermon, he inevitably talked of the Christian duty of all to unite and struggle and that El Padre and all the bishops of Latin America believed peasants should organize cooperatives. The weekly cooperative meetings would begin right after the service.

These weekly meetings became important social occasions, times to get together with people from other parts of Jaida Arriba whom one did not see all week, to discuss publicly problems that long had been suffered quietly and individually, and to hear news from the outside world. They often were preceded by pick-up music—someone on the *tambora* (drum), someone on the *güira* (cylindrical tin tube whose rippled surface is scraped with a metal rod), and others singing and clapping merengues or the lively new songs learned at the catechism classes. Sometimes men actually took up the women and began to dance.

Interest and confidence in the cooperative were heightened by two actual economic successes in the early spring of 1968. A few large-holding members were able to pool 300 quintales of coffee that had not been obligated before the harvest and sell it directly to Fenacoop. The price they received was $3 more per quintal than the compradores were offering. Here was visible proof that by organizing they could indeed get a better price, and evidence, too, that the people from Fenacoop could be trusted. The cooperative also began to make small loans to its members—$10 to buy a small pig, $30 for a mule, $25 for a family illness. By late summer of 1968 the cooperative had more than eighty members.

But the growth of the cooperative also brought intensified verbal attacks by the middlemen. They warned their peasant clients that the cooperative had no money to advance them before the harvest, nor to pay them for their coffee at harvest time: "only we have the money to help you." They dismissed the idea that this new venture would bring benefits. Pointing to the failure of the cooperative centered in the pueblo and tried twenty years earlier, the middlemen foretold new doom: "These city folk with all their learning are going to suck you dry, you who don't even know the letter 'o'." They warned, too, against the peasant leaders: "This cooperative is only for the clever ones. Your money is going to stay in the hands of these sharp characters. The big fish always eat the little ones."

Rumors that the cooperative was communist also appeared (although no one was clear where they originated). The word "communist" raised the fearful specter of absolute evil: the communists were antichrists who would destroy the churches, suppress Catholicism, confiscate all land and houses and chickens and coffee, take away one's children; and, according to news on the radio, people in the capital and other cities who were accused of being communists often were found beaten or dead or missing. But such rumors were difficult to sustain in the face of the church and government backing for the cooperative.

The middlemen coupled their warnings with appeals to self-interest. They tried to lure large-holding coffee growers with promises of abundant cash advances and special deals. Their main target was Puro, whose initiative, business know-how, and organizational abilities were crucial to cooperative success. Arturo frequently gave him "friendly" advice. Shaking his head despairingly, he would talk with foreboding about the inevitable failure of this peasant group as others elsewhere had failed and warn Puro: "What they're going to do when they fail is criticize you—they'll even call you a thief!" Calling Puro to the back of his store, he would offer him special deals: "Why do you want to put yourself at the head of this movement? This cooperative is for people who don't have enough coffee to protect them- selves. But you can defend yourself by buying the coffee of others. Look—I might even be able to help you make contact with some of the big ex- porters." But Puro, looking squarely at Arturo, would respond calmly: "I'm not in this as a business, but in the service of others. I'm like an apostle. What little I know I want to give to others as a way to love God. When I live a comfortable life, without thinking about others, my life is empty."

"These words," Puro told me (a wise twinkle in his smiling eyes), "fell a bit hard on Arturo, because the words of the church can be pretty convincing." Indeed, Arturo's attitudes changed dramatically over the ensuing months. He gradually grew less antagonistic toward the cooperative. Possibly it was his rapidly failing health and the new importance religion took on for him, an importance heightened by his participation in a Cursillo de Cristiandad. He stopped trying to dissuade Puro and others and even began to talk favorably about the cooperative. In September of 1968, he actually rented his processing factory to the cooperative for $700 for that year's harvest. And the next year, not long before his death, he sold it to these peasants.

The economic power of the comerciantes did not become a serious threat to the cooperative until the last months of 1968. Until that time, cooperative members continued to receive the credit they needed at the comercios of Manuel, Puro, and Arturo. The cooperative itself was able to meet most of the small, preharvest cash needs, formerly met selling a la flor, with loans from the fund of savings. But the approaching harvest demanded enormous amounts of ready cash: the pickers had to be paid weeks before the coffee was ready for sale. The cooperative also needed cash to give members when they delivered their coffee. Their cash needs were too pressing to wait another one or two months while the cooperative processed and finally sold their coffee. While the compradores offered cash on the line, the cooperative had no money: by September of 1968, most of the $2,000 it had accumulated through member savings was already circulating in small loans. Capital had to be obtained from another source or the peasants would be forced to turn back to the compradores.

The promotores and Presidente Administrador of Fenacoop long had promised the cooperative cash advances. As late as September, when Fenacoop officials helped draw up the agreement to rent Arturo's factory, they spoke confidently of a $40,000 or $50,000 loan. They promised that the loan would arrive in early October. But October came and went and no money arrived. Those whose coffee was ripening were in desperate need of money. A few sold cows and pigs, sacrificing their precious livestock to get the cash needed to avoid having to turn to the compradores. A few turned to the compradores out of necessity. By the first week in November "the situation was desperate." A group led by Puro went to the Idecoop offices in Santiago and there placed a call to the Presidente Administrador of Fenacoop in the capital, explaining the urgency of the situation. Finally, in the third week of November, $4,000 arrived. Far from sufficient to meet the cash needs of the anxious members, it vanished in loans to members the same day it arrived. At the end of November, with no more money forthcoming, Fidel (himself only just recently hired as an official promotor by Idecoop) interceded. Personally visiting the Presidente Administrador of Fenacoop in Santo Domingo, he was able to obtain another $3,000 in early December. Again, a few days before Christmas, after another series of urgent calls, $3,000 more arrived. But this, like the small amounts that had arrived before, lasted no more than a few days as peasants, the coffee harvest upon them, faced losing their harvests or turning back to the compradores for money.

The first harvest season, the loans from Fenacoop eventually totaled only $13,000. Although some members were forced to go back to the compradores, the cooperative itself pulled through. What the peasants themselves had saved had not been enough to challenge the control of the compradores; the cooperative's very survival had depended on gaining access to capital outside the campo. But this new source, we will see in Chapter 9, prove a mixed blessing: economic freedom from the local middlemen was to bring a costly dependence on new, national-level brokers.

The difficulties the cooperative had with the first harvest were compounded by new pressures from the compradores, particularly from Manuel on whom so many in Jaida Arriba depended for credit. During the initial nine months of organization, his attacks upon the cooperative had been largely verbal. He continued to advance food to all his clients, confident that they would, as always, pay him with their crops. But the Fenacoop loan changed everything: Manuel saw that the cooperative was indeed going to market coffee directly and that his clients might not sell their coffee to him.

His first move was to threaten withdrawal of credit and loans. "I can't help those who sell to the cooperative with anything," he would say. "I certainly can't give them food or money, because how are they going to pay me back if they sell it to the cooperative." He would tell those who gathered evenings in his store: "When that cooperative fails, they better not expect that they can come running back to me for help." To such threats he added dark hints of foreclosure: "He who leaves me had better be prepared to pay his bill immediately!"

When the first of his clients began to sell their coffee to the cooperative, Manuel made good his threats, refusing them additional credit and demanding payment of existing debts. Demanding such payments was an open challenge: not being able to pay was considered shameful; being asked to pay, insulting. And such actions posed a serious economic threat to peasants continually short of funds: families had to be fed and coffee had to be harvested.

Manuel's actions polarized the situation in Jaida Arriba; one was either "with Manuel" or "with the cooperative." "Hearing these threats made us mad, and we struggled even more so we wouldn't have to return and kiss his hand, to humiliate ourselves." Puro, Salvador, Pucho, and other leaders intensified their attacks on these middlemen who were exploiting the peasants, overcharging them for food, underpaying for crops, and reaping great profits "from the sweat of peasant brows." Although most of their public attacks never mentioned any comprador by name, Pucho tended "to put things very clearly." He personally attacked Manuel as "a man who is sitting on top of us, forcing us under his yoke. He is an enemy of the cooperative, an enemy of society. Manuel is like a pig that we have fenced into a pigsty and here we are feeding him our crops to fatten him!" In a public confrontation in front of Manuel's store Pucho told him: "We're going to gather our force, fall on top of you and destroy your business."

Manuel's threats and sanctions were motivated by more than simply a desire to frustrate or destroy the cooperative. As a comerciante in a profit-based economic system, he was rational not to give credit or cash advances to those who sold their crops to others. His only way of insuring against losing money advanced to peasants whose severe economic needs threatened to absorb immediately any cash entering their hands was to be paid directly with produce. Yet the cooperative was now publicly attacking him, advising its members (many of whom owed him money) not to sell their coffee to him, and openly threatening to drive him out of business.

The conflict grew more open and severe in the ensuing months (the spring and summer of 1969) when the cooperative threatened to challenge Manuel's control not simply of coffee but of consumer goods too. Peasant leaders (against Fidel's advice) began laying plans to form a consumer cooperative—a comercio like Manuel's, but one that would sell basic staples to members at lower prices, dividing the profits among all.[8]

Events came to a head in the summer of 1969. The cooperative, seeking a site to build a store, arranged to buy a piece of land and a small general store directly across the main trail facing Manuel's comercio. The owner of the store agreed to sell the land and structure for $150. But then Manuel made a counteroffer: $150 without the structure, and he pressured the owner not to sell to the cooperative. The open conflict fired heated cooperative meetings. Manuel's actions were presented as proof positive of his exploitation of the peasants.

The cooperative met Manuel's offer and finally convinced the store owner to sell to them. A spirit of *lucha* (struggle), long growing among the more dedicated cooperative members, had come to the surface. Meetings were called to plan the construction of the new cooperative general store. The large and middle holders volunteered money, wood, nails, and tin roofing; the small holders and day laborers, their labor. When the building began a few weeks later, everyone in the cooperative pitched in. For three weeks, the small center of Jaida Arriba buzzed with activity; women and girls carried cans of water on their heads for mixing cement and cooked breakfasts and lunches; men with carpentry skills worked with hammers and saws while those with mules or oxen hauled logs to be cut by others into planks.

As the store neared completion, a meeting was called to plan administration. Long debates were held over whether or not the cooperative should give credit. With Puro arguing persuasively against such a policy (there was not the capital to do so), it was decided that all payments must be in cash. Then an administrator (a twenty-year-old with a seventh-grade education) was chosen.[9] Finally, a list was drawn up of those officially entering and how much capital each was willing to contribute for initial purchases of goods. Thirty-six members entered with a total of $400. The meeting that began at 2:00 in the afternoon ended, the hall still filled, at 11:00 that night. A week later, Puro (who since had closed his store and sold his goods to the cooperative) went to Santiago to make the first purchases. In late September 1969 the store was opened.

The opening day fell on a fiesta day. Hundreds of people came to the chapel in their Sunday best for the Palabra de Dios. Women prepared food in the small kitchens near the comercios. A gay, festive spirit prevaded the air as the doors of the cooperative were opened. People jammed into their own comercio to see and touch and talk loudly of their new building, the comercio they owned.

That day, Manuel's comercio seemed nearly deserted. But far fewer actually left Manuel than the numbers filling the cooperative on opening day. Once again, Manuel leveled the economic sanctions at his disposal: foreclosure on debts and denial of credit to those who joined the consumer cooperative. To Manuel, it made sense to refuse further credit to those who joined the cooperative and bought there: why should he be advancing credit to those who had the cash to buy at the cooperative store? But the cooperative defined his actions as evil efforts to destroy it.

The struggle over the consumer cooperative affected all the noncoffee growers in the community, the small holders and day laborers who had been unaffected by conflicts over the sale of coffee. They were now forced to decide between Manuel and the cooperative. If it was difficult for the larger peasants to survive without credit to pay up debts to Manuel, it seemed impossible to most of the poorer peasants. But the consumer cooperative, with the support of many of the large- and middle-holding coffee growers (who had the good fortune of extra cash from an unusually high price for coffee during the 1969–70 harvest) managed to survive and grow its first year. Not until a year later, when more normal coffee prices plus difficulties obtaining outside loans caused a severe cash shortage and pressured the cooperative to start giving members credit, did the consumer cooperative begin to run into severe economic difficulties.

In Jaida Arriba in early 1970 there were two cooperatives, the Cooperativa Agropecuaria and the Cooperativa de Consumo. The consumer cooperative had about fifty members, the large majority of them middle and large holders. The Cooperativa Agropecuaria had about eighty-five members, about half of whom were small holders or day laborers. Its funds were pooled with the two other cooperatives in the neighboring campos that had joined with Jaida Arriba in mid-1968 to form a district cooperative.

Headquarters for the central office were in El Río, at Arturo's old factory, bought late in 1969 with a $5,000 loan.[10] But this district cooperative was still only a provisional organization; it had not yet had an official constituting assembly nor had it been legally incorporated. Toward this goal another series of short courses with Fidel and Padre Miguel were organized in San Juan de la Sierra in mid-1970. With their help, peasant leaders from the three districts examined constitutions from other cooperatives, discussing the meaning of each point and deciding the rules they wanted for their cooperative. One serious problem had to be solved before the assembly: if what was being constituted was a Cooperativa Agropecuaria that would market coffee and procure loans from other institutions on the basis of the members' production, then those members without coffee production had to leave the cooperative. In Jaida Arriba, peasants with or without coffee, day laborers as well as large holders, always had been encouraged to join the cooperative, put in savings, and make loans. But the day laborers and small holders would now be forced to leave. A decision was made at the courses with Padre Miguel and Fidel to form a new and separate savings and loan cooperative, open to anyone, to absorb these poorer peasants. Although a few middle and large holders agreed to enter into the savings and loan cooperative to help it get started, most leaders poured their energy and excitement into the Cooperativa Agropecuaria (and the consumer cooperative). This left the savings and loan cooperative, as one small holder described it, "a dead thing."

The constituting assembly for the Cooperativa Agropecuaria held in August 1970 was an event of great import and excitement. The cooperative was still to face severe difficulties in the coming years: the central problem of gaining access to the large amounts of capital needed to survive against the competition of the compradores still had not been successfully resolved. But for most of the more than one hundred members who came with their families and friends, by mule and by foot, to the former factory of the largest comprador in the region, the assembly was a symbol of great hope.

A special mass was held by the bishop in the church on the knoll above the cooperative factory. Then the hundreds of people present proceeded down to the factory, packing the enormous wood-frame warehouse. At the long table in front sat the leaders from the three districts. At the front left of the head table, sat the guests of honor: the bishop, El Padre, the regional director of Idecoop, and Fidel. But these outside dignitaries spoke only briefly, The assembly was a peasant assembly. Few minded that much had been rehearsed. All had come to the meeting ready to vote for constituting the cooperative on the basis of the constitution formulated in the preceding courses. They quietly listened as Antonio, a tall, gaunt, forty-year-old peasant from one of the districts, slowly and nervously called the meeting to order and led the assembly point by point through the prepared agenda. Despite the rehearsals in the courses, this was the first time he had ever addressed so enormous a group, let alone directed a meeting of such proportions and with such dignitaries present. Antonio's hands shook visibly as he brought down the gavel to call the meeting to order. He spoke haltingly, his voice quavering. But the assembled peasants were attentive and respectful. The leaders who sat before them and talked were friends and neighbors, campesinos just like themselves, not people from the city who had come to talk down to them and tell them what to do. They, the peasants, were voting and deciding on serious matters.

Antonio gradually grew calmer. Finally, as the assembly drew to a close, he put aside his prepared agenda and drew a crumpled sheet of paper from his back pocket. Explaining to those who watched that he had something of his own he wanted to add, he unfolded the paper and read:

Compañeros,

Today, the day of the Constituent Assembly, we've taken the first step—it is such a transcendental step that it will leave a page written in the history of the cooperative movement in the Dominican Republic.

That's why we are inviting you to forget about the Dominican custom of not doing anything, and of waiting for help. A lot of times, I've been with people, who tell me: "I'm okay, because my compadre takes care of things for me." Other times, I've been with people who tell me: "We're lost here, because the people up there in government, don't do anything for the campesino." And I ask myself: "And you, what do you do for yourself and for your country?" Let us not forget, *compañeros,* that if someday we hope to see development, everyone of us has to do something.

Gentlemen, if we are trampled on today by the higher-ups, we ourselves are to blame. Why? Because we have been used to asking for help, to not doing anything to solve our own problems. Each one of us is responsible for our problems. And also, for the problems of our country—because this is your country, because this is my country, because this is the country of all of us.

Gentlemen, I speak in my own name and in the name of my companions in battle. We invite you to continue fighting—forgetting hatred, bitterness, selfishness. It doesn't matter what class you are, what race, what color, nor what political ideology you have. We invite you to continue fighting: first for yourselves, for your children, for your *compañeros,* and for your country.

Gentlemen, the seed has been sown. The first to be born was the Agropecuaria. Then, we saw the birth of a group of consumer cooperatives. Third, we saw the birth of a group of savings and loan cooperatives. And the seed has sprouted. Now we have to help the tree along; it's up to us to take care of the tree; it's up to us to defend the tree. Let's not forget, *compañeros,* that there are only two things that depend on us: victory or defeat.

This two-room house of a small holder is built of hand-sawn, whitewashed pine boards and has a pine shingle roof. The kitchen is in a separate building behind it.

The families in Jaida Arriba all live on their plots of land, separated from each other by steep slopes and ravines.

Mule teams are the principal means of transporting goods in and out of Jaida Arriba.

The one-room schoolhouse in Jaida Arriba offers only a third grade education. The children barely learn the fundamentals of reading, writing, and arithmetic.

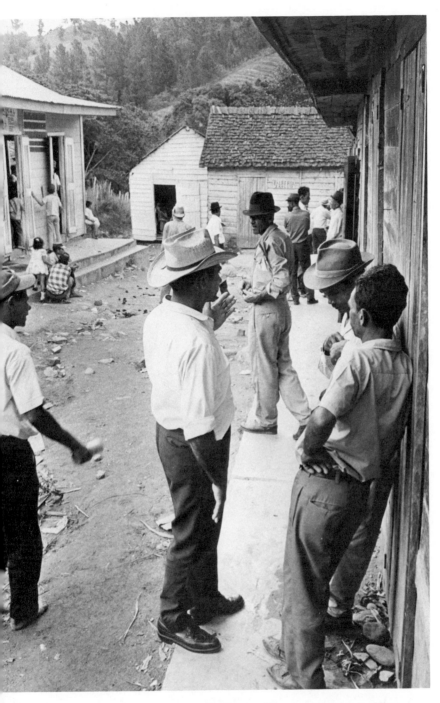

The commercial center of Jaida Arriba, normally nearly deserted, fills on Sundays with people who go to chapel and spend the afternoon catching up on news and socializing with friends and relatives they seldom see otherwise.

The cooperative store, typical of small rural general stores, sells everything from food, hardware, and kitchen utensils to cosmetics and shoes. It also serves as a social center where people gather to visit, play dominoes, and, in the back room, drink and dance.

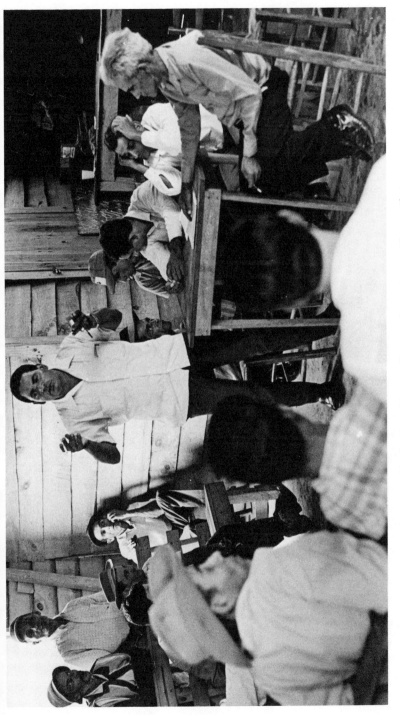

A cooperative leader addresses the members at a weekly meeting.

Some of the less steep land can be plowed using teams of oxen. Steeper land is sometimes turned by hand, using a pick.

Threshing beans is one of the jobs often still done by exchange labor teams, or *juntas*. Some of the men still keep time by singing traditional changes (*decimas*) while they work.

111

PART TWO

CONCIENTIZACIÓN
AND THE CREATION OF POWER

CHAPTER 6

THEORETICAL APPROACHES

> When human society is considered with calm and disinterested attention, it seems to show at first only the violence of the powerful men and the oppression of the weak: the mind revolts against the harshness of the former; one is prompted to deplore the blindness of the latter.
>   —Jean-Jacques Rousseau, *The First and Second Discourses*

The peasants of Jaida Arriba faced constant problems meeting basic economic needs and a consequent dependence on middlemen, which resulted in high prices for consumer goods and low prices for their crops. The cooperative offered them new hope: the continual money shortage could be solved by a fund built on personal savings and government loans that could be lent to members. With this fund, coffee could be protected from preharvest sale at low prices; direct access to the marketing system would bring higher prices for coffee, further relieving money shortages; and a consumer cooperative could provide the peasants with needed goods more cheaply and give them a share of the profits.

Presented this way, the acceptance and growth of the cooperative seems almost natural. Indeed, certain theoretical approaches might quickly point to the "objective" interests the peasants had in freeing themselves from the control of the middlemen, show how these interests were reflected in the cooperative ideology, and thus explain the peasant cooperative organization. Other theoretical approaches might point to the strains the peasant undoubtedly faced in his various roles: his obligations as a father demanded that he meet the economic needs of his family, although he often had neither harvest nor money; as a producer, his crops needed soil and care which he often lacked the land or money to provide; as a seller, he often had to sacrifice crops cheaply, and as a consumer, to buy goods dearly; as a debtor, he was continually faced with the need to find ways to pay back credit and advances from the comerciantes, although harvest times were distant and yields poor. Such approaches might then explain the acceptance and growth

113

of the cooperative ideology by pointing to its importance as a symbolic outlet for these strains.

But such explanations of the seemingly natural development of the cooperative out of objective interests or role strains avoid certain central questions: (1) Why did no ideology or movement aimed at collective action either to alleviate existing economic difficulties or to struggle against the control of the middlemen arise in Jaida Arriba before 1967? (2) When the cooperative ideology was introduced into Jaida Arriba, why was it accepted by some peasants and rejected by others? (3) How was the cooperative able to create the power necessary to break the control of the middlemen? This chapter will explore and develop theoretical approaches that will be used as guidelines for examining the first two questions in Chapters 7 and 8. It will build on two theoretical approaches that claim to deal with the causes and effects of ideologies: "interest theory" and "strain theory." In Chapter 9, I will turn to the problem of creating power.

"INTEREST" AND THE INTEREST THEORY APPROACH

Historically, interest theory stems from the notion that people's consciousness is determined by their social being.[1] A person's ideology, a particular form of human consciousness, is tied to a particular form of social being, economic, or class position. Men and women in particular class positions have particular "interests" that are rooted in these social situations; people in the dominant or ruling class, for example, have certain interests in maintaining their position and continuing to benefit from those subordinate to them, while those who are dominated have an interest in changing the nature of their condition. Ideology, then, is conceived of as both a "weapon" and a "mask" for social interests (Geertz 1964:52; Berger and Luckmann 1967:6). Those who rule use ideology as a weapon to protect their social interests by masking might as right and class interest as the general good; those who are governed see ideology as a weapon to unmask such interests and to provide a guide to changing the nature of that control.

In the framework of interest theory there exists an often implicit or hidden theoretical link between class position and ideology. That link is "perceived" interests: people perceive and feel the particular social "interests" that are inherent in their class positions and are motivated to act on the basis of these interests. They make a calculation of their personal advantage and on this basis accept or create ideologies as weapons or masks.

How much does interest theory help us to answer the first two questions posed above? To be useful to us, interest theory must help to explain change in ideologies (in this case, why at one particular time people did not believe in cooperative action against the compradores and at another time they did). And interest theory must also explain differences in the ideologies held by different persons (why certain men accepted the cooperative ideology and others rejected it, often in favor of the counterideology that middlemen presented).

To explain change in ideologies and differences among ideological positions, interest theory points to the variable of class position, the source of ideology. Different class positions have inherent in them different interests. But how do we explain a change in ideology among a group of people in the same class position? Or how do we explain different ideologies among those in the same class position? Or similar ideologies among people in different class positions? Interest theorists may recognize the existence of such possibilities.[2] But can they explain such differences within their conceptual framework? They might respond that men perceive and feel their social interests differently and thus may create or accept different ideologies despite similar objective class interests. The scarcity of ideological activity in Jaida Arriba before 1967 could be explained by the peasants' lack of perceiving the interests they had as peasants and the threats to these interests posed by the compradores. But a central question is still begged: how are these different perceptions of interest to be explained? The theoretical framework of interest theory provides little help. Part of the problem is the very way that "interest" is conceptualized simultaneously as both a psychological and a sociological concept, "referring both to a felt advantage of an individual or group of individuals and to the objective structure of opportunity within which an individual or group moves" (Geertz 1964:53). Conceptually, no distinction is made between "social" interest and "perceived" or "felt" interest. This not only makes it difficult to talk about "different ways that social class interests are perceived and felt," but it allows one to slip easily from one meaning of interest to another, often covering important differences. What does it mean to say that an ideology "corresponds" to a class interest? Does this mean "objective" class interest or "perceived" class interest? There is another danger, too: one might assume that these are really the same thing—that objective class interests are what men perceive as their interests.

Assuming, however, this conceptual distinction, could the difference between "objective" class interest and "perceived" interest be explained within the interest-theory framework? The only independent variable to turn to would be class position. One might then explain changes in "perceived" interest by exploring changes in the class position of a particular group.[3] But as long as "class position" is the only independent variable, explanations are severely restricted. The situation in Jaida Arriba comes close to being inexplicable: changes in ideology without changes in class position, differences in perceived interests among those in the same class position, and similar perceptions among those in different class positions.

In actual practice, a number of authors who might be thought of as interest theorists do introduce the possibility of a change in perception of interests without a change in social position[4] or suggest that the way a person perceives his interests may be shaped by factors other than his class position. These authors are, however, forced to step outside the conceptual framework of interest theory to introduce new concepts, such as "culture."[5] But they do suggest a different perspective: how people perceive their class position must be conceptually (and analytically) separated from that position; and one must allow for the possibility that perceptions may be shaped by factors other than class position. The meaning of class position for a person in terms of his perceptions of interest thus would be seen as a mediating factor between ideology and class position, analytically independent of either ideology or class position.

This new perspective will be explored later, but it would be well to point out now one further problem with "interest theory." It often implies that the link between class position and ideology is through some calculation of self-interest. Although some ideologies may indeed be no more than products of a calculation of personal advantage, this narrow utilitarian view of human motivation runs two risks: excluding other ways in which men come to relate their ideas to their social position, or merely reducing all ideologies to products of self-interest by definition.

A way out of this problem might be to expand the notion of interest. Interest could be conceived of as including nonrational action and the pursuit of any psychological satisfaction. But such a broad conception severely reduces the explanatory power of interest theory because we are led to say merely that ideologies are motivated. Instead of "men act in their own interests," we are left with the tautology, "men act as they are motivated to act" (Sutton et al. 1956:13, 304).

Another possible solution offered is a vague historicism that avoids using the term "self-interest" and instead links social class position to ideology by saying that ideas "express," "reflect," are "determined by," "molded by," "conditioned by," "penetrated by," "correspond to," or "emerge from" class position. But such links are not incisive. They are "question-begging," and "they hide inadequate analysis" (Mills 1967:425). The concept of "interest," then, clearly presents severe limitations. How might these limitations be overcome?

FROM "INTEREST" TO "STRAIN"

An alternative approach, "strain theory," also links social factors to ideology, but the link is people seeking relief from anxiety and tension, not people acting in their own interests. Further, the social factors it conceives of are broader than simply class position.[6]

Strain theory sees people's social position in terms of the various roles they play in society's institutions. These institutions must cope with a variety of functional problems that any society faces—such as dealing with the natural environment, allocating resources, maintaining order. But such problems are only imperfectly met in any society. The different institutions in which men act—the economic, political, religious, educational, familial—have different and sometimes discontinuous norms. And there may be discrepancies in the goals of these different institutions, "between emphases on profit and productivity in business firms or between extending knowledge and disseminating it in universities, for example" (Geertz 1964:55). And within social roles themselves there may be contradictory expectations, such as those a woman may face as wife and as professional. Strain theory argues that "individuals living in societies experience these imperfections as *strains*; they must at times face situations where the expectations they have learned to view as legitimate are thwarted, or where they must wrestle with conflicting demands" (Sutton et al. 1956:306). The contradictions, discontinuities, or strains in a person's position in the social system are felt as strains by individuals themselves. Tensions within an individual's personality deepen this sense of strain (Geertz 1964:54).

Strain theory holds that the strains to which society's members are subject are not random, but patterned: people are conceived of as being in social roles in institutions that pattern their activity; thus the strains to which these roles and institutions subject people should themselves be patterned (Sutton et al. 1956:307). The patterned strains which people experience generate emotional energy that needs an outlet. Herein lies the basic psychological assumption of strain theory: people seek to get away from anxiety, to reduce strain, to cope with tension. They may have many reactions to strain. Among these are "psychosomatic and neurotic symptoms . . . less spectacular character disorders, crotchets, idiosyncrasies," "nailchewing," and "alcoholism" (Sutton et al. 1956:307, 308). But one patterned response is ideological: "Ideology is a patterned reaction to the patterned strains of a social role . . . . The general mode of relation between strain and ideology is that of symbolization: ideology is a symbolic outlet for the emotional energy which the strain creates" (Sutton et al. 1956:307,308).

What limits would a strain theory approach place on answering the first two questions about Jaida Arriba—the lack of ideological activity before 1967 and the acceptance or rejection of the cooperative ideology by certain groups once it was introduced?

To explain change and variation in the ideologies held by various groups of men, strain theory would direct us to the different kinds of conflicting demands and social strains of men in different social roles. Businessmen would thus have different ideologies than students and military officers. Groups of men who changed from coffee-growing peasants to rural wage laborers or to local store owners would change their ideologies in response to the new strains in their new social roles. But as we found with the use of class in interest theory, this approach would not account for changes in ideologies among groups of men for whom the conflicting demands of a social role had not changed. Nor would it explain differences in ideology among groups in the same social role, nor similar ideological patterns among groups who faced different social strains in different roles.

Implicit within the framework of strain theory, however, is one possible explanation. The differences in the way people feel or experience similar social strains can account for variation in ideologies. Here ideology is linked to the social strain of a social role by the mediating factor of "felt" strain. Changes or variations in how the conflicting demands of a social role are *felt* can explain, for example, the changes or variations in the ideologies of men facing the same conflicting demands of the same social role.

But even if strain theorists followed this avenue, their framework could not *account* for differences in the ways social strains are felt because "social strain" is the only independent variable. Furthermore, the very concept of "strain" (like that of "interest") has a theoretically dangerous vagueness about it. It is both a sociological and a psychological concept; it refers both to such social phenomena as the conflicting demands and expectations of a social role *and* to how a person experiences or feels such social pressure. Using the same word to mean two different phenomena makes analysis of the relationship difficult. The strains of the social role and how these strains are experienced are different matters; to combine them conceptually yields a vagueness in any theoretical statements.

ORIENTATIONS: THE MEDIATOR BETWEEN IDEOLOGY AND SOCIAL SITUATION

Both interest and strain theories thus face similar difficulties. Implicit in both is the notion that the particular meanings social situations have for men (in terms of "perceived" interest and "felt" strain) mediate between ideology and its sources in these social situations. But, explicitly, these orientations toward social situations either are not mentioned or ideology remains as a direct response to the social situation itself.[7] If these meanings were explicitly considered, variations in such orientations could help explain change or variation in ideologies. How, then, are changes and variations in "perceived" interest or "felt" strains to be accounted for in a way that will allow us to explain (1) changes in the ideology of a group of men in the same social situation (for example, the nonexistence of ideological activity in Jaida Arriba before 1968 and the occurrence of such activity afterward with no change in class structure or social roles); (2) variations in the ideological positions of groups of men in similar social situations (why, among peasants in the same class position in Jaida Arriba some men accepted and others rejected the cooperative ideology); and (3) similarities of ideologies of men in different social situations (why, for example, the cooperative ideology was accepted by groups of men in Jaida Arriba with different "class interests")?

"Perceived" interests and "felt" strains must first be freed from "determination" by class position or social strain. A clue to the direction we might look is provided unwittingly by certain strain theorists themselves. They occasionally imply that the kind of strain, if any, experienced by men facing the conflicting demands of a particular social role will be shaped by the particular orientation *they bring to* that role (Sutton et al. 1956:330). And they suggest that similarities in these orientations exist because they are cultural orientations (Sutton et al. 1956:309, 327). Implied, then, is that the culturally patterned variety of definitions men bring to their particular social roles will pattern the variety of strains experienced—and the variety of ideological activity that occurs.

For my purposes, the following formulation may prove useful: the particular meaning a social situation has for people must be thought of as analytically independent of that social situation; various perceptions of interest or feelings of strain are among such meanings; and such meanings mediate between ideologies and an "objective" social situation. This formulation is not a new one. Its history goes back at least as far as the distinction Max Weber makes between an empirical occurrence and the "meaning" people give to that occurrence when he posits these as the two moments of a "social event." The meanings that a particular aspect of a person's material existence has are not inherent in this existence itself, but do mediate between existence and "consciousness." C. Wright Mills writes:

> The consciousness of men does not determine their material existence; nor does their material existence determine their consciousness. Between consciousness and existence stand meanings and designs and communications which other men have passed on—first, in human speech itself, and later, by the management of symbols. These received and manipulated interpretations decisively influence such consciousness as men have of their existence. They provide the clues to what men see, to how they respond to it, and how they feel about it, and how they respond to these feelings. Symbols focus experience; meanings organize knowledge, guiding the surface perceptions of an instant no less than the aspirations of a lifetime (1959:415—16).

This theoretical stance is found in recent research, too. In their investigations of attitudes and behavior of certain British workers, Goldthorpe et al., for example, emphasize the lack of direct association between the strains and pressures imposed by certain kinds of work situations and worker attitudes and behavior (1968:182). They stress "the explanatory relevance of the wants and expectations which men *bring to* their work" which can be regarded as *mediating* between features of the work situation objectively considered and the nature of the worker's response" (1968:182).[8]

This approach, however, only defines the problem: if we want to use the orientations people have toward their social situation to help explain particular ideological responses to those situations, we first have to explain the variety, stability, and change in these very orientations. There is a serious theoretical problem here, one of the core problems of the sociology of knowledge: how do we explain such meanings and orientations? While this chapter will not tackle this theoretical problem, some of its assumptions should be made clear.

Meanings and orientations are rooted in a "culture" into which men are born, parts of which they learn (what some social scientists call socialization) and parts of which they change. I conceive of culture, with Geertz and others, as a symbol system: "Culture is the fabric of meaning in terms of which human beings interpret their experience and guide their action . . . the framework of beliefs, expressive symbols, and values in terms of which individuals define their world, express their feelings, and make their judgements" (Geertz 1957:33). Culture, however, cannot simply be taken as a "given" and then used to "explain" particular beliefs and attitudes. A particular culture has itself been created, sustained, and changed: it has a historical context. It is possible, for example, that certain symbols have been forcibly excluded by those in power.[9] Furthermore, a culture does not determine the particular meaning men give to an event nor the particular orientation they have toward some aspect of their social situation: men are no more solely products of culture than they are solely products of their social class or social role.

Within a culture, people apply a variety of symbols in different ways to give meaning to a particular event or situation. An ideology (as I will discuss below) is a particular set of symbols men use to give meaning to a situation; it provides a guide to thought, feeling, and action. Implicit here is a certain flexibility within a culture. Cultural symbols may be logically inconsistent or contradictory, and different culturally available responses may be combined and applied to a variety of situations. I am not, then, conceiving of culture in a "holistic" sense—as, for example, a well-integrated set of norms and values necessary for the maintenance of a particular social system.[10] Rather, I am conceiving of culture as a "toolkit" from which people may draw symbols and use them to shape meaning and to which new symbolic "tools" may be added.[11]

Why, then, do certain events or social situations have particular meanings for certain groups? An answer to this question should involve consideration of at least two factors. Because a culture has a particular historical context, it offers only a limited number of symbolic alternatives. Not only are there obstacles to the introduction of new symbols but also barriers to the very creation of new symbolic alternatives and definitions.[12] Second, how people apply particular symbols to give meaning to certain situations is not simply a matter of intentional choice or purposive action. Here the notion of man as

the creator and maintainer of culture comes together (dare I say dialecti-
cally?) with factors that shape what he creates.

Two factors seem particularly important: personality (or character) and
life experiences. The first is largely absent in the following analysis since its
usefulness in explaining group phenomena is somewhat questionable.[13] But I
will touch on the importance of life experiences in shaping the meaning men
give an event or situation. The particular orientations they have are "socially
generated and sustained" (Goldthorpe et al. 1969:185). And to understand
why men have adopted particular values and motivations, these orientations
"must be traced back so far as this is possible, to typical life situations and
experiences" (Goldthorpe et al. 1969:185).

Three kinds of life experiences seem especially relevant: individual, historical-generational, and social experiences. The first I will touch on briefly in
those few places where individual personalities are dealt with.[14] Historical-
generational experiences such as the impact of living under Trujillo's dictatorship and the concomitant fear of opposition to authority and lack of
participatory and organizational skills will be mentioned briefly.[15] More
emphasis will be put on the effect of other experiences such as common
family histories and school experiences and shared hardships in the early
pioneering and settling days of Jaida Arriba.[16] Related to the historical-generational experiences are an important set of social experiences such as the
everyday experiences peasants have in their class situations and in their
various social roles in institutions such as the church, the family, and
extended kinship groups. Such experiences will be brought to bear (often
tentatively and implicitly) in explaining how particular orientations are generated, sustained, weakened, or threatened.[17]

The above approach suggests certain things I should know about Jaida
Arriba. I should try to understand the "objective" social situation in the
community, particularly the social strains and conflicting demands imposed
on various classes of peasants and the kind of control exercised over them.
This indeed has been the task of the first five chapters. My next task should
be to identify the different meanings groups of peasants give their social
situation and to explore, using the limited information I have, how these
orientations are generated, sustained, weakened, or threatened. This will be
the central focus of Chapter 7. Orientations of particular concern would seem
to be those of "perceived" interest and "felt" strain because such meanings
may give us a clue to the lack of a cooperative ideology before 1967 and its
eventual acceptance or rejection.

FROM A "MALAISE" TO A "PROBLEM"

Understanding the sources of the orientations people have to their social
situations is an important first step in explaining particular ideological re-

sponses to those situations. The next step is to understand how such orientations link ideology and social situations. Here conceiving of orientations only in terms of interest is limiting: it implies that "self-interest" is the only orientation people can have toward their situation. But the concept of "felt" strain—if refined and clarified—might be more useful.

An initial formulation might be this:

People "feel" strain when they see the conflicting demands placed upon them as things that must be wrestled with, as problems that must be solved. To be sure, there are many difficulties in society, but often they are not seen or regarded as problems. It is when people feel their situation as a problem and are looking for solutions that ideologies become important in offering them guiding principles.[18] But this formulation would serve as a more useful analytical tool if it were refined to allow for different kinds of felt strain. As outlined, difficulties in society either are felt as strains, or they are not.

A peasant in Jaida Arriba unwittingly suggested the following refinement. I asked him why everyone claimed "blindness" to what the compradores were doing before the cooperative was organized, yet many *did* know something about what was going on. He explained: "Well, before things were *mal* (bad) and everyone knew things were bad, but after the cooperative came everyone could see more clearly the problem." This seems an important distinction: the difference between seeing things as bad—as an inchoate, undefined malaise—and seeing one's situation as a problem needing a solution. Formulating this distinction more clearly will prove useful.

I will say that a situation is "bad" when people experience certain "difficulties" (a lack of medicine, money, or clothing) or experience certain of its aspects as "wrong" (particular actions of a comerciante). Such a situation is seen as a vicissitude of life, a near-permanent hardship, unchangeable but for the grace of God. When a bad situation comes to be seen as problematic, people begin to question it, to think in terms of causal relations, perhaps conceiving of strategies to deal with the problem of so and so or asking how to cope with such and such. In regarding a situation as problematic, they may see no solution or believe that existing strategies are weak and inadequate; but at minimum they are thinking of the situation in terms of what can be done.

One further specification to this malaise-problem distinction should be added: a public-private dimension. People may experience a particular wrong or difficulty as a personal malaise that they, as individuals, are suffering or enduring; or as a common, public malaise that others in their class or community or kin group also suffer from. Problems, too, may be experienced as private matters, as personal troubles whose statement and resolution are questions of individual responsibility. The statement and resolution of public problems, on the other hand, lie within the larger institutions and social structures of a historical society.[19]

These distinctions will prove important later: when people come to see a *malaise* as a *problem,* change through human action may begin to be conceived as a possibility; when personal problems are seen as public ones, collective action may become possible.[20]

Such distinctions also allow more precision about "interest." One kind of strain people may experience is that of conflicting demands inherent in their class positions. One meaning they may give to this situation is a *problematic* one: certain interests they have, given their social location in a particular class, seem thwarted (perhaps by the power of those in the ruling class) or endangered (perhaps by the organized struggles of the working class). If they experience their thwarted or endangered interests as class interests, they experience a *public* problem. If they experience personal troubles (for example, seeing high credit rates and personally decreasing real income in the face of individual cash shortages), their problems are felt as *private* ones. They may, however, have no clear perception or understanding of their interests, but experience a certain undefined *malaise,* feeling certain things are bad or difficult or wrong. People in a particular class may experience neither problems nor malaise. They may, for example, accept the ruling class's definition of their interests (for example, continued individual initiative and personal struggle leads to betterment) and see neither difficulties nor problems with their position, nor even identify it as a class position. Interest thus becomes one kind of strain that may be experienced in various ways.

The distinctions outlined here also permit the identification of problems beyond thwarted or endangered interests and the examination of social situations other than those defined by economic class. It is possible to explore the malaise or problem (public or private) that people experience given their political or social position, or given particular roles in religious, political, or familial institutions.[21]

THE CONCEPT OF "IDEOLOGY"

I first suggested that the mediating factor between a social situation and the ideological response to it is the orientation people have toward that situation. Above I elaborated two kinds of orientations, "malaise" and "problem" and further added a "public"/"private" distinction. A remaining task is to establish some theoretical links between orientations and ideologies in order to explain why new ideologies are created and accepted. To do this, some clarification of the concept of "ideology" would be useful.

We need a notion of ideology that allows us to link it back to the kinds of orientations that may have encouraged its creation or acceptance; we need to know why a particular orientation was conducive to a particular ideology. The concept of ideology in the strain theory approach is not very useful here. By defining ideology as "a symbolic outlet for the emotional energy which strain creates" (Sutton et al. 1956:308), we can only analyze an ideology in terms of how well it provided an outlet or drain for the emotional energy of the strain: the ideology that was created or accepted would be that which provided the best outlet. This approach also excludes the possibility that people may act as purposive beings, who create or accept ideologies because they make some sense and because their guidelines seem useful. People are conceived of as thoughtless responders-to-stimuli; any ideology is explained (and dismissed) by merely classifying it as some "symbolic outlet."

The concept of ideology in interest theory is somewhat more useful. Ideology is seen as a weapon (or, from another perspective, as a mask) for the struggle or defense of class interests. People articulate or accept ideologies for a purpose. But the notion of "ideology as a weapon" is still too narrow. Geertz makes this point well: "The battlefield image of society as a clash of interests thinly disguised as a clash of principles turns attention away from the role that ideologies play in defining (or obscuring) social categories, stabilizing (or upsetting) social expectations, maintaining (or undermining) social norms, strengthening (or weakening) social consensus, relieving (or exacerbating) social tensions" (1964:53). We could, however, widen the explanatory usefulness of the concept of "ideology" by broadening it to mean an explicit set of ideas or symbols that can guide people's thoughts, feelings, and behavior. Such a notion of ideology has a certain theoretical justification, the outlines of which are provided by Geertz.

The defining proposition of his approach is "that thought consists of the construction and manipulation of symbol systems which are employed as models of other systems, physical, organic, social, psychological, and so forth" (Geertz 1964:61). Thought (conceptualization, formulation, comprehension, understanding) is "a matching of the states and processes of symbolic models against the states and processes of the wider world" (Geertz 1964:61). Symbolic models are thus extrinsic sources of information in terms of which both the cognitive and affective sides of human life can be patterned. Based on this notion of thought as the construction and manipulation of symbol systems, we have some basis for conceiving of ideology as one kind of symbol system which has in common this important quality with other symbol systems: "They are extrinsic sources of information in terms of which human life can be patterned—extrapersonal mechanisms for the perception, understanding, judgment, and manipulation of the world. Culture patterns—religious, philosophical, aesthetic, scientific, ideological—are "programs"; they provide a template or blueprint for the organization of social and psychological processes, much as genetic systems provide such a template for the organization of organic processes" (Geertz 1964:62). This quality of ideology as a set of explicit symbols that can guide men's actions, thoughts, and feelings provides us with the conceptual tools to begin a discussion of how ideologies link to their sources.

THE CREATION AND ACCEPTANCE OF NEW IDEOLOGIES

The central question now is: under what conditions are new ideologies—symbolic guides to thought, feeling, and behavior—created and accepted? Using the distinction between a problem orientation and a malaise, I will argue the following: when people experience a particular social situation as problematic, they feel the need for explicit symbolic guides or ideologies; when existing guides seem weak or inadequate, the circumstances are right for the creation or acceptance of new ideologies.

When people merely experience a malaise and not a problem, they do not yet have a need for an explicit ideology, an explicit set of symbols to serve as guides. "Uneasiness and indifference," wrote Mills, are "not yet formulated in such ways as to permit the work of reason and the play of sensibility" (Mills 1959:11). It is exactly when people experience a problem yet find "institutionalized guides" to be inadequate or absent that cultural-symbol systems like ideologies come crucially into play. And people come to question the validity of such "institutionalized guides"—the common knowledge or everyday maxims or strategies that guide their lives—when they fail "to deliver the goods": "The validity of my knowledge of everyday life is taken for granted by myself and by others until further notice, that is, until a problem arises that cannot be solved in terms of it. As long as my knowledge works satisfactorily, I am generally ready to suspend doubts about it. . . . Only when my maxims fail 'to deliver the goods' in the world to which they are intended to apply are they likely to become problematic to me 'in earnest' " (Berger and Luckmann 1967:44).

A necessary condition for the rise of a new ideology is the simultaneous existence of a "problem orientation" (my formulation of what Geertz calls "socio-psychological strain") and the absence of a set of symbols to serve as guides. "It is a loss of orientation," Geertz argues, "that most directly gives rise to ideological activity, an inability, for lack of usable models to comprehend the universe of civic rights and responsibilities in which one finds oneself located" (1964:64). When people have a problem orientation toward their situation *and* they lack guides (institutionalized guides or sets of symbols like ideologies) to thought, feeling, or action, a new ideology is most likely to be created or accepted.[22]

This formulation can be improved by replacing "loss of orientation" or "absence of cultural symbols" (which imply a sense of total disorientation) with a notion of "weak orientation" or "inadequate cultural symbols." In those problematic situations where people doubt the validity of existing knowledge or question the usefulness of the explicit symbolic guides or ideologies, they most readily accept or create new ideologies. "Loss" or "absence" then becomes only one possibility.

This formulation allows us to move away from a linear model which first posits the failure of existing ideologies as guides and only then deals with the emergence or acceptance of new ideologies. It offers the possibility that a new ideology or symbol system may itself affect the way people feel toward existing ideologies or symbolic guides. This formulation would then present an alternative by which ideologies may be linked to their sources: not only do they serve as symbolic guides, but they may actually intensify the need for such guides by undermining the validity of existing ideologies and by heightening the doubts about the adequacy of existing sets of symbols as guides for coping with the problems.[23] Indeed, the actual presentation of an alternative may move some people to perceive the inadequacy or absence of existing symbolic guides or to reject these guides.[24]

Reformulating the link between ideology and problem orientation we thus have the following: it is when people both experience a problem orientation toward their situation *and* find the available institutionalized guides or sets of symbols or ideologies to be lacking, weak, or inadequate as guides to thought, feeling, or action that new ideologies are most likely to be created or accepted.[25]

I have mentioned two possible ways in which ideologies may be linked to problem orientations: as explicit symbolic guides in situations where such guides are lacking; and as a way that existing symbolic guides, such as current ideologies, are weakened. But there is also a third consequence: ideology may affect the very meaning men give to their social situations, in some cases actually helping to create the problem orientations to which they respond. Ideologies may "create problems" by introducing new sets of symbols (or applying existing symbols in new ways) and thus giving new meanings to existing situations. An ideology may change "justice" into "injustice," convert "right" into "might," transform a malaise into a problem or turn a private trouble into a public problem.[26]

The various ways that ideologies are linked to people's existing orientations helps us better to understand important connections between *ideology* and *leadership*. Ideologies do not somehow appear as responses to strain and get mystically diffused. They must be created and propagated. In situations where people regard their world as problematic and have even begun to doubt existing institutionalized guides, there still may be no ideological activity. We are thus led to at least pose the questions: Why do people not create alternatives? What are the obstacles to the creation of new sets of symbols? In Chapter 7, I will explore what some of these obstacles were in Jaida Arriba. They throw light on a phenomenon noted in much of the literature on peasant movements: that ideologies come from outside the peasant communities. Because of the difficulties many peasants may have in reconceptualizing their world, "brokers" and leaders come to take on great importance. These people often create ideologies, or bring them from the outside to the peasant, or modify new conceptions to fit local needs. And they use ideologies to make people "see clearly" the problems they have, to see the failures of existing guides to action, and to see the usefulness of these new ideologies as guides. The above theoretical approach also suggests an approach to a problem pointed to by Wolf: why organizers and leaders are or are not successful in promoting a new ideology.[27] Those who introduce or encourage an ideology, like the ideology itself, will be perceived and judged in terms of existing orientations.[28]

One important question still remains: given various ideologies, all of which seek to mobilize thought and action regarding an existing social situation, why do some take hold and others not? This problem is discussed by Geertz. Interest theory, he writes, talks of interests "corresponding to" or "being reflected in" ideologies; strain theory about emotions "finding a symbolic outlet" or becoming "attached to appropriate symbols"—but there is "little idea of how the trick is really done" (1964:56). "The link between the causes of ideology and its effects seems adventitious because the connecting element—the autonomous process of symbolic formulation—is passed over in virtual silence." (1964:56–57)."

How ideologies actually function is beyond the scope of this chapter, but the directions such an analysis might take can be suggested. A new ideology will face this fundamental problem: the symbols it presents will be interpreted and judged in terms of the existing culture. Just as the orientations people have toward an aspect of their social situations are important in determining whether or not they feel a need for an explicit symbolic guide, so too are existing orientations important in shaping people's reactions toward the symbolic guides, definitions, and solutions offered by a new ideology. A new ideology must be perceived as acceptable within the culture. We can then ask: what effects are preexisting orientations going to have on the acceptance or rejection of an ideology? I will explore two ways in which ideologies may gain acceptance in the context of existing orientations: by reformulating and using existing cultural symbols, or by formulating new symbols or ideas, "nesting" them into the symbolic bed that already exists.

An example of the first was the cooperative's use of existing symbols of prestige in its struggle for acceptance. The social standing of those who introduced, promoted, or criticized the cooperative proved an important factor in the acceptance or rejection of the cooperative ideology.[29] Furthermore, a variety of orientations often exists within a culture which might be applied to give different meanings to a particular situation. By applying available meanings or symbols differently, an ideology can shape a new understanding of a given situation. If, for instance, both a Catholic Ethic and a Protestant Ethic are orientations available in a culture (that is, in some situations people argue that one should accept God's will and in others that

God helps those who help themselves), then by reapplying these symbols to situations where they were not before applied, people may be encouraged to think about them differently.

The second way ideology may function to gain acceptance—through formulating new symbols and "nesting" them within an existing culture—is touched on in various ways by a number of authors. In examining why "certain cultural systems and values multiply, move, and spread successfully (become 'best sellers') while others do not spread at all or spread little," Pitirim Sorokin argued that two of the conditions that explain the differential spread are "the nature of the system or value" and "the nature of the culture of penetration and diffusion" (1959:620–21). The more complex, refined, and difficult to understand the cultural system being introduced, Sorokin argued, the more difficult will be its spread (Sorokin 1959:622). This same rationale lies behind Converse's argument that "what" information is more easily transmitted than "why" information—that "it is easier to know that two ideas go together without knowing why" (1964:212).

As to the existing culture *into* which the new cultural system is diffused, Sorokin wrote that, other conditions being equal, "the more congenial to a given value the culture of its penetration and diffusion is, the greater the diffusion, the more chances it has for becoming a best-seller" (1959:527). But Sorokin remains vague about what congeniality means except some comments that indicate certain kinds of logical relationships ("consistent," "casual," "contradictory") among values.[30] It is doubtful, however, that the people's perceptions of the new ideology are based on such criteria.[31] In my analysis, I will focus on how people understand the new symbols, the meaning they give to these symbols; hopefully, this will provide some understanding of how new symbolic elements in an ideology do or do not "fit" into a given culture.

An ideology may not always be "congenial" with all the orientations in an existing culture. A culture suspicious of outsiders will pose obstacles to an ideology "brought in" by outsiders; a culture in which people are suspicious of each other will pose difficulties for an ideology that argues that each must trust the other with his money. One must recognize the possibility that any ideology may encounter "resonance" or "dissonance" given existing orientations, and then pose the questions: In what ways were existing orientations conducive to or obstacles to the acceptance of an ideology? And how, if at all, did the ideology function to overcome existing obstacles? In exploring how the peasants in Jaida Arriba viewed an action-oriented ideology based on collectivistic and solidaristic principles and introduced by people outside the community, I will examine the kinds of orientations that existed toward action, toward collectivistic activities, toward others in the community, and toward outsiders.[32]

A clue for exploring how new symbols are formulated and gain acceptance is also provided by Geertz. He does not present a detailed explanation of the process of symbolic formulation, but he does suggest where to look: at the efforts of those who have attempted "to construct an independent science of what Kenneth Burke has called 'symbolic action' " (1964:57).[33] What is needed is a notion of "how symbols symbolize, how they function to mediate meanings" (1964:57). Geertz gives an example of how one element of style—metaphor—functions to give meaning, transforming, for example, false identifications (like that of "slave labor laws") into analogies (like the labor policies of the Republican party) that can guide thought, feeling, and action in a particular way.

Geertz further emphasizes that the meanings metaphors attempt to spark are socially rooted and "the success or failure of the attempt is relative not only to the power of the stylistic mechanisms employed" but also to the social, psychological, and cultural contexts (1964:59). Geertz's suggestion to explore stylistic elements such as metaphors to understand how symbols symbolize or function to mediate meanings may be useful in understanding both how ideologies formulate new symbols and "fit" them into the existing culture and how they reformulate and use existing symbols.[34]

In the following two chapters the theoretical suggestions made above will be applied in an effort to answer the first two questions posed at the beginning of this chapter. In addition to the class position of various groups in Jaida Arriba (discussed in Chapters 3 and 4) we will have to understand how their particular orientations toward the social situation shaped their acceptance or rejection of the cooperative ideology. Further, we need to explain the variety, stability, and change in these orientations—how they were generated, sustained, weakened, or threatened by certain life situations and experiences. We shall see if the orientation they had before 1967 was one of a malaise or of a problem; whether they thought about difficulties or problems as private or public; and, in situations felt as problematic, how they judged existing strategies, ideologies, or symbolic guides for thought, feeling, and behavior. We will then explore the extent to which the cooperative ideology was created and accepted in a situation where people both experienced a problem orientation toward their situation *and* perceived available institutionalized guides or ideologies to be lacking, weak, or inadequate.

CHAPTER 7

WHY NO NEW IDEOLOGY?

In this chapter I will explore the question: why did no ideology or movement aimed at collective action, either to alleviate existing economic difficulties or to struggle against the control of the middlemen, arise in Jaida Arriba before 1967? One answer is this: before 1967 no one introduced to the peasants the idea of forming a cooperative. But this assumes that ideologies and movements only arise when they are "brought to" the peasants from outside the campo; it avoids an exploration of why an ideology or movement did not arise from among the peasants themselves. This is what I wish to explore, examining first how the peasants thought about their economic situation and their relations with the middlemen.

THE ECONOMIC SITUATION: MANY PROBLEMS, FEW SOLUTIONS

The discussion in Chapter 3 showed how pressures deriving from particular forms of production, growing families, and inheritance patterns confronted the peasants with an increasing scarcity of productive land, a lack of work, and a near-continual money shortage. These pressures, we saw, had a differential impact on different classes. But we have little notion of how the peasants themselves saw either their economic situation or the strategies available to meet basic needs.

DAY LABORERS AND SMALL HOLDERS. The lack of productive land and the continual money shortage made existence a constant problem for day laborers and small holders. Each peasant regarded these problems as personal ones. Each was tormented by the doubts arising from these insecurities:

> My head is tortured when I can't find food for the kids—and with such bad land, my harvests don't help at all. One lives suffering each day. Perhaps today I'm able to eat, but perhaps tomorrow no. And knowing that the children are going to have to spend the day sick with hunger.

130

Me, I'm tough—I can stand it. But little children! I'm not even able to sleep. Sometimes I lie down, exhausted, and perhaps I get the first little sleep. But afterward I toss and turn, thinking how poor one is—unable to give food to the family, clothes to the family, give them a proper education.

Given this continual problem of sustaining self and family, what traditional guides or strategies could the day laborer or small holder follow? How did he think about them?

The most common strategy to earn money for food was to sell personal or family labor. But these peasants saw this strategy as far from adequate. Work was scarce, except during the coffee harvest. When they found work, the peso a day it paid seemed barely enough to feed their families that day, let alone the following day when no work could be found. Further, they had difficulty earning the money they needed to work what little land they might have. The continual search for scarce, low-paying work instead of working their own land or having a steady job was experienced as a personal problem, a severe obstacle to survival.

My biggest worry is having to spend the whole day looking for work and not being able to find it and feed the little ones. Perhaps at night, when I'm desperate, I'll just go to anyone and say: "Pay me a day, because I don't have anything with which to give food to the children." I get a peso, and I go and work the next day. This peso goes. But the next day I wake up in the same bind: who am I going to get another peso from. . . . Working by the day, hoping to eat at night, maybe getting a peso—I don't see how I can climb out of this.[1]

The comerciantes sometimes provided another temporary strategy for survival. The poor peasant who awoke with no food to feed his family often could go to Manuel or Puro for a pound of sugar and rice and a few plantains on credit for a day or two. But such credit was only a stopgap, a way to eat that day. Sometimes obtaining credit was difficult or impossible since the comerciante hesitated if he was unsure of being repaid.

After credit or a small loan was secured, the day laborer or small holder faced a new problem: with little or no production, scarce work, and low wages, how was he going to pay back the money? The immediate strategies the day laborers and small holders applied to meeting their basic needs thus were seen as inadequate or nonexistent. But what of strategies for future improvement?

One of the cultural norms in the community prescribed that one build now for a better future. But the actual economic situation of the day laborers and small holders made the institutionalized routes recommended for improvement seem impossible if not barred. The common way to get ahead was through agricultural production with the harvest earnings being applied to family needs and new production costs. Working one's land, however, required some capital. Yet with little land, poor soil, and meager harvests, few were willing to provide such capital to a small holder. The peasant was thus caught in a bind:

> Here one is completely caught. You can't work this waste land. You want to plant beans, but they cost $2.50 a box for planting. And they probably won't produce enough to pay it back. So what store is going to give you credit for food for all these days that you are working your own land? The land doesn't yield. Look, to make a conuco I'd have to plow. Without plowing it would be useless. But I'd have to pay $1.50 for a team of oxen. But where am I going to get the money? Anybody would be afraid to lend me this money because they are afraid that the production wouldn't give enough to pay them back.

If the small holder did plant and harvest his crops it would still be difficult to put aside any earnings: that not already owed to whoever financed the harvest was instantly absorbed by urgent family needs.

Another common way to improve one's situation was buying and raising animals. By selling a fatted calf, a peasant earned the money to buy land to expand production or purchase more animals to build up his livestock. But day laborers faced extreme difficulty in accumulating even the small capital needed to buy a pig ($10 to $15) or a calf ($30 to $40). Sometimes they could share the cost (a medias, or half and half) of purchasing the animal with someone, but this mechanism offered only limited future improvement. The animal was difficult to hold in the face of continual needs for immediate cash for bills or medicine. And when the day laborer or small holder sold an animal bought a media, one-half of the gross profit went to the person who first supplied half the initial capital; and the remainder often was earmarked for past debts.

The strategies for solving the problems of everyday existence and for improving one's future situation were thus felt by the day laborers and small holders to be inadequate at best. A lack of land, scarce work, low wages, continual money shortage and debt: this was the situation the peasant daily experienced as a crisis, the everyday face of the personal problems he saw engulfing him.

When existing strategies failed, these peasants often expressed a sense of resignation toward their misery. A day laborer, whose youngest child died a few days after we spoke, told me of his ongoing tragedy: the acceptance of a fate against which he saw himself powerless.

> So here I am today with neither health nor funds. What I'm most worried about at this moment is my situation—I simply can't meet all needs at the moment—but I'm resigned. All I have are my own two arms and the grace of God. My hope is that God'll give me some way to

earn something, even if it's only enough to keep my family alive. If they deserve it. If not I'm resigned to whatever God wants. The only thing that has kept me going is that I'm a person who has always had faith in God and in the Virgin Mary. And no matter how down and out I am, I never lose my faith in God.

Many wondered if there were any way out of their dilemmas—except, perhaps, through the grace of God, El Presidente, or a rich patron. Such solutions are a characteristic of what Richard Morse, following Weber, calls a Catholic society: "In a Catholic society . . . people's positions and their hopes for improving them (or of achieving salvation) are determined by institutions or authority figures" (1969:13).[2] Many students of peasants have noted their fatalism and resignation to existing conditions, their hope for change residing in the hands of powers above.[3] But it is important to recognize that such beliefs are *not* simply the products of a culture, transmitted through a socialization process, that has stamped its members with a fatalistic and resigned orientation toward life. Rather, such beliefs are socially generated and sustained; they help make sense of near-permanent poverty and dark futures.[4] If they were resigned to never having enough to eat, it was because they had no land and could think of no way to get it. If they knew not where to turn, except to God or some patron for the money they needed to eat, it was because they saw nobody who would give them work. "What a guy is most worried about here is that he won't find anything to latch onto— worried sick because he goes out looking for a buck or two and he just can't find it. We're really living in a crisis now. I live in such a state that I don't even want to think anymore about how I'm going to spend the rest of my life—if you have nowhere to go, to earn a peso or two. The only thing you can count on is God's will." If they saw debt was inevitable, it was because they saw no way to pay without falling further in debt. "You borrow $5 and pay it off little by little, and while you're paying off, you have to go out and borrow some more. Then you're trapped. You're going to end up spending the rest of your life in crisis and poverty." The day laborers and small holders were not unaware of the cultural value placed on hard work, struggle, and self-help as against merely waiting for divine intervention. Many still tried such strategies despite continual failures; but often they saw no way to help themselves. The only cultural alternative then available for making some sense of seeming futility and impossibility was hope for help from above:

Here I don't. . . . I don't. . . . I don't even know where to turn. But I always think that God will help me. One has to make an effort yes. Because God says: "Help yourself, and I will help you." But here in the campo, it's got to be something done by the hand of God. The best we can do here is try to find a day's work. And where are you going to get with this? You earn a peso, you eat fifty cents and you put the other fifty cents to work. But if you don't have any food, you're going to have to eat this fifty cents too. No matter how much economizing you do with a peso, the most you're going to have left is five cents. Right now I'm trying to find someone who can help me. And I am asking God for a better future for my family. Without land, how are you able to work? The only exit I say is New York. Here there is no way to rise. Maybe if God helps me. If God does not wish it, I'm not going to get out of this situation here or in New York.

THE MIDDLE AND LARGE HOLDERS The middle and large holders in Jaida Arriba shared with their day laborers and small holders this continual or near-continual shortage of money. This mutual problem gave the cooperative an appeal across class lines. There was, however, an important difference: most middle and large holders had land and production sufficient to meet subsistence needs without having to sell their labor or that of their families. Their major problem was how to get money between harvests. The three traditional strategies open to them—credit from comerciantes, sale of animals, and preharvest selling of their coffee—were all inadequate.

The credit they could get (on the basis of their coffee production) temporarily solved their immediate money problem but put them into near-continual debt. They worried constantly whether their harvests would yield enough to repay loans. "You spend the year working, and the harvest arrives, and what happens? You find you owe more than the harvest produced. How are you going to pay all those debts? You have to hope that the comerciante will give you more credit—that he'll let you pay him back the next year. But the next year you find you owe twice as much. And what happens if the harvest isn't enough again? Better to throw a lasso over the branch of a pine tree and hang yourself!" Not being able to pay one's debts was a cause for *verguenza* (shame). One might be thought an untrustworthy person. And unpaid debts lessened the chances for getting credit again. The threat was real for these peasants: "I couldn't sleep at night thinking of all the money I owed. When you take credit it's because your fields don't have crops yet. You live with a tremendous debt, an enormous debt, realizing all the time that you owe money and don't have a cent to pay with. And you're terrified that you're going to default."

The second strategy available to these peasants (especially some of the larger holders) was the sale of a pig or a cow. Although few had much livestock, they had more salable animals than did the day laborers and small holders. But this strategy was also felt to have severe limitations. Only a handful of large holders had sufficient livestock to absorb such sales without sacrificing their efforts to maintain and increase their herds. Most were struggling to develop their livestock, and the sale of one of their three or four cows was a severe blow.

The third strategy was to sell their coffee before the harvest. But the effects of this strategy were considered onerous because the peasant faced future debts and sacrificed much of his earnings. "To sell the coffee at half price we had to be absolutely against the wall, desperate to find a way to defend the family." Pre-harvest selling was done only in cases of absolute necessity: to save a life, bring a child to the doctor, to pick ripe coffee which threatened to fall to the ground and rot. How to avoid preharvest selling was a problem the peasants experienced each time urgent cash needs arose.

Faced with the frequent problems of how to pay debts, meet cash shortages, avoid sacrificing animals, and escape preharvest selling, many of the middle and large holders sought some means to improve (or at least maintain) their present situations. But they were aware that the traditional strategies for improvement—increasing livestock and expanding agricultural production— were severely limited.

The large holders (and to a lesser extent the middle holders) had more possibilities than did poorer peasants to develop their livestock; their money from coffee harvests, more available pasture, and more food from their conucos enabled them to fatten at least some animals. Nevertheless, serious pressures impeded this strategy. The open forests where their fathers had grazed large herds were becoming settled and enclosed. With lands being subdivided among families, pasturing land was growing increasingly scarce. And urgent cash needs continually threatened attempts to develop a herd.

The large and middle holders also faced severe limitations on expanding agricultural production. The unlimited forests their fathers had cleared and planted were dwindling quickly; even those few with money to buy new land saw that there was little for sale. Mamón put the problem this way:

> You know, I have nine boys. The little land I have is not enough. How are they going to make a living on a few tareas? But the most serious thing is when the little ones begin to cry because they don't have enough to eat. The ones that are a bit older, it's not as bad. At least they'll know why they're going hungry. But the little ones aren't going to understand the why. In the old days, one never had to buy staples. There was always land to plant them. But now it's different. You have to buy everything except water and firewood. When you have to buy plantains and sweet potatoes you know things are bad! In the old days we never thought much about the future. If you wanted to clear a conuco, you cleared it. But since then things have gotten tighter and tighter.

Most of the large and middle holders, then, did not see any effective strategies for coping with dwindling resources or with the everyday problems of near-continual debt, frequent cash shortages, losses from preharvest selling, and forced sale of animals. These problems appeared as "given" facts of life. Many rarely even conceived the possibility of now being in debt. They could struggle to solve these problems, but their failures had to be accepted with sad patience and anxious resignation. But like the day laborers and small holders, their fatalism did not come from being a "fatalistic people" created by a "fatalistic culture." Indeed, many of the large and middle holders saw certain spheres of life where one could and should change the world through human action: they and their fathers had been the pioneers who had cleared and planted the land and created what they had today; they believed that one got ahead in agriculture through hard work, that one lives by the sweat of one's brow; they thought many day laborers were poor because they did not work hard enough, did not put their earnings into pigs or animals or land, did not struggle to plant and weed what little land they had: "If you like fish, you have to get your ass wet to catch some. But some people like others to catch the fish for them and to bring the fish to them. They like a low-hanging mango that's easy to pick."

But despite this work ethic, their situation of money shortage and continual debt often supported a fatalism when they saw no way out. They incurred the debts buying on credit because "your daily needs simply forced you to." They did not want to sell their coffee a la flor, but they saw no other way. "That was really something. . . . I get the shivers just thinking about it. No matter how much you thought, there was no way out of those problems! They were so big you don't know which way to turn. Your head became cloudy—your mind fogged up. Your wife was sick and you didn't have a cent to take her to the doctor. You just couldn't beat those problems, so you were forced to sell a la flor." One peasant explained: "We conformed with this slavery, living in the problem, but not trying to find a solution." Such problems were burdens that had to be borne: "We were like the mules in a pack train: you put a burden on them and they don't shout." This orientation is perhaps most vividly captured by the metaphor of "blindness" which they use today to characterize their former beliefs. "We were blind, not thinking about anything. There was no road open to us to get out. We lived like slaves, thinking this was our destiny. We didn't have this knowledge that man can change with his actions, with his ideas."

The problems felt by the day laborers and small holders were in certain ways felt by the middle and large holders: all were concerned how to get the money with which to meet certain needs, all felt existing strategies were wanting. But for the middle and large holders the problem was getting needed money to hold them until their land produced its harvest; for the day laborers and small holders the problem was how to get land that produced or steady work. For the middle and large holders the problem was not "how to eat that day" but "how to pay back the money that always seemed owed." Improving, or even maintaining, their existing economic situation was also of great concern to all the peasants. But if traditional strategies seemed inadequate for the middle and large holders, they were nonexistent for the poorer peasants.

The peasants of Jaida Arriba thus faced certain problems in meeting their most basic needs; and the strategies or guides suggested by their culture and experiences seemed to most either inadequate or useless. Why no ideology arose or was created in such a situation before 1967 (despite the existence of conditions seen as necessary in the theoretical approach in Chapter 6) will be the subject of the final section of this chapter, "Obstacles to Problem Definition and Ideology Formation." But here two additional points should be made about what the peasant did not perceive.

The problems felt by the peasants were seen as private, not public, and the strategies they followed recommended individual remedies. The cooperative ideology transforms these private problems into public ones. Further, these problems were not unified into any simple, accepted, well-defined orientation. The peasants felt themselves faced with a variety of problems: how to get more land, how to get work, how to get the money to eat or buy medicine or bury a family member, how to pay back debts, how to avoid selling a la flor. But in no sense did the peasants share an overriding concern with the creation of a fund to meet their present and future needs. Thus the drive toward forming a cooperative crystallized and unified these various problems into a common desire for a collective fund to meet money shortages.

THE MIDDLEMEN: JUST OR UNJUST?

Understanding peasant attitudes toward the comerciantes also helps explain why the peasants did not organize to challenge these middlemen before 1967. Did the peasants feel wronged by the injustice of these men or helped by their favors? Did they see them as honest or dishonest, trustworthy or suspect? Did they even conceive of these men as exercising control? Was their relationship to these comerciantes felt as problematic?[5]

PROJIMIDAD VERSUS *POR INTERÉS.* One central dynamic in the peasant-middleman relationship centered around the exchange of goods and capital for crops: the comerciante provided the credit or preharvest advances the peasant urgently needed; in return, the peasant sold his crops to the comerciante. This relationship drew the peasants into near-continual debt. The payment of such debts was a constant problem. But we have not yet explored the sets of moral criteria by which the peasant actually judged the comerciante's actions. One criterion derived from traditional notions of exchange and obligation; another from money-based economic relations. The first centered around the concepts of *projimidad* and *por interés*.

Projimidad literally translated means neighborliness. A *prójimo* is not merely a geographical neighbor, but one who helps out in times of need by giving assistance with work, sending food to a hungry neighbor, or lending money (without interest) to help someone facing a crisis of illness or death. "If I'm able, and I see a person in need, I have to help him out, I have to give him something. If you see a guy who doesn't have any beans, you have to give him some." Much of this traditional notion is captured by the term *caridad* (charity), a word with a more religious aura.

One important response to such projimidad is *agradecimiento* (gratefulness). One is thankful and appreciative for the help offered. Further, the receiver becomes obligated to the giver. One who receives help from a neighbor on an exchange labor team must reciprocate likewise. A peasant who sends food to a neighbor who is sick or short of food would expect the same if he were in need. Or he might later receive a sack of sweet potatoes or a few bunches of bananas. When I was given food and shelter by the families I visited, I gave the family photographs to express my agradecimiento. When one reciprocates, however, what is given should not imply "repayment." Thus a peasant gets "invited" to help on an exchange labor team of one who has helped him; one sends a sack of sweet potatoes or a photograph as a gift, not as payment.[6] If, however, repayment is implied in the reciprocity, this infers that the person who originally did the giving acted por interés (out of self-interest) and he would feel *avergonzado* (ashamed). This would be an insult! Acting por interés is the frowned-upon opposite of acting out of projimidad or caridad. When someone acts out of self-interest he gives to receive, not to help.[7] Further, when someone capable of giving refuses to help someone in need, he too is acting por interés.

Such giving and reciprocating defined the traditional relationship between the peasants and the comerciantes: the comerciante was a projimista if he provided "help" (credit and advances) and was willing to "hold out" until the peasant could get the money, or harvest the crop, needed to pay; the peasant reciprocated with his crops and business. The comerciante was acting por interés (and thus wrongly) if he refused to give credit or advances or pressured a peasant to pay a debt.

Because all the peasants received at least some credit or advances from the comerciantes, their judgment of these men as projimistas received frequent support. The peasants, in turn, "grateful" to the comerciantes, loyally sold their crops and bought their goods from the comerciante who had been "helping" them.[8] Many would have felt deep shame at leaving a comerciante who had been helping them for years in order to find a better deal elsewhere; such would be acting por interés and ungrateful. These traditional relationships, however, were often undermined when economic considerations forced the comerciantes to act by different rules.

The comerciantes supplied the peasant with commodities bought on the market and sold for profit; in turn, the peasant exchanged his crops with the comerciante not simply in gratitude but as commodities with a money value that were "owed as payment of a debt." Although the comerciantes often thought of their actions as "help," they also thought about "profit and loss." If the comerciante acted as "neighbor," credit and advances should have been given to all in need for however long they were in need; but if the comerciante acted as "businessman," he needed to deal only with those who surely could "pay back" and to limit the term of loans. One comerciante explained: "Charity and business are two different things. If you mix charity with business, you go broke." Such capitalistic economic criteria were, from the traditional frame of reference, "wrong": such was acting por interés. The conflict manifested itself in a number of ways.[9]

Skeptical of the ability of some peasants to pay, the comerciantes might refuse or limit credit or ask when payment could be expected. The peasant would judge these actions as por interés and often bitterly resented them. Instead of being treated as "a Christian" who had real needs, the peasant was treated as a commodity and valued for what he owned: "What you're worth is what you have." One peasant remarked: "If I go into a store and ask for some help, they'll ask me: 'And how are you going to pay it off?', And I'd tell them: 'I'm hoping to get work so I can pay it off.' And they'll tell me: 'I can't give you credit.' Then they may give me a few grains of sugar, to boil a tea. Here there's no help for anybody." And one small holder laughed at the suggestion that the comerciantes were projimista: "If you're in front of a pine tree, and they're behind you, and they can push the trunk over on you to get rid of you, they'll do it. They've got their money, so it doesn't matter to them if you die."

All the comerciantes in the region of Jaida Arriba suffered such criticisms, but some of Manuel's actions were particularly resented. Set on doing a good job as manager of Pedro's comercio, Manuel was extremely careful to whom he gave credit and advances, avoiding many of Pedro's "charitable" actions that had contributed to his economic difficulties. But it was just such projimidad of Pedro against which Manuel was judged.

Although many of the middle and most of the large holders had little difficulty with credit, they too were not blind to the interés behind it. They knew that the comerciantes often gained benefits from the crops the peasants sold to pay for credit advanced. "Whenever I'd go into someone's store to get a pound of sugar or rice and he'd let me have it, I knew damn well he let me have it because he had his eye on my crop." Some also noticed that prices on credit were often higher. This was not "the rightful cost one paid for credit," but the comerciante "taking advantage" of one's lack of cash, or perhaps even trying to deceive. The credit relationship itself, however, was rarely seen as a form of control (a way to "bind" clients or to "get a hold of" crops) and almost never as a problem needing a solution. Few people asked themselves: "How can I avoid buying on credit so I don't obligate my crops, or have to pay higher prices." Whatever the difficulties, credit buying was still the only strategy for meeting everyday food needs; and the peasants, who always received at least some credit some of the time, were grateful for this "help" despite the interés they saw. A large holder explained: "We felt grateful to those people, because naturally, we were hungry and we didn't have any money. Then we'd go to him, and he'd tell us: 'Sure! With pleasure. Anything you need.' But we knew that they were the ones that came up on top, not us."

There was, however, one sphere where the link between debt and the control of the price of one's crops was clear to all: the preharvest advances made for coffee a la flor. The peasants saw how great were their losses—and the comprador's gain. "There was no doubt about it—from $20 to $30 ... that was unfair, since you knew he was really making a lot of money. His profits were really too much!" But even here resentment was mixed with, and often tempered by, gratitude. The peasant in urgent need of cash before the harvest to cure his wife or weed his crop was grateful to a comerciante willing to advance money a la flor despite the loss. "With your wife sick—even if you were losing money, you were grateful to them for buying your coffee a la flor. There was no other choice, when you needed the money so badly."

The peasants, then, viewed the comerciantes with mixed feelings; they were not seen as simply "right" or "wrong," "good" or "bad," "just" or "unjust."[10] This ambiguity later proved important. The ability of the co-operative to define the middlemen as a "problem" and to weaken their control depended on its tapping already existing currents of resentment toward the self-interest of the comerciantes and turning them against the bonds of gratitude for past help.

THE HONEST MAN VERSUS THE CROOK. Although the peasants criticized the purely economic criteria used by the comerciantes, such criteria did have some legitimacy.[11] The peasants themselves frequently were involved in business dealings such as raising cash crops for the market, buying and selling labor. They recognized that one must "make money" to get ahead in this world. But only certain ways of making money were "right." And "rightness" meant "honesty" and "trust" (confianza). A good comerciante was one whom the peasants could trust: they could depend on him to "give what was just or fair" for their crops. He was "an honest man" who would not try to overcharge them on provisions. On the other hand, one was wary of the possible deceiver or crook.

Many peasants suspected certain comerciantes, such as Manuel, of some-times trying to deceive them, although there was no public admission or statement of this. Publicly these comerciantes were deemed honest. Indeed most peasants who sometimes felt "taken" did not think of the comerciantes as systematically deceiving them. "Perhaps," they would say, "it was an error." If the peasant felt he had been overcharged, he raised no questions, accepting such actions quietly, resignedly. They were timid about biting the hand that fed them and knew that if they complained, the comerciante would simply explain the error as the peasant's. Many peasants also suspected that the comerciantes were taking advantage of their urgent needs by offering an unfair price, although before the cooperative accusations such as the following rarely would have been stated publicly: "All these negociantes rob you blind. If you have a plantain grove that is worth $200, and you have to sell it, they'll only pay you $100. And because I'm hard up, I have to let them have it. He's the only one who has money. I have to go to him because I'm hard up." A common practice of the compradores further underscored this suspicion: they would offer certain of the larger coffee growers "special deals" of fifty cents or a peso more per fanega to get their coffee, and the peasant was told "not to tell anyone."

Some peasants also resented not being treated with trust by the comerciantes. When they asked for credit or an advance, they did so with every intention of paying it back. But the comerciante might refuse 'such requests on purely economic grounds. Not only was such an action wrong as self-interest, but the peasants saw it as a challenge to their honesty, implying that they were not "trustworthy people" and were trying to deceive the comerciante. Such a refusal was resented as an insult, a cause for verguenza. One small holder explained: "I take credit from Manuel. He may give me stuff on credit, but he makes a face, like he doesn't trust me. But if somebody with money walks in, he's all smiles. With me, since I'm a poor man, he makes a face. You feel ashamed when you see the face he's making but you still have to ask for credit. You feel like two cents if he refuses you, and you crawl back again that afternoon to see if maybe he's changed his mind. That's what you call feeling like two cents. We aren't trying to trick anybody; sometimes, we're just not producing anything."

These "grievances" were thought of as personal difficulties, not public problems, and were heard only in the intimacy of one's own kitchen. They were perceived as an inevitable part of life. And after all, despite these difficulties, the comerciantes were the only source of credit and cash advances. Thus few ever conceived of the comerciantes as a problem. Few asked the question: how can the comerciantes be avoided or eliminated?

EL PEJE GRANDE (THE BIG FISH). Thus, the middlemen were judged by at least two important contrasting sets of values: projimidad versus por interés and "honesty" versus "crookedness." Although the relationship with the comerciantes was not itself seen to be problematic, certain actions of particular comerciantes were judged as bad or wrong precisely because they were acting por interés or dishonestly. But a certain malaise also permeated the relationship with the comerciantes that was related to, but not completely described by, these criteria.

The peasants often bore a resentment, sometimes bitter, sometimes mild, toward those who were "better off." Words like *los ricos* (the rich) or la gente grande always carried an inference of resentment and envy: "Here are we poor struggling to eat or have a house with a roof that does not leak while these rich folk have life so easy." There were only vague notions of "classes" of people whose power was based on the control of certain scarce resources and who were part of a larger system. But an undercurrent of resentment was plain.[12]

This quiet resentment for los ricos often was matched by a deep current of suspicion and distrust: a "powerful man" was likely to take whatever advantage he could of the poor (a belief with considerable grounding in everyday life). "The big fish always gobbles up the small fish." Such people lived "mounted on one as if one were a mule," leaving the peasants with "the yoke placed."

The gente grande were also seen suspiciously as "intelligent people," *gente que sabe* (clever or wise people). They knew how to take advantage of a business transaction; they knew how to get ahead and would very likely take advantage of *un campesino bruto* (a stupid, ignorant peasant). "The guy who knows something lives off those who don't know anything; I'm talking about people who have a good head, either for business or for swindling."

These beliefs continually underlay peasant dealings with the comerciantes: however grateful they were for the help of these men, however honest a particular comerciante seemed to be, there was still resentment of their better position and a suspicion that they might be using their savvy to take advantage. "The comerciante never figures that he's going to end up in the bottom someday, he thinks he's always going to be on top. And he climbs up over the small men." In any dealings with a comerciante, one thus had to be wary, suspicious.

While this suspicion and resentment against the comerciantes rarely took public form, it nourished a certain malaise; certain things were "bad" about one's daily relationship with the comerciantes despite surface cordiality and often deeply felt gratitude. But until the cooperative ideology harnessed this current, the actual relationship with the comerciantes itself was not questioned as problematic.

LACK OF PERCEPTION OF CONTROL. The nonproblematic orientation toward the middlemen was supported in another important way: most peasants had only vague perceptions of the comerciantes as exercising "control." They conceived of control only in this limited sense: the comerciantes could decide whether to give credit or advances, or could tinker with prices on credit purchases. Few thought of the comerciantes as a group who "controlled cash and credit" or "controlled access to markets" and used such control to "set prices" on coffee or on consumer goods. This lack of a clear understanding or conception of control was sustained by a geographic and cultural isolation from the business world of the pueblo.

With little contact with retail prices in the pueblo (and no contact with wholesale prices), the peasants had little systematic idea of price differences. Some were discontent when they noticed higher prices for credit purchases, but such discontent was never publicly stated nor were price differences clearly defined.

The peasants, furthermore, did not perceive the comerciantes as controlling access to the market—as standing between them and substantially higher prices for their crops at the exporting houses or on the international market. The word *intermediario* (intermediary or middleman), connoting the control exercised by a comprador in his position between the peasant and the market, was not introduced into everyday speech until the cooperative was organized. The lack of such a perception was in part maintained by the comerciantes themselves. They would agree among themselves not to reveal to the peasants the prices in their contracts with the exporters. Instead they would explain that they were getting but a peso more than they were offering. The peasants had little way of knowing otherwise. They might suspect that the comerciante was taking some advantage of them, but they had no clear idea of exactly how much. Indeed, the peasants had little notion of how the market system worked: many did not know that exporting houses even existed. There was, instead, some vague thing "out there" called the "market"; the local comerciante had access to its mysteries.

The few large holders who did know something of the kind of control being exercised over prices did so because they were given special deals. But such deals were conditional on their keeping things secret. Puro himself discovered how much the major compradores were getting only in 1966.

> Arturo trusted me a lot, and once he invited me to take a trip with him to Puerto Rico when he went there to make a contract with an exporting firm. He showed me the contract and he told me: "I'll let you see the contract but don't tell anybody about the prices. You have to watch out for me, protect me from the other negociantes. I'll take 200 quintales from you and make only 50 cents on each one. But if the others come and ask you how much you're selling for, tell them it's $28." And Arturo paid me $33, and he sold for $34. From that time on, I was on my guard because I realized that we were pretty much in the dark in these matters. Most people knew nothing, absolutely nothing. The buyers would offer us a price and we'd say "amen."

Credit itself was not viewed as a mechanism of control—as a way in which the comerciantes "captured" peasant products by obligating debt payment with crops at whatever price they set. At most there was a certain uneasiness when a peasant felt obligated to sell his crops to a comerciante despite better prices elsewhere. Furthermore, credit itself was not a problem; it was a traditional way of life. A peasant worried about the debts he was incurring, but he could not conceive of living without such credit. Often he merely sent his coffee to the comerciante as each fanega was harvested and dried without even asking the price. Only at the end of the harvest would he go to see if his debts were paid and there were anything left over. "At that time, we weren't really aware that we weren't being paid enough for our crops, that the buyer was paying us whatever he wanted. We didn't realize anything—we took on credit, we paid with the harvest, and we really weren't thinking about what we were doing. All we worried about was how to pay off the debts, worried that what we produced was less than what we spent."

Just as there was little awareness of the losses incurred by selling through the comerciantes, little thought was given to the comerciantes' use of their capital as a mechanism of control. One important exception existed: the buying of coffee a la flor. The peasants, we saw, viewed such a strategy as a problem in itself. They saw how much they were losing on each fanega of coffee. And they consciously perceived the comerciantes using their control over money to exercise control over prices. The fact that control was perceived and resented in at least one sphere was to play an important role in the concientización of the peasants by the cooperative.

Most peasants, then, viewed their relationships with the middlemen in terms of the help these comerciantes provided. Particular actions might seem wrong, and there was a certain malaise: there was a general suspicion and resentment of the middlemen as *peje grande*; overcharging on credit purchases was often considered crooked; and at the same time as credit and preharvest buying were gratefully received as acts of projimidad, strong undertones of por interés were present. But the middlemen were not seen as a problem. This in part explains why there was no ideological activity or movement aimed at collective action against the control of the middlemen before 1967. Conversely, it helps to explain one of the ways the middlemen were able to maintain their control: their control was hardly perceived as such, let alone thought of as problematic. How these orientations toward the middlemen were socially generated and sustained were touched upon briefly in this part, but an important question still needs examination: why was the existing malaise not transformed into a clearly defined problem before 1968?

OBSTACLES TO PROBLEM DEFINITION AND IDEOLOGY FORMATION

In the first part of this chapter we saw that the peasants felt a number of problems in meeting basic needs and viewed existing strategies for coping with these problems as inadequate or impracticable. Although such a situation (the theoretical approach implies) presents at least necessary conditions for the rise or acceptance of a new ideology, no such ideology formed within the community. Further, as we saw in the second part of the chapter, the malaise often felt toward the relationship with the middlemen was not transformed into a clearly defined problem. It is important, then, to explore some of the major obstacles to problem definition and ideology formation within Jaida Arriba in the years before a cooperative ideology was introduced from the outside.

LACK OF PUBLIC SPACE AND DISCUSSION. One of the major obstacles to problem definition or ideology formation was the lack of peasant discussion, particularly public discussion, of their daily difficulties and problems.

Until the adult catechism classes and the cooperative were founded, there were no public forums for discussion: no town meetings, community councils, action committees, or even clubs where people got together to discuss common or shared problems. There were few occasions when the peasants from the various parts of Jaida Arriba even gathered together to chat or become acquainted. One opportunity was the priest's visit for mass, but the priest came only once every six to eight weeks.[13]

Perhaps the most common public arenas for discussion and conversation were the local comercios. Here the women would come during the day and the men in the late afternoon. Sometimes families would come on Sundays to buy supplies and to see friends, compadres, and relatives. There were tables and chairs to sit on, and people would drink beer or rum and play dominoes. But the conversation at the comercios rarely touched on common difficulties or encouraged the public discussion of personal troubles. People joked over beer and rum, sharing tales of the olden days, or stories of women, womanizers, priests and nuns who had fallen to temptation, cocks, pool, dice, and the lottery. With the comerciante present, one was not encouraged to complain about difficulties with him. Further, each was cautious about confiding in others the particulars of his economic dealings. "Before the cooperative there was a lot of mistrust—nobody trusted anybody but himself."

When people did talk about difficulties or wrongdoings, it was often through the traditional form of *chismes* (gossip). "Did you hear what so and so did . . . or what happened when so and so said such and such?" Such chismes rarely involved the public admission of personal troubles or the definition or analysis of any problem. But they did often spread and reinforce discontent. One might not admit that he had been forced to sell a quintal of coffee for $18 or had been turned down by a comerciante when he asked for help, but hearing of others' experiences created the impression that one was not alone in his suffering. Such gossip helped sustain notions that the peasants were always deceived by the ricos. But such gossip also brought mistrust and divisiveness. "Was it true that so and so got a better price than I did? Can anybody, even my own brothers, be trusted when it comes to money?"[14]

People might gossip in the quiet corners of the comercios, but the most frequent arenas for such gossip were the privacy of the trail or conuco, or around the kitchen hearths among brothers, neighbors, compadres, or close friends. Those who shared close bonds of trust and friendship might even share their personal problems. But even here, such conversations often took the form of complaints and commiseration. Things were bad for the peasants, bad for oneself. There were many problems. But that was the way things were. Such complaints were cries of pain and agony against the difficulties and problems that were felt daily. If strategies were discussed, they were individual actions: a way to borrow money to pay a debt; an interest-free loan from a friend to avoid selling coffee a la flor to buy medicine.

As the peasants today look back over this time (seeing it through their experiences in the cooperative), they describe it as a time of little *ambiente* (ambience) and much isolation; one suffered the problems and difficulties of everyday life alone. "Back then, you hardly ever used to talk about your problems. We visited a neighbor's house, but only to have a good time. Everybody had their own problems suffering like sheep—you can kill a sheep and it won't cry out. Everyone wanted to take care of their own problems by themselves. And when you're by yourself what problem can you possibly take care of? We used to be blind. We couldn't come up with a new idea. Now we know that we share all our problems." It was only after the cooperative was organized that people began publicly to share their problems and feel the universality of what they once thought were private troubles particular to them. Their complaints and gossip regarding the comerciantes were brought into a public arena; the cooperative ideology provided them with a language that allowed expression of complaints and criticisms.

LACK OF KNOWLEDGE AND POOR CRITICAL ABILITIES. A "crucial weakness" of the Chinese peasants as a political force, wrote William Hinton, was their "lack of vision. . . . They were in the position of a man trying to survey the sky while imprisoned at the bottom of a well" (1968:55). Such a lack of vision characterized most peasants in Jaida Arriba. They had neither the knowledge nor the critical abilities to transform the malaise felt toward relations with the middlemen into clearly defined problems or to create new ideological alternatives. Such inabilities were sustained by their limited experiences with the world outside Jaida Arriba and by the kind of education (if any) they received.

Most peasants only left Jaida Arriba occasionally, perhaps to see a doctor or a relative in the pueblo. Such "forays" into an often strange and unknown world, peopled by "clever folk" out to deceive the ignorant peasant, were rarely illuminating experiences. Constantly wary and on the defensive, the peasants stayed close to the few areas they knew: the market where the jeep left them off, houses of friends or relatives who had moved in from the Sierra.

Radios provided the peasants with some contact with the outside world after 1961. (Before Trujillo's death, radios had been prohibited.) But before 1967 the peasants learned little from the radio that was applicable to their daily problems and difficulties.[15] Further, nobody ever read newspapers or books—newspapers were never even brought to the campo.

The peasants' vision was restricted further by critical and conceptual inabilities that hindered them from using what knowledge they had to create new alternatives. Their formal education always had been by rote: as children, their catechism classes had taught them through memorization and repetition; and those who had attended rural schools (which offered classes only through the third grade) had learned how to read, write, add, and subtract in the same way.[16] They had little encouragement to define problems, let alone find solutions for them. They were not trained to apply existing ideas and possibilities to a new area or to create new possibilities. They were not accustomed to defining a difficulty as a problem that might then be broken down into smaller, more solvable problems. They were not encouraged by their education to ask, inquire, suspect, doubt, seek clarification. Unable to see what existed as but *one* possibility, the peasants were left in hopeless awe of the inevitability of their situation.

The kind of education they received did not completely crush creativeness or inventiveness among the peasants in Jaida Arriba. But it did pose severe obstacles to visionary thinking, problem definition, and ideology formation.

LACK OF SELF-CONFIDENCE AND TWO WAYS OF "KNOWING". The obstacles posed by such inabilities were compounded by the peasants' lack of faith and confidence in themselves: they felt ignorant.[17] One of the most common explanations given for poverty, for the failure to question the comerciantes before the cooperative, for the failure to take many kinds of action is this belief in their own incapability: "we peasants, we're stupid." The peasants were aware of another world of written words with which educated people had contact. But for them it was a dark mystery, for they could read and write poorly or not at all. "The only letter I know is the O, and only because it's round." "I'm ashamed to get together with educated people because really and truly, I'm kind of dumb."

Such a lack of self-confidence and feeling of inferiority did not support an atmosphere of inquiry, questioning, and problem definition. Few thought to ask such questions as: "Where does this difficulty come from? What can be done about this problem?" Rather, they felt that "you can't get anything out of ignorant or stupid people." "When you see that somebody else knows more than you do, you don't even care to find out—because the other one already knows more than you anyway."

Their lack of self-confidence, compounded by weak critical abilities, encouraged two seemingly contradictory ways of understanding the world. Both these ways of knowing posed further obstacles to the definition of problems and the conceptualization of new solutions. The first way of "knowing" was not through abstract reasoning or logical argument, but through "seeing." "For us," explained one peasant, "it's like Saint Thomas said: you've got to see to believe." People believed true what they saw to be true: "the proof was in the pudding." They often hesitated to experiment because this meant trying something that had not yet been seen and was therefore "unknown." Such a basis for belief makes sense for the peasant: feeling unequipped to judge new ideas and plans with which he has had no experience, he feels incapable of knowing without seeing.

The attitude of "seeing is believing" presents further obstacles to new ways of thinking about one's situation because it often supports suspicion toward new ideas. The peasant is sure about what exists; why take a chance of upsetting his already precarious existence by trying something new? He feels a negativism about anything new and untried, an assumption that something new cannot work. And often such an assumption can be broken only by showing that it can work. Further, if new ideas are presented by government officials or men from the pueblo, there is even more reason to be suspicious: these people long have tried to take advantage of the peasants at every opportunity. Better to wait and see before believing.

Given this common-sense epistemology, the second way of knowing may seem surprising: one knows because someone who knows (*uno que sabe*) says that "such and such" is true. But if one is skeptical about believing without seeing, how then can he simply believe in what someone "who knows" says? For the peasant, however, it is just *because* he feels unable to "know" without seeing that he may be willing to trust the word of someone else who does seem "to know."[18] Thus peasants facing problems and lacking confidence in their abilities and judgment often went to others "who knew," accepting their advice without question: "We can't figure out things for ourselves because our minds haven't been developed very much. Our minds were buried in the ground and couldn't grow. When someone comes along who can speak openly and clearly and who knows how to explain things, he creates a favorable image and we campesinos respond: 'Right. That's the way it is. Yes, sir! Just as you say!' That's because we used to have a habit, which was very common. You hardly ever hear anyone protesting and saying: 'No. What you're saying is not true. It's this way for this or that reason.' "

If someone had an economic problem, he went to the comerciante for advice. "You used to think that they were the people to go to. I figured that, since they had money, if I had to get involved in some business deal, so-and-so would know what to do. And for any little problem you'd go to them and ask their advice." The meaning of this lack of self-confidence is dramatically expressed by one cooperative leader who talks of the change the cooperative brought about inside of him: "Before the cooperative, my son told me that he wanted to be a priest. And I told him: '*Coño, carajo*! What are you talking about being a priest?' I thought that was impossible. But just a few months ago, when the chance came up, even though I didn't know how I was going to pay the costs of his education, I gave him my permission. Now I have faith, faith first of all in myself and then in God. When God said: 'Help yourself, and I'll help you' who did he put first? He put man first." Given this lack of self-confidence and deference toward the sabios, it is not surprising that there were few peasants who came to define their situation as problematic or to create new ideological alternatives.

FURTHER OBSTACLES TO PROBLEM DEFINITION AND IDEOLOGY FORMATION. There were some important exceptions to the general patterns discussed above—men who not only defined a central economic problem to be a lack of cash, but who also saw comerciante control of credit and marketing as a problem and who even conceived of an alternative through cooperative action. Why this alternative was never formulated into a coherent ideology and publicly propagated among other peasants illustrates some of the specific obstacles to problem definition and ideology formation faced by a group of potential peasant leaders.

Of the handful of coffee growers in Jaida Arriba who saw control by middlemen as problematic, only three felt the problem as a public one in need of a communitywide solution. Foremost among these was Puro, whose position as large holder and comerciante put him in a unique situation for understanding how control worked. The strategy he thought of for solving the problems of continual money shortage and comerciante control was the formation of a cooperative. He did not "invent" the idea. In the early 1950s, a Cooperativa de Ahorros y Crédito had been founded in San Juan de la Sierra. He had heard of it from those who had been members, and he saw that, despite its failures among the peasants, it functioned successfully among the people in the pueblo. Puro applied this idea to the situation in Jaida Arriba. If the peasants could form a cooperative fund, they could loan each other money in times of need. Puro reckoned further that a cooperative might help with the problem of comerciante control: preharvest selling could be eliminated, coffee could be sold directly in the pueblo for higher prices, and members could buy consumer goods jointly at lower prices.[19] Puro discussed these ideas with two other coffee growers, Pucho and Darío. Both of them had been members of the Cooperativa de Ahorros y Crédito in La Sierra; and Darío had found it beneficial.[20] The three often stayed late at night in Puro's store discussing their problems. They all agreed that the problem of cash shortage, and the advantage the comerciantes took of it to control prices, could be solved with a cooperative. But they took no action. Why?

For one reason, they were hindered by their lack of knowledge and self-confidence. They did not know exactly what to do. "We used to think about a cooperative, but we didn't have the faintest idea of how to go about organizing ourselves into a cooperative. We didn't have any idea of how to begin, how to save, how to educate ourselves. . . . We used to have goodwill, but we just didn't know how. And since we couldn't see things too clearly, we didn't want to go out on a limb."

The obstacle was not merely a lack of knowledge about cooperatives, but a lack of knowledge about any form of permanent, collective organization. The very notion of "calling a meeting to organize a community group" was still foreign. Their few experiences with collective action were limited. One was the traditional junta. But an exchange labor team was task-specific, and once the task was done, it dissolved. No formal organization was involved: no need for choosing leaders, resolving problems, making decisions, disseminating information. The work tasks involved were traditional ones known to all.

Another experience with collective action had been the building of the chapel in 1963–64. People from all over the community participated, but the direction was the work of one peasant, Pablo. He organized labor teams to cut and haul wood, prepare cement, and level the ground. He called no meetings, discussed his plans with few people, made all decisions himself, and personally collected the money needed to pay for nails, cement, roofing, and carpenters by going around from house to house asking for contributions.

The lack of both organizational experience and knowledge of cooperativism created another obstacle to action: a lack of self-confidence. And lacking confidence in their own knowledge and abilities, they feared acting and failing. Puro remembers: "At that time I used to talk a lot about the problems but I could never make up my mind to tackle them, head-on. I was kind of afraid that I'd begin forming a cooperative not knowing anything about the movement and that I'd fail." That lack of self-confidence also is reflected in the feelings of some of the peasants like Salvador who initially were elected leaders: "They made me the interim president but I didn't think that I was going to be a leader—because I had hardly any education or any experience. At that time, I had only gotten to the third grade, and all I knew how to do was farm. The first day that I spoke at a meeting, I couldn't calm my nerves. My nerves were like trembling inside me. I had never spoken in public before!" Before the cooperative was organized, such fear and lack of confidence hindered Puro and the others from even calling a meeting.

Another obstacle to taking action was the atmosphere of mistrust and suspicion in the community. Puro's compadre Pablo had faced such suspicion when he had collected money to build the church. Pablo remembers: "Back then, what hurt most was the gossip that was running around. When I was collecting money for the chapel, some people would say that I was using it for my own family. And when you're out working without self-interest, when you're doing it for love, it hurts you to hear that." Puro knew of the criticisms that had been made of Pablo: "There was so much individualism back then. We didn't dare put any of our money into someone else's hands because of all the failures that had come about after placing your money in someone else's hands for some sort of private business. And that's why you don't want to take a chance." And he was particularly hesitant because he knew what they might think of him, a comerciante, organizing such a group:

"And I also had to think that I was a negociante. I thought the others were going to say that I was collecting money to take advantage of them."[21]

In this context the bishop's visit to Jaida Arriba in late 1967 took on great importance. It gave Puro the self-confidence and courage actually to step forward: "Everybody was really happy with what Monseñor said, and that gave me the courage I needed."

Puro, then, was not "blind" as many others now feel they were before 1967: he did see the situation with the comerciantes as problematic and he had an idea for a strategy, but he did not know exactly what to do and lacked self-confidence. Given the link between the acceptance of a new ideology and a problem orientation formulated in Chapter 6, Puro might be expected to have been "ready" for a new ideology: it is when people both experience a problem orientation toward their situation *and* perceive the existing institutionalized guides or sets of symbols or ideologies available to be lacking, weak, or inadequate as guides to thought, feeling, or action that new ideologies are most likely to be created or accepted. Puro expressed this notion well:

We were kind of like in a dream and we wanted to open up our eyes and solve those problems. We dreamed of what could be done but we didn't know how to do it, we didn't know how, we didn't know what to do. When somebody comes along who can see things a little bit more clearly, who can explain what can be done, how our problems can be solved—it's like when a bottle with a top on it gets opened up: that's the idea. We can do things here. For example, I always used to want to discover, but I was ignorant. Someone else came along and he told me how. And this mind of mine, which wanted to learn but wasn't able to, all of a sudden opened up.

When the promotores came and told us about their ideas—about forming groups, saving, speaking—we suddenly saw the light, our eyes were opened, and we could see clearly. We had been willing for a long time, and with that little bit of light we took the first step.

CHAPTER 8

ACCEPTANCE
AND REJECTION
OF THE COOPERATIVE

Only a few peasants in Jaida Arriba supported the cooperative when it was first organized. Acceptance came slowly; for some, it never came. The central question explored in this chapter is: why was the cooperative accepted by some peasants and rejected by others?

The group that was founded late in 1967 had twelve members, eleven middle and large holders and one day laborer. Although many more came to weekly meetings, after six weeks there were only twenty members, fifteen of them middle and large holders. By late summer of 1968, the cooperative had grown to over eighty members; thirty-five were large and middle holders, the remainder day laborers and small holders. In mid-1969, the Cooperativa de Ahorro y Crédito was formed to absorb peasants who did not grow coffee. The Cooperativa Agropecuaria was left with forty-three middle- and large-holding coffee growers (from Jaida Arriba). The Cooperativa de Ahorro y Crédito had fifty-eight members, fifty-one of whom were day laborers and small holders. The other seven were large and middle holders who also stayed in the new cooperative to help it get off the ground.

If the act of joining the cooperative (which involved a commitment of scarce, hard-earned money) is taken as an indicator of some initial "acceptance" of the cooperative, clearly acceptance was gained somewhat slowly. Further, most of the initial members were large or middle holders, although the cooperative did draw members from every class. After nine months the number of day laborers and small holders had grown to about forty-five, or 39 percent of the total number of day labor and small holders. By this time, 55 percent of the large and middle holders had joined.

Taking the marketing of coffee through the cooperative as an indicator of "acceptance," cooperative acceptance appears somewhat less among the middle- and large-holding members because many did not sell their coffee through the cooperative during the 1968–69 harvest. By the 1969–70 harvest, however, all members were marketing their coffee through the cooperative.

From May 1969 to February 1970, the first nine months of consumer cooperative organization,[1] thirty-five large and middle holders joined, all of them already members of the first cooperative. But of the more than fifty day laborers and small holders who were already members of the first cooperative, only twenty-seven joined, and of these, many did not actually leave Manuel's store and begin buying at the consumer cooperative until mid-1970.

By late 1971, four years after the first cooperative group was started, the Cooperativa Agropecuaria had forty-five members from Jaida Arriba, all middle- and large-holding coffee growers (forty-three of whom had joined by mid-1969). The Cooperativa de Consumo had grown from sixty-two members in February 1970 to more than ninety members. A little over half were large- and middle-holding peasants; the others, day laborers and small holders.

The above data, although sketchy, indicate that the "acceptance or rejection" of the cooperative was not a simple act that occurred at one point in time; further, certain patterns of acceptance and rejection need some explanation:

(1) Why did the cooperative gain acceptance slowly? What were some of the obstacles to acceptance and how, if at all, were they overcome?

(2) The data make clear: (a) The cooperative initially drew most heavily among the middle and large holders; but it did draw some people from every class. (b) In the months following the initial organization, the cooperative began to attract more day laborers and small holders, although proportionately to the population, the percentage of middle and large holders always was greater. (c) Peasants in similar class positions reacted differently to the cooperative: many middle and large holders waited much longer than others to join, and a few never joined at all; a few day laborers and small holders were initially involved in the cooperative, about 44 percent eventually joined the first cooperative, but most others never became members of either the Cooperativa de Ahorro y Crédito or the Cooperativa de Consumo. Why did class position seem at least partially to influence acceptance or rejection of the cooperative? What factors other than class might be important in explaining acceptance and rejection?

(3) Why did some people accept the cooperative to the extent of joining it and committing their money to it, but at first hesitate to break with the middlemen and market their coffee through the Cooperativa Agropecuaria or buy their goods from the Cooperativa de Consumo?

THE COOPERATIVE IDEOLOGY:
TACKLING BASIC ECONOMIC PROBLEMS

THE COOPERATIVE AND EVERYDAY PROBLEMS. Through the initial cooperative ideology, the multitude of everyday problems and inadequate strategies of the peasants merged into a new, clearly defined public problem: how to create a cooperative fund from which people could draw to meet their everyday needs.

Money shortage and the inadequate strategies for meeting it were blamed on the lack of a common fund. As soon as you make a fund in the cooperative, Puro and the promotores would tell the peasants, you can begin borrowing money to cover your necessities. When your children are sick and you do not have the money to buy medicine, you can borrow it from the cooperative; if you need money to fence in your conuco, weed your crops, harvest your coffee, you can come to the cooperative and a fund will be available.

The cooperative ideology struck particularly strongly at the dissatisfaction caused by forced, preharvest selling losses. Everybody, at some time, had suffered these losses; but ashamed of having these needs and embarrassed by the low prices they had received, few ever had made these problems public. Puro used the weekly meetings to get people to talk, and gradually this quiet, personal suffering was transformed into a public, collective problem. The solution, insisted Puro, was "a common fund to protect our coffee from the middlemen."

The cooperative strategy made sense to many of the large and middle holders. They imagined that the cooperative would be like their own bank. Pooling their money made sense. If a wife or child fell sick they would not have to sell a quintal of coffee for $20 instead of $30. Nor would they have to sell off scarce animals they had been struggling to raise to build up a herd. And as the cooperative got under way and the common fund grew at each weekly meeting, it provided them with visible proof that such collective action could solve their cash needs without the sacrifices of former strategies. "When we had been in the cooperative for three or four months, something came up that I needed $15, and I had a calf. And I went out one Friday to weigh the calf to sell it. But when I was on the way, I got the idea: 'What am I doing? Let me borrow the $15 from the cooperative.' I borrowed it and I didn't have to sell the calf. And afterward, I sold that calf for $78!"

The cooperative also fired the imagination of some of the day laborers and small holders. Some saw the cooperative fund as a source of the money they desperately needed when they could get neither work nor credit. Again, the cooperative backed up its verbal claims with actual loans. "I went in for this one reason: that if you had saved $5 they'd lend you $10; when you had saved $10, they'd lend you $15. And all the time the money was together, earning interest. When I had $5 saved up, and they lent me $10, I became even more enthusiastic." But to most day laborers and small holders the cooperative did not seem an adequate solution. It did not loan money for daily food needs; its loans for production costs or livestock purchases were severely limited. It loaned money according to a person's ability to repay. Most day laborers could only borrow as much as (or a little more than) the pittance they had already saved. Given these limitations, the cooperative seemed to favor only those who were better off: "They say that the cooperative benefits you, but that's only for people who have more money. When you get in, you begin earning a little money and saving it up. Then a poor man who is sick goes in and says: 'I need $100.' And they tell him: "We'll see if we can get it for you.' But then what happens? They pay you, a man with money, but not me. So who is going to end up getting helped, you or me?"[2]

THE COOPERATIVE AND FUTURE CONCERNS. Beyond their daily problems, the peasants of Jaida Arriba bore a deep concern for the future.[3] But they felt that their strategies for improving their situation and leaving their children something were severely limited.

Puro and the other leaders brought these problems into the public arena, continually insisting that the cooperative was the only solution: land was scarce, soil deteriorating, families growing. Through a cooperative, people could save their money to buy land, or to educate their children, or to leave to their families if they died. Puro would tell the early meetings: "I can see that we are heading into misery within a few years: the land is getting scarcer and we are all farmers without any other profession. The fallow plots that we are clearing and burning are producing very little. When all the land here has been worked, when there is nowhere else to farm, and when your children are looking for somewhere to farm—they need a place to work—then, where are they going to work?"

The people in the meetings began to talk publicly of these problems, each telling how much land there used to be when he was growing up and how little there was now. Personal troubles were transformed into public problems; and Puro presented the cooperative as a way they could do something. Many remember joining because the cooperative gave hope in the face of a bleak future: "I entered saving pennies but thinking of dollars." "When I joined, I was most interested in taking care of tomorrow—to have something to fall back on from now on." A middle-holding coffee grower was taken by the success stories he was told: "I went in thinking of examples of all the other cooperatives in other countries that had progressed. I never forgot the example of England, where a cooperative began with twenty-seven men and one woman, saving four cents a week." Many who entered saw the cooperative as a way to leave something for their children. "I entered thinking that I would pave the way for my family to take care of themselves." Or, as a number of peasants put it: "I entered with the hope that if perhaps I should die at least I'd have the money to be buried."

The cooperative's public definition of the future as problematic made a deep impression upon the day laborers and small holders, as well as on the middle and large holders. These poorer peasants, we saw, unsuccessfully tried available strategies for improving their situation. The cooperative seemed to be a solution, a way to get the capital to buy and raise livestock, or to save money to buy land. "My interest came, I entered thinking that since I was a person that was working only a tarea and a half of land . . . I went in with the hope that if God helped me to put together some money, I could buy a little piece of land for my family." Perhaps most appealing, the cooperative held out the same promise it did to many of the middle and large holders: a way to create a personal fund to provide some security and future for one's family. One small holder remembers: "When I joined . . . they said that a poor person, saving 25 pennies a week, could put together $100. And that the cooperative would be the only way that a poor person could put together that much money. When I joined, I was only thinking about saving money, for my family's good. Because if you die, what do you have? But if you begin saving 25 pennies here and there, maybe you can put something together."

But most day laborers and small holders did not see this cooperative strategy of accumulating a fund through slow saving as feasible. They barely had the money to feed their families from day to day. How, they thought, were they going to get even 10 cents to put into the cooperative each week? The cooperative leaders saw a different reality. They pointed to the money these poor peasants spent each week gambling (particularly buying lottery numbers). The poor could "save" this money instead of "throwing it away." Some were convinced, but most saw the lottery as a necessity, not a luxury; every few weeks someone won $14 or $28 or more; and just by putting down twenty-five or fifty cents! How many weeks of savings would it take to earn this much? The cooperative leaders responded that much more was lost over the weeks than ever was won; the cooperative was a surer way. But their arguments often had little effect. Indeed some of the poorer peasants who entered with high expectations became disillusioned when their savings did not grow. "I joined the cooperative only thinking about tomorrow, about the future—not mine, but of those two boys you see over there. But I can now see that it's not going to work. I joined thinking that if I died tomorrow, I could leave them about $100 so they could protect themselves." Some withdrew; others maintained their faith that someday, somehow, the cooperative would bring them a better future.

THE COOPERATIVE VERSUS THE MIDDLEMAN:
FROM A MALAISE TO A PROBLEM

THE COOPERATIVE VERSUS CONTROL OVER COFFEE   After the first few months of organizing, another thrust in the cooperative ideology became increasingly important: the cooperative was not simply a way to meet everyday needs or future worries, but a solution to the problem of middleman control over prices of coffee and consumer goods. Few peasants initially saw "middleman control" as a political problem. The leaders' task, then, became to define middleman control as a public, political problem and to present the cooperative as the solution. They did this by publicly revealing to the peasants the huge profits the comerciantes were making, by defining these profits as "losses" to the peasants, and by presenting the cooperative as a way that something could be done.

From the first meetings in La Loma and El Río, the promotores made clear how much money the compradores were making. They would ask the peasants how much they were selling their coffee for. "$29 or $30," the peasants would reply. And the promotores would respond: "These compradores are selling your coffee in Santiago for $35 and $36 right now. And what the comprador is earning for himself, you can earn for yourselves."

Most peasants were surprised that the compradores were receiving such high prices in Santiago; but it made sense. Everyone knew that the compradores were gente grande who got rich at the expense of the poor. The angry reactions of Arturo against the promotores in El Río seemed a confirmation of what the promotores were saying.[4] And these promotores seemed to know what they were talking about: after all, they were intelligent agronomists from the pueblo and had been sent by El Padre.

Weekly cooperative meetings in Jaida Arriba made middleman control even clearer. The special deals and favoritism in prices were revealed. Puro continually formulated the control of the comerciantes in a simple, cogent form and related everyone's individual case to one central fact: the lack of union, the lack of a cooperative.

Because they were not struggling together a comprador might buy five fanegas from one peasant at $28 and then two fanegas from another at $26. Because everybody was divided, the compradores could pay whatever they wanted to pay; but by organizing a cooperative the peasants could all get the same price. Puro further explained to them how they lost money by selling coffee in fanegas: each fanega weighed more than a quintal—they were losing five or ten pounds of coffee on each fanega they sold. On 20 fanegas, one might lose two whole quintales! But if they sold together, through a cooperative, these extra quintales would not be lost.

Time and again—in meetings, in encounters on the trail, in neighbors' kitchens—Puro explained how the market worked, how the compradores were earning so much money. He helped popularize the word intermediario (intermediary or middleman), emphasizing that these intermediaries were obstacles between the peasant and the higher prices in Santiago. He used the metaphor *cadena* (chain) to describe the market system: it was a chain of people through whose hands the coffee had to pass, each one taking out a profit that the peasant himself could have if he sold directly through a cooperative. The wealth of the compradores, already clear and visible to all, was presented as something the peasants too could share: "If other people have become rich with your products and your sweat, why can't you yourselves become rich?"

The discussion of such problems in meetings and the sharing of tales of personal sufferings and losses helped create a sense of a common, public problem. So too did much of the imagery. Puro charged, "We are the intermediaros' slaves." The slave metaphor characterized not only the peasants' common need and dependence, but a common enemy: the comerciantes. The cooperative offered a way to freedom. "Through our savings we can become freer men. We will be able to protect our products better instead of giving them out so cheaply before the harvest time. The intermediarios won't just pay us whatever little thing they want." The comerciantes were also drawn as the *dueños* (owners) of the peasants' coffee because the peasants "gave" it to them to sell at whatever price they wanted. Puro's experience as a commerciante gave credence to his claims. Puro also explained how they could sell directly, gaining these profits for themselves and freeing themselves from the slavery of the intermediaries: unite in a cooperative and sell their products together. "I told them: 'I'm a negociante. I earn a peso for every quintal of coffee that I buy. And I sell it to Arturo. He earns three or four pesos more. Those are three or four pesos of profit that each of you is losing on every quintal. But if we were to sell our coffee together in a cooperative, we ourselves could earn that money. If we get together, we can all get out of this slavery.' "

In seeking to define middleman control of the coffee market as problematic and to present the cooperative as a good guide to action, the leaders and promotores thus often worked very closely with existing orientations. They built on difficulties already felt with the comerciantes and added a clear definition of a "control" which previously was, at best, ill-perceived. But the impact of these efforts at concientización during the initial months and years of the cooperative is hard to judge. To what extent did people actually come to accept the cooperative because they accepted this problem definition and solution?

Very few initially saw the cooperative as a way to get better prices for their coffee or to keep the profits that the comerciantes were earning. Indeed, when I explicitly asked if better prices were a motivation for joining,[5] most said no, they did not imagine this would be possible when they first entered.

"They said that we would be able to sell our coffee through the cooperative, but I was dubious." But after some people joined and committed their savings, and everyone saw the cooperative's early successes in making loans and marketing coffee, many seem to have been more receptive to the arguments about control of the middlemen and the benefits of marketing through the cooperative. Puro, reflecting on these early days, remembers: "In every meeting, I would make a lot of analyses of that sort. And that caused them to open up. There was a type of triumph in the meetings—a tremendous joy. These examples were crystal clear to them—as though their blindfold had been taken from them." One senses from Puro's description that the peasants were coming to see the world in a new way—to understand certain causal links between price and middlemen and market, to see this as problematic, and to see the cooperative as a solution.[6]

Peasant reflections about the impact of the cooperative on them also indicate that at least some peasants came to accept the cooperative because they came to see the middlemen as problems and the cooperative as a good strategy. They saw themselves, for example, as having been "ignorant" and "innocent", and the cooperative as revealing how things really were and giving them knowledge. They also described themselves as being "blind" before the cooperative—not seeing the kind of control the middlemen actually exercised, not seeing the earnings they were making as wrong, not seeing any way to change the situation. "Before the cooperative was organized, I was completely blind. I knew they had benefits, but I didn't realize it was that much." "We were like blind. We lived like slaves, working for somebody else, and taking only a little piece for ourselves." This metaphor of "blindness" helps capture the meaning the cooperative ideology seemed to have had: it brought them a certain light, clarity, vision. The cooperative ideology helped them see their relationship with the middlemen as problematic and the cooperative itself as a solution.[7]

THE COOPERATIVE VERSUS CONTROL OVER CONSUMER GOODS. Few peasants perceived that the comerciantes exercised any comprehensive control over the prices of consumer goods. They did not realize that the comerciantes bought cheap in Santiago and sold dear in Jaida Arriba; they had little idea of what the price differences were.[8] Only certain specific actions of particular comerciantes were interpreted as control over prices and sometimes judged to be wrong: overcharging and higher-priced credit. But these were seen as the selfish or dishonest acts of individuals who acted por interés or tried "to cheat." "Comerciante control over consumer goods" was not itself seen to be a problem.

Little mention was made of forming a consumer cooperative during the first months of cooperative organization. But two of the cooperative leaders, Puro and Pucho, soon decided to challenge middleman control over consumer goods by presenting it as a problem which a consumer cooperative could solve.[9] They began to promote the idea in early 1969 after the Cooperativa Agropecuaria was successfully processing its first coffee harvest.

Pucho and Puro clearly outlined the prices paid by the comerciantes in Santiago and the increase they charged in Jaida Arriba for these necessities. Through a cooperative, the peasants could get these lower prices and would not have to pay "whatever these comerciantes felt like charging." As the major thrust of their argument, they pointed out that the comerciantes were "making themselves rich with the peasants' money." Comerciante profits came from the peasants, and they rightfully belonged to the peasants. In the meetings Puro would point out the wealth of the comerciantes like Manuel and would ask: " 'Where did all that money come from?' And they answered: 'From us, from what we bought there.' And I told them: 'That's right. One man has gotten rich from profits he has made on all of us. And if we were to form a consumer cooperative, we ourselves would be the ones to earn that profit.' " Puro drew a vivid image of how much the peasants could earn and save for their children's future by explaining what would have happened if their fathers had formed a consumer cooperative: "I gave them a type of example. Now let's imagine that my father and some of the other old men had had a cooperative when they got married. They've been married now for twenty or thirty years. And let's suppose that every year they have been able to make a profit of $20. In twenty years, they would have had $400. And with one hundred families here at $400 each, they could have had $40,000 in twenty years. And our children will end up thanking us and they'll never have to criticize their parents, to blame their parents as we blame our parents, because our parents haven't done anything for us."

Few peasants ever conceived that prices could be lower, or that these profits were "losses" that were being "taken from" the peasants to whom they rightfully belonged.[10] But this traditional, never-questioned "fact" of the comerciantes was now set off as a problematic form of control by its very contrast to a new alternative way of doing things.

It would be interesting to know how the peasants saw the Cooperativa de Consumo in 1969. To what extent did they come to join this consumer cooperative (committing new funds) and eventually leave Manuel because they accepted the cooperative definition of the comerciantes' control of consumer goods as a problem the consumer cooperative could solve? I have little information on this question. I do know that no one who was not already a member of the Cooperativa Agropecuaria joined the consumer cooperative when it was first organized. Further, a split formed along class lines: very few day laborers and small holders actually left Manuel and began purchasing at the consumer cooperative during its first nine months. They might have seen the consumer cooperative as bringing them lower prices and new earnings, but they did not see it as solving their daily cash crises: one had to pay cash at the cooperative. If the amount of credit offered by the middlemen seemed inadequate, the cooperative strategy seemed impossible: "The cooperative didn't used to sell on credit, and since Manuel sold on credit, I'd say: 'What kind of help is that?' "[11]

The many middle- and large-holding members of the Cooperativa Agropecuaria who did join the consumer cooperative in its first months were probably attracted both by the cooperative's critique of the middlemen and by the promise of its alternative guide to action; also important, their funds in the Cooperativa Agropecuaria and their greater cash crop production made the cash payment demands of the new cooperative seem at least possible. The initial successes witnessed in the Cooperativa Agropecuaria likely strengthened the credibility of this new cooperative. Further, its highly visible, concrete imagery might well have had great appeal: unlike the control the comerciantes exercised in the coffee market, their control over consumer goods (that Puro and Pucho sought to define as problematic) was vividly clear in the tangible wealth that was displayed daily before the peasants' eyes. The comercio's shelves bristled with row upon row of rum bottles, soft drinks, fruit juices, and tomato paste; shoes, belts, machetes, and hats hung on the walls; kerosene-driven refrigerators and lanterns purred in the customer's ears; and behind the counters the bins were always filled with salt, sugar, rice, beans, onions, garlic, coffee, and corn.[12]

After the Cooperativa de Consumo began functioning, visible evidence of lower prices helped attract new people and probably served further to convince those who had already joined. It made clear by example both the extent of previous comerciante control over the price of consumer goods and the fact that the cooperative strategy was a way to cope with this problem. Many peasants talked of having been "blind" or "ignorant" before, but then "seeing" the problem they had been living earlier, "discovering" there was another alternative.

> Before the cooperative, no one had discovered that they could be living better. At that time there were negociantes selling a pound of rice for twenty cents, a pound of spaghetti for twenty-two cents, and a pacifier for ten cents. We were all blind then, and we had to do as they said. If they said a pound of rice was worth twenty cents, we had no other choice but to pay that price because they were all selling for the same prices. It was a chain. But now the cooperative is selling rice for fifteen cents, spaghetti for seventeen cents, and pacifiers for five cents. The cooperative means progress. It's something that has been created so that people with a head on their shoulders can begin to move ahead.

ACCEPTANCE OF THE COOPERATIVE: FOUR YEARS LATER

Methodologically, I faced difficulties discovering how people had felt one or two years before I first talked with them. Theoretically, the definition of "acceptance of the cooperative" was questionable: I used "joining the cooperative" and "marketing through or buying from the cooperative" as indicators and asked people what motives they had for their actions. Yet when people committed money to, sold through, or bought from the cooperative, they may not yet have "really" believed that their situation was problematic or that the cooperative was a good strategy. Further, one may not wish to say that people have "really" accepted a new ideology until they have come both to believe it and to act upon it for some period of time in case that acceptance proved only tentative or temporary. Serious epistemological problems are posed here: do you know that a person has accepted a new ideology, or any new belief, when he says that he has? Or only when he also acts upon it? Or when he both acts upon it and says he believes it? And how many times, or for how long, does he have to so act or believe?

I have no answer (if indeed there is an answer) to these questions. But in this section I will present another meaning of acceptance and examine such acceptance in early 1972, four years after the first cooperative group was formed. I will define acceptance both as being an active member (saving in, buying from, or selling to the cooperative) *and* as believing that the cooperative is personally important. The central theoretical question here is: was such acceptance based on the belief that the cooperative was a good guide for action, thought, and feelings in a problematic situation?

To explore this acceptance, I chose active members and asked them five "scale" questions.[13] I considered the cooperative "personally important" if they themselves brought up its importance in any of the open-ended questions: as an explanation of a change for the better that had occurred in their situation (question #5) or that they expected would occur in their situation (#4); or as an element in their hopes and fears for the future (#1 and #2).[14] Finally, I examined the reasons given for such acceptance to see if it were based on the belief that the cooperative was a good guide for action in a problematic situation.

THE DAY LABORERS AND SMALL HOLDERS. My sample of small holders and day laborers was too small to make any systematic generalizations. Of the five peasant cooperative members from these classes to whom I asked the scale questions, only two expected their lives to improve in any significant way in the next five years. Interestingly, both of them saw themselves at #1 on the ladder four years ago, before the cooperative was founded, and felt that they were still on #1 today, but thought that they would be on #10 in five years. And both of these peasants saw the cooperative as playing an important part in their future improvement in two ways. The cooperative was a way they could continue to avoid the previous debts to the *comerciantes* that had always plagued them. (See Table 8.1.) This was not because the cooperative provided them with the money they needed to buy with cash; but because in demanding cash buying, it had taught them such was possible. Their economic

TABLE 8.1
Answers to Question #3 of Scale Questions for Day Laborer or Small-Holder
Cooperative Member

Day Laborer or Small-Holder Cooperative Member	Self-placement on Ladder Four Years Ago	Self-placement on Ladder Today	Self-placement on Ladder In Five Years	Cooperative Mentioned As Important
Member 1	1	1	10	Yes
Member 2	1	1	1	No
Member 3	1	1	10	Yes
Member 4	2	1	2	No
Member 5	3	2	2	No

SOURCE: Personal interviews.

situation promised to be "a lot more under control than it used to be." Somehow (and they were not sure exactly how) their lives since joining the cooperative did not seem as hopeless and confused, and debts did not continually lurk behind them: "It's this mysterious thing that makes me so thankful to the cooperative. It's all progress with the cooperative. Today my work is a lot easier. Now I don't spend all my time floundering around, and I can handle my debts a little bit better. And I don't have to work so hard all the time. I'd say that the cooperative has set an example for all family fathers." Further, they saw the cooperative as a way in which they would eventually accumulate savings. With $6.25 saved in the savings and loan cooperative and $24.15 of savings and earnings in the consumer cooperative, one small holder commented: "Now my future looks brighter. And what I'm hoping is that every day it keeps getting a little bit brighter."

The other three small-holding and day-laborer peasant members, however, saw their situation neither as having improved nor as improving more than one "rung" over the next five years. The cooperative was "a good thing," they said, because it helped them save money for the future, and it gave benefits unlike the comerciantes who kept the earnings for themselves alone. But these benefits were only for "the coffee growers," those with money to save, crops to sell, and cash to buy at the store. The splitting of the Cooperativa de Ahorro y Crédito from the Cooperativa Agropecuaria was seen as an effort by "those who have" to exclude the "unfortunate ones" from the benefits of the greater capital and resources available to the Agropecuaria. And when the consumer cooperative started giving some credit at the end of 1970, these day laborers and small holders began to resent the restrictions placed on their credit while "those with coffee" (who, it seemed, needed much less "help") received much more. Bitterly disillusioned over the cooperative "solution," one day laborer told me:

I joined the cooperative because people told me that if I joined the cooperative and I needed a pound of salt, they'd let me have it. But ever since I joined the cooperative, I've been having a harder time than I ever had before. Because before I joined the cooperative, when I was broke, the other pulperías could help me out with a pound of salt, or some rice, or some spaghetti. So now, it's the cooperative who has that responsibility toward me. Imagine: there I was sick at home, and I sent to ask the cooperative to let me have some food, but they refused to sell it to me on credit. So, where is all that unity that people were talking about? Where is the sense of community?

THE MIDDLE AND LARGE HOLDERS. I asked the scale questions to eighteen of the forty-five members of the Cooperativa Agropecuaria. Fourteen of them felt their situation had improved in the last four years, and ten of these saw the improvement as three or more rungs. Sixteen of the eighteen saw their situation as improving in the next five years. Most significantly, all but four mentioned the cooperative as being at least in part responsible for their past improvement or their expected future improvement or both. Chaguito expressed the feeling of many: "The only thing that I hope for in the future is to do what I can to help the cooperative progress. That's what we all hope here. Try our best to keep that cooperative growing all the time. Because that's the only thing there is around here. There's nothing else. By yourself you can't do anything." The particular explanations these middle and large holders gave for seeing the cooperative as important reveal the great extent to which they saw it as a necessary strategy to cope with the "problems"—now well defined—facing them. (See Table 8.2.)

The cooperative, many felt, provided them with a good way to solve the money shortages to meet urgent cash needs. They felt they no longer had to incur the sacrifices of such previous strategies as selling off scarce animals or selling a la flor. When they told of their hopes for the future, some mentioned that they hoped "each day the cooperative will be better able to help its members." And in the face of the continual difficulties the cooperative had in getting the funds it needed to finance preharvest and harvest needs, the fears some mentioned for the future were the inability of the cooperative to continue to make such funds available and a return to their former situation. "A worse type of future would be if what we have going for us right now would end up failing—the cooperative, the united community. And also, sickness. When there is a lot of sickness around, and you don't have the money to buy medicines, that's a pretty tough situation. If we don't stay united, things would get that way. But if we stay united, everything will work out all right."

Not only did the cooperative help solve money shortages, but it also transformed the malaise of credit into the problem of control and provided at least a partial solution. Although the cooperative did little more than educate its members with new norms—it is bad for you and for the cooperative to buy on credit—many middle and large holders credited the cooperative with

Table 8.2
Answers to Question #3 of Scale Questions for Middle- or Large-Holder
Cooperative Member

Middle- or Large-Holder Cooperative Member	Self-placement on Ladder Four Years Ago	Self-placement on Ladder Today	Self-placement on Ladder In Five Years
Member 1	4	3	5
Member 2	3	7	8 or 9
Member 3	4	10	10
Member 4	1	6	10
Member 5	4 or 5	1	5
Member 6	2	5	7
Member 7	4	1	6
Member 8	1	5	9 or 10
Member 9	2	5	9
Member 10	4	7	10
Member 11	1	10	15 or 20
Member 12	1	3	8
Member 13	0	2	5
Member 14	1	3	10
Member 15	2	1	1
Member 16	4	6	7
Member 17	1	3	6
Member 18	2	3	4

SOURCE: Personal interviews.

"freeing" them from the constant debts and control they previously had suffered. Not being in debt eliminated many of the tensions and worries that plagued so many lives before the cooperative transformed the constant concern over continual debt into a solvable problem: "When you're in debt, that's something that really frightens you. A person who owes money has all sorts of worries. Right now, I only owe about $5, but once I owed $100. It was terrible. You were sick with worry, buying your food on credit, month after month. Now I feel like a rich man. That was really a terrible situation. I spent all my time asking God to help me find a way out. That's why I am grateful to the cooperative. After joining the cooperative, that was it. After God, it is the cooperative that I'm most grateful for."[15]

Furthermore, to depend on themselves, and not on the comerciantes—not to have to "go through the verguenza of asking for credit"—was a source of pride to many: "Ever since the cooperative, there are a lot of us poor people who have begun to feel proud because we used to have to buy on credit and now we don't have to. We can buy with our own money, without owing anybody a cent." One of the greatest impacts of the cooperative was in dealing with the acute concerns the peasants had about the future. Those who mentioned the cooperative as having made, or as holding out the promise of, improvement in their situation usually pointed to their savings. The cooperative was a way to educate their children—"perhaps even let them reach the eighth grade." The cooperative was a way to save for one's old age, or for the future of one's children and wife in case of death: "And maybe by saving money in the cooperative, you are taking care of your future. And if you should die, that money is there for your wife, for your children."

By late 1970 the cooperative was also helping the peasant improve his future situation in a way not originally foreseen by the organizers. The cooperative (through Fidel) enabled its members to get long-term loans for fertilizers through a new government assistance program for stepping up coffee production. Yields increased rapidly, and the cooperative was credited by many with another promising strategy for the future.

The comments of these middle- and large-holding members also revealed that the cooperative had transformed their relationship with the middlemen from a customary one marked by certain wrongs into a problem. And the cooperative, they felt, was the solution. The consumer cooperative not only gave them lower prices but also the profits "unjustly" kept by the comerciantes. Perhaps most important, the cooperative made clear the control exercised by the middlemen and gave the peasants a way to break free. Thus the greatest fear of a number of large holders was that the cooperative might fail and they would be back at the mercy of the middlemen. "My biggest fear is that the struggle will fail. Here there are many times when money is scarce. If it weren't for the cooperative, these people would buy coffee at whatever price they wanted. If we're not able to get some capital, we'll have to live under their thumbs again, selling at half price. And at their prices I can't even feed my family! And they're getting away with half my money!"

CLASS AND IDEOLOGY

The cooperative leaders, we have seen, crystallized or created a problem orientation (toward both the economic situation and the middlemen) and undermined what few strategies were considered adequate. Further, people came to accept or reject the cooperative based on some decision about the adequacy or inadequacy of the cooperative strategy vis-à-vis their particular situation. But to what extent did such acceptance or rejection depend on class position?

Class position did not "determine" people's reaction to the cooperative in any simple sense, either in the early months or after a few years: among middle and large holders with the same economic resources and potential for gain, some initially accepted and others rejected the cooperative (though most are members today); some day laborers and small holders who I thought had little to gain from the cooperative (given their lack of resources) nevertheless joined and remained members.

The theoretical approach in Chapter 6 did not suggest any simple relation between class and ideology, but it did suggest a relation in the following sense: the orientations people have toward their situations are at least in part generated and sustained by the particular historical experiences they share by being in the same class; and these orientations mediate between a person's class situation and his response to a new ideology. Thus in cases of certain common orientations across classes we might expect similar ideological responses; in the case of different orientations, different responses.

One of the reasons why the cooperative was accepted by at least some peasants in all classes was that the problems and solutions it defined crystallized orientations shared by all classes, and these peasants perceived the cooperative as providing a good strategy to get out of their problematic situations. All of the peasants felt a lack of cash, and the cooperative seemed to provide them with a way to meet urgent cash needs; all the peasants were concerned that existing strategies for improving (or even maintaining) their economic situations were inadequate or nonexistent, and the cooperative seemed to provide a way for a better future through savings and loans, even for those with no coffee; all the peasants were concerned with ways they could save or earn money, and there was thus some appeal across classes for a consumer cooperative that would offer lower prices and share the earnings that previously were made by the comerciantes.

Those small holders and day laborers who *rejected* the cooperative ideology based their judgment, at least in part, on exactly those class-based orientations that differed from those of the middle and large holders. They felt money shortages as the more immediate daily problem of how to feed their families, and they did not see the cooperative as helping them here; they saw that the cooperative loaned money in accordance with the amount one had, and, having little, felt they would get few benefits; they saw the cooperative's promise for a better future dependent on what they could save today, but felt they had no money for food, let alone to save; they saw the cooperative as giving better prices for coffee, but felt that this would be of little use since they had no coffee; they saw the cooperative as promising lower prices and a share of the earnings on consumer goods, but felt that their continual lack of cash made impossible that cash buying required in the cooperative. Thus the orientations that peasants in different classes had toward their economic situation and toward the middlemen did affect their reaction to the cooperative ideology. But because the cooperative appealed to certain orientations that were shared, and not to others, there was no clear-cut division across classes.

There is, however, something that the theoretical framework does not explain. Given the fact that some orientations were shared across all classes, and others were particular to certain classes, why did some of the peasants in each class respond differently? Implicitly, the explanation I have offered is this: people actively make decisions and judgments based on an existing set of orientations; and the particular ways the peasants felt about their economic situation and their relationship with the middlemen were neither so uniform nor "determining" that they "channeled" everyone into the same response. Rather, given a complex set of orientations that defined certain limits of choice, the peasants themselves decided how they thought. And the judgments of many in the same class were different.

SHAPING THE MEANING OF THE COOPERATIVE: FURTHER STRUGGLES

Even within this "activist" posture in the explanatory scheme, I can specify still further some of the criteria by which people made their judgments. So far I have looked only at how orientations toward *economic* situation and the middlemen, generated and sustained by experiences common to particular classes, affected the meaning people gave to the cooperative ideology. But other kinds of orientations will shape the meaning given to a new ideology like that of the cooperative: the ways people think about new ideas, particular modes of action, each other, those who bring them the new ideas, and so forth. These orientations may be shaped, generated, and sustained by factors other than experiences common to particular classes. Indeed, there may be certain shared situations (being in the same community, the same kin group, the same neighborhood) and shared historical experiences (having gone through school together, having lived through the era of Trujillo, having been rooked by the comerciantes, having been in the same catechism class) that cut across class lines and support certain sets of orientations that are independent of class. And just as the orientations the peasants had toward their economic situations had a certain variety (even among those in the same class) upon which very different decisions could be based, these other orientations had a richness and complexity and could support different responses to a new ideology. This set of orientations defines other ways in which the cooperative was judged, and the potential symbolic weapons that the middlemen could use to maintain their control and the cooperative leaders could use to break it.

THE THREAD OF COLLECTIVISM. Among the generally weak traditions of community organization and action in Jaida Arriba, one common experience helped explain the new cooperative idea: the traditional exchange labor teams or juntas. The bishop used this "explanation" on his visit in 1967 by emphasizing that the power and benefits of working together in a cooperative were like those of a junta. Fidel, too, found it a powerful image, a way he could let the peasants "see" a cooperative far better than through explanations of its philosophical purpose and complex organization:

I'd tell them: "There are a lot of ways that we can speak about cooperativism, but we don't have to get involved in all that. You know what a junta is? When I was a child, we invited all the neighbors to our house so they'd help us to put on a thatched roof. And in just one day, we put the entire roof on. That's what a cooperative is. It comes from cooperation. So two or three people cooperate, to solve the problems that one or two of them have." And then I'd ask them: "You people have that system of a junta here in the conucos, don't you? And then they themselves began explaining to me how juntas worked. I always thought that you should avoid fancy words. As soon as I started talking about the junta, they knew what I was talking about right away.

The benefits of collective action captured by this metaphor were stressed continually by Puro at the weekly meetings: "I used to say that if a man harvested three quintales of coffee and went to some company in the pueblo to sell it, the company would laugh at him. And he'd lose more in costs than he'd make selling here. But if we were a hundred men and got together a hundred quintales, then we could really make something. Uniting together we could put together a fortune in a little while—and leave the exploitation of these middlemen." The application of the already existing symbol of the peasants' motives for joining the cooperative were most often expressed in these terms.

SELF-INTEREST VERSUS SOLIDARITY. One of the central orientations with which people viewed the cooperative was that of self-interest: what can the cooperative do for me? The leaders answered: the cooperative will provide you with savings for the future of you and your family; with low-interest loans; with higher prices for your coffee and lower prices for your foodstuffs; and with the money you need to avoid selling a la flor. And the peasants' motives for joining the cooperative were most often expressed in these terms.

Yet a purely instrumental orientation hardly serves to build and then sustain an organization.[16] Each year, for example, as the harvest season approached and the cooperative's own funds ran out, the peasants— desperately in need of money—had a short-run interest in returning to the comerciantes.

The comerciantes constantly appealed to the peasants' immediate self-interest, offering them "easy credit" during the difficult preharvest times when the cooperative often had no money to loan. The comerciantes also used the lure of "special deals." One large holder was told: "What do you think you all are going to do? You have no money. What chance do you think this cooperative has? You'll never be able to get together more than smidgen of coffee, and no one is going to buy that. Listen. You'll be much better off with what I can offer you." And, too, there was the intense, and potentially most serious, effort to buy off Puro.[17]

Ideologically, the cooperative leaders responded in two ways: they tried to strengthen and manipulate the caridad-projimidad orientation and to build on the solidaristic ties that did exist in Jaida Arriba.

From Caridad to Comunidad to Cooperativismo. Many peasants in Jaida Arriba described social relations in the years before the cooperative as marked by egoism and self-interest. "Everybody just worked for himself. Everyone went his own way—pulling in his own direction. Nobody was worried about anyone else."[18] But coexisting with this instrumental orientation were certain institutionalized patterns of mutual assistance defined in solidaristic terms. After a woman gave birth, family, neighbors, or compadres would come to help clean the house, cook, and take care of the children while the mother was in bed. Family and friends visited to see the child, chat, and bring gifts of eggs, coffee, canned juice, condensed milk. If there were a serious illness, close family or friends might offer to loan money for a trip to the doctor. For the poorest peasants, someone might take up a collection for medical aid. If a person had to be moved, mules were lent readily. In serious cases a group of twenty or thirty men would take turns carrying the invalid in a litter down the steep trails and across the rivers to the jeep road. When someone died, those who came to pay their respects brought sugar and coffee and often some food to help serve the visitors. If the family was poor, relatives and neighbors might help provide food and candles for the "ninth day" when many gathered and coffee and food had to be provided. A carpenter might volunteer a coffin. Such solidarism was characterized by one large holder: "All our lives, we had always given help to those who had needed it. If someone was sick, if he needed a little money, he found it. If he didn't have any food, we gave him some plantains. If he didn't have beans, we gave him some beans. And on Christmas Eve, we used to take up a collection to give food to the poor people. And also, if a poor person died, we'd take up a collection to bury him, and for the wake."

Such actions were seen as the charity (caridad) or neighborliness (projimidad) discussed earlier; the help (ayuda) given to another in need.[19] It was only proper that a good neighbor be concerned with "the good of others." Acting otherwise was acting por interés—and criticized as self-interest.

The new church teachings introduced by the bishop and El Padre built upon these solidaristic orientations, and church and peasant leaders used them to support the cooperative effort. The new catechism—itself seen by the bishop as a way to create a "sense of community," a mystique upon which organizations like the cooperative could build—introduced the concept of *comunidad* (community). It proved a powerful metaphor. "La comunidad" defined a whole organic body that had a certain reality, a certain life for which one could struggle and sacrifice. It encompassed everyone, eliminating distinctions of wealth or status. Familiar as a geographic concept, its new use was understood quickly. Struggling for the "comunidad" was continually linked (in mass, in catechism, in Cursillos de Cristiandad) to existing notions of caridad and working for "the good of others." It was infused with an almost sacred, religious meaning. The "community spirit," the bishop and El Padre stressed, was the living expression of Christ's words: struggling for the "comunidad" was the way in which one "loved one's neighbor," the way in which one actually lived "a Christian life." Amor, they emphasized, was not merely the relation between sweethearts (as the peasants commonly used the word), but the basic element of human interaction, the true word of Christ.

These notions were then used to bestow a semisacred aura on the cooperative itself. "Those who are concerned with the good of the others," El Padre would say, "are those who are struggling for the community. Selfishness means to do nothing for others. The cooperative is the best way to live. That's the true Christian community. There are people who want to knock the cooperative down. Those are the selfish ones." This notion was stressed by Fidel when he came to give talks, by Padre Rodolfo and Padre Miguel at their cursillos, and by the cooperative leaders at meetings. Puro would argue: "The best Christian is the man who puts himself in the service of others. When you're not aware of other people's problems and don't fight to solve them, there's no true charity, no love. And where there's no love, there can be no Christianity. To solve our problems together, we have to join in a cooperative."

It is doubtful, however, that many people initially joined the cooperative out of solidaristic motives. Of thirty-one people whom I asked about their initial motives for joining, only Puro and Pablo (organizer of the church-building efforts) mentioned what they could do for the community among their motives—and this despite all the socialization into a solidaristic orientation in the years since they entered. Even more revealing, given the cultural "sanction" against admitting acting por interés, were the five who frankly admitted that when they first entered it was just for themselves and they were not thinking of anyone else. They made such comments as: "To tell you the truth, when I joined I was only looking for my own—and my family's—benefit." "You went in just thinking about yourself." But despite the initial unimportance of a solidaristic orientation, many members came to define their actions, at least in part, in such terms. With the constant definition of their actions as "Christian" and "good for the community" (and the existing orientation against acting por interés) many came to think of their actions in terms of the common good. Working out of a sense of "love," for the good of the "community" became a common part of the language of those in the cooperative. Personal sacrifices—putting in more money to build the fund of capital, temporarily selling coffee at a lower price to the cooperative, buying at the cooperative store even though Manuel might be underselling on some items, waiting it out when loans were delayed in arriving—were phrased in this idiom of sacrifice and struggle for the community. "From an individualistic point of view, you live for yourself. If I have enough to live on, I'm not going to worry whether the other guy is working or not. That's not the way it is in the cooperative. All of us are united, and we all have our money there. It doesn't matter if one person has more than the others. We are all the same. There's more charity being practiced there. When a person is in the cooperative, everyone is fighting all together. You have to look at it as though I'm helping you and you're helping me." A young large holder (who previously had been getting special deals from the *compradores*) explained to me how his orientation had changed: "When I entered the cooperative it was because I saw it would help me. It was a way I could get some money. But after one of the courses, I suddenly got this real interest. I began to go to the meetings and work with my *compañeros.* And then, something happened inside me, in my heart. And from then on I've been willing to do anything for the cooperative."

As more people came to perceive their actions in terms of comunidad and amor, solidarism did not "replace" self-interest, nor was it "more" or "less" important than self-interest. But it did become one way in which people oriented their thoughts and behavior, judged the leaders and other members, and understood the need for certain personal sacrifices for the good of the group. This solidaristic orientation became particularly important for a number of the leaders who sustained frequent personal sacrifices—long periods of time away from their families and fields, paying out-of-pocket expenses themselves, constant meetings and trips. Coming back on mule with a group of leaders who had been to a neighboring campo to help them organize a cooperative, I listened as Salvador broke the silence, asking the others how they felt after spending a day like this. And then, answering himself, he said: "I really feel good inside. I feel like one of the apostles, preaching the words of Our Lord. We are preaching the words of cooperativism to other people, teaching them, helping others to start some sort of peasant organization."

Using Existing Ties of Solidarity. The cooperative tapped yet another important element of solidarity: traditional ties of kinship, fictive kinship, and friendship. Particularly important were the ties among what I will call the "Las Barrancas" group, many of whom lived in the Las Barrancas section of Jaida Arriba.[20]

Importantly, neither geographic proximity alone nor bonds of kinship or fictive kinship automatically created the sense of solidarity among the families in this group; rather, such solidarity was created by particular personal and historical experiences. The Las Barrancas group centered around the children of four families, but also included two people from other families. The children of three of these families had been born and reared together in El Río. Because their fathers or mothers were brothers or sisters, they were related as first cousins (see Chart 8.1). They were childhood friends and later

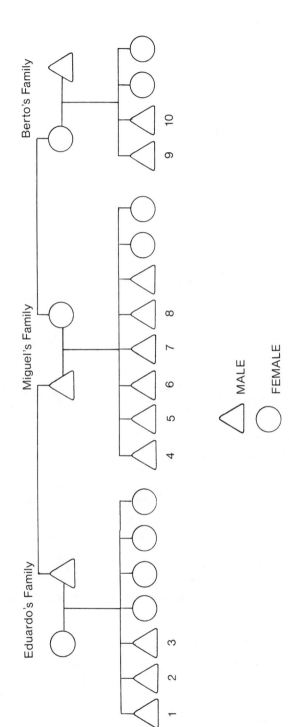

Eduardo's Family   Miguel's Family   Berto's Family

1 2 3   4 5 6 7 8   9 10

△ MALE

◯ FEMALE

Numbers indicate male family heads living in Jaida Arriba at the
time the cooperative was formed

CHART 8.1

Kinship Ties among Three Central Families in the Las Barrancas Group schoolmates at the three-year rural school. When their fathers settled in Jaida Arriba, they continued to visit with each other on Sundays, often gathering at one house to eat, play baseball, "dolls," or "hide and seek." When they married, the bonds among them were strengthened still further. Two of Eduardo's sons married women who not only were sisters but also were first cousins to all of Miguel's children. Eduardo's third son married a woman who was the sister of the wives of two of Miguel's sons. And one of Eduardo's daughters married another of Miguel's sons.

Rafael's family was the fourth family around which the Las Barrancas group was centered. Rafael was father of five daughters and three sons, one of whom was Puro. They came to Jaida Arriba long after the others had settled and married (Puro was already in his early twenties) but came with a reputation for being "of good stock." They purchased forest land and settled in the midst of the other three families. The others immediately offered help. They gave Rafael food before the harvest, lent him animals, helped him build his house, clear his fields, and plant. Rafael and his children were accepted quickly, and the new friendships were soon strengthened by bonds of ritual and fictive kinship.

Such bonds of fictive kinship reinforced ties among all the families in the Las Barrancas group since they often chose the baptismal godparents from among themselves. Compadres were chosen on the basis of "affection, on the friendships that you have formed with your closest friends. *Compadrazgo* (coparenthood) comes from those friendships, from those friendly relations. In Las Barrancas, it was always the closest neighbors. There are always closer friendships among people who have always lived together, almost like family relationships. And since you love your children, you want their godfather to be a person whom you feel some affection for."

If we look at those people from Jaida Arriba chosen by the families in this group to be the godfathers of their children, the percentage chosen from within the Las Barrancas group itself makes clear both the strong bonds of trust and friendship that existed and the extent to which such bonds were reinforced by these fictive kinship relations (see Table 8.3).

Another factor helped sustain the solidaristic ties among these families. The lack of great disparity in their economic class position (they were all middle- or large-holding coffee growers[21]) meant that they could both give money to one another in times of need and repay such (interest-free) loans at harvest times.

The strong solidaristic ties among the Las Barrancas group became an important basis upon which to build the early cooperative organization. Of the four initial leaders of the cooperative, Puro was Rafael's eldest son, Pucho and Mamón were Miguel's two oldest sons, and Salvador was Eduardo's youngest son. Further, of the twelve peasants who stepped forward to put in money at the first cooperative meeting in the chapel, eight were from

TABLE 8.3
Compadre Relations among Families in the Las Barrancas Group[22]

Family in Las Barrancas group	Godfathers from Jaida Arriba	Number of these godfathers in Las Barrancas group	Percentage of godfathers from Las Barrancas group
Family 1	4	4	100
Family 2	0	0	
Family 3	7	7	100
Family 4	4	4	100
Family 5	4	3	75
Family 6	7	7	100
Family 7	7	5	71
Family 8	6	5	83
Family 9	1	1	100
Family 10	4	2	50
Family 11	2	2	100
Family 12	4	3	75
Family 13	0	0	
Family 14	3	3	100
Family 15	6	5	83
Family 16	5	4	80
Family 17	6	3	50

NOTE: Families 1–10 are those so numbered on previous diagram. Family 11 is Rafael's family; 12, 13, and 14 are the families of his sons. Family 15 is headed by nephew of Rafael (first cousin of 12, 13, and 14). Families 16 and 17 have no kinship relation to the others.
SOURCE: Personal interviews.

the Las Barrancas group. And of the twenty-seven peasants who were members when the first promotores came to Jaida Arriba three months after the initial organization, sixteen were Las Barrancas families. One of them, looking back at these first days of organization, explained: "When I joined the cooperative, I thought it was just us people from here in Las Barrancas, and that we weren't going to try to deceive each other. I didn't have any idea of why I was joining the cooperative. I just trusted my compañeros."

LACK OF SELF-CONFIDENCE AND THE TWO WAYS OF "KNOWING". The peasants' lack of self-confidence also posed a serious obstacle to acceptance of the cooperative. Many in Jaida Arriba were skeptical of their abilities actually to organize a cooperative and make it work. This made them leary of committing their hard-earned pennies and pesos. "At first, when they were just starting the cooperative, I was sure that we couldn't make any progress. I just thought that such stupid, ignorant people couldn't make any progress, couldn't keep any sorts of records." Many remembered the stories of the cooperative in the pueblo that had failed many years before because the "clever ones" from the city took advantage of the "ignorant people" of the country. "How are we peasants to know what to do? How are we to defend ourselves?" Lacking confidence in themselves, many of the peasants relied on one of the fundamental cultural ways of knowing the truth or possibility of something. "Let's wait and see how this works," many thought to themselves. "Let me see it, then I'll believe it." But such a way of "knowing" clearly was an obstacle to cooperative action: the cooperative demanded action to create something that did not yet exist except as an idea.

Unable to "believe by seeing," the peasants were particularly susceptible to a second important way of knowing: listening to what those "who knew" (the sabios) said. The advice of the comerciantes, who manipulated these doubts, thus appeared all the more convincing. They warned the peasants that the sabios in the pueblo would take advantage of their ignorance, and reminded them: "You should never drop what you already have for something new."

Such advice strengthened already existing doubts based on the peasants' sense of inferiority and their lack of anything concrete to judge. "They [the comerciantes] advised me not to enter—they told me that it was going to fail and I'd end up losing my money. So I didn't dare join."[23] Arturo's advice caused more than one peasant to pause and doubt. "That used to be the custom here. The comerciantes thought they were your parents. And we did whatever they told us, like a teenager obeying his father. Arturo told me: 'Don't do that. Don't you join the cooperative.' It was like a piece of advice. For me, Arturo was like an adviser. And I was torn inside because he advised me not to join. I didn't believe him, but I didn't doubt him either. I was on the borderline."

The cooperative's rapid organization and early successes helped overcome doubts with visible results. Many peasants began to come to the weekly meetings to listen and watch, to see "if the first people that had entered would drown." They listened to Puro give talks on cooperativism. They listened to others ask questions. They watched each week as the group slowly grew in size. Each week they saw the amount of capital in the fund increase.

When the consumer cooperative was formed this same phenomenon occurred. People hesitated to enter and commit themselves to buying with cash: it was inconceivable to many that this was possible because buying on credit was all they knew. But people saw it was possible: "And that's when people were shocked: we were still alive, eating, and we were not buying on credit." The lower prices were also visible proof. "That's when everybody started getting interested."

As the cooperative actually began to do things—organize a small group, accumulate a fund of capital, make loans, and sell coffee for higher prices and consumer goods for lower prices—more and more people could believe by seeing. Their way of knowing, initially an obstacle, became a source of support for the cooperative. Puro, reflecting on what he learned in organizing the cooperative, summed this up well: "Now I realize that it is only when things are going well that organizations can attract more members. There's so little education that people around here can become aware of things only when they see, and touch, and they are looking directly at it, and not when they are being told about theory. It's when they see reality. That's because our minds haven't been trained. We don't know how to figure out in our own heads what a business is—we can figure things out only when things are actually happening."

The cursillos (especially those given by Padre Miguel and Fidel) also helped overcome the obstacles posed by lack of self-confidence and feelings of inferiority. One such obstacle was fear of speaking in meetings, a fear that inhibited not only a sense of participation but the public clarification and solution of important problems. Believing themselves to be uneducated and ignorant, most peasants felt they had little to say and feared others might criticize their ill-formed ideas or poorly pronounced words. "I was kind of ashamed to express an idea, to speak in front of other people. It was my nerves—I'd get nervous and I couldn't say a word. Or I didn't have any ideas to put into words. Even if I did have good ideas, my embarrassment, my nerves, would get ahold of me, and I couldn't speak. Even to you, Ken. I felt such verguenza. I was afraid I would make you mad with some stupid remark—I was afraid that my own conversation would make you mad."

There was a sense of shame in front of others lest they think badly of one's ideas. And even if they did have ideas or opinions, they tended to downgrade them, believing they were ignorant and that others—leaders like Puro, Pucho, and Salvador—were much more knowledgeable than they:

I kept still, since they knew more than I did. But when I went home, I saw things the other way: I thought we hadn't made the best decision in the meeting, my knees were trembling [he stood up to illustrate, his legs and knees shaking violently]. And my nerves! I couldn't get ahold of myself. I felt like my nerves were all trembling inside me. And when they told me that I had to go to Santiago to speak to all those exporting houses—with a lot of gente grande! [His hands drew a big belly over his thin frame.] And to see other people in—Idecoop, and to go to the bank, and write a check. I was trembling all the way. I was really afraid.

The peasants remember how the courses helped them overcome this fear. Since everyone was forced to speak, they all shared the fears and nervousness of each speaker. They came to understand that their "personal" problem was a common one and that each had to help the other by listening quietly and giving encouragement. Each presentation was greeted by applause. After each session, all laughed and joked about how nervous they had been. With continual practice in the courses, and then at the meetings in Jaida Arriba, their fears began to disappear.

We campesinos used to be afraid to speak out. But now, if something has to be said, we say it. Some person from the outside would come, and we wouldn't say anything, afraid that our way of speaking was bad. Maybe that's why we were the way we were. The gente del pueblo speak well, but up here we speak any old way. But now, with the cooperative, if you have to defend your rights you defend them, even if what you say comes out wrong. If you have to defend your rights, even if you say "majiz," [instead of maiz] go ahead and say it—because we have to defend our rights.

The cursillos also fought the peasants' sense of inferiority by pointing to the abilities they did have—"the bishop himself was a peasant!"—and by attacking the whole sense of deference toward the sabios so deeply rooted in peasant culture. Fidel told them, "You shouldn't go along with something just because it's a priest that says it; you should think about it, talk with others, ask questions. But don't let yourselves be impressed just because the priest sent me, and the bishop sent the priest. You can't go to me or to the priest to solve your problems. You have got to discuss them yourselves, ask each other about them. In this cooperative you are going to manage your own money and solve your own problems." Such admonitions and encouragement did not, of course, make years of deference and inferiority evaporate from the peasants' heads and hearts. But a traditional attitude was now a public problem: at least someone was beginning to tell them that they were not incompetent brutes, at least to suggest the possibility that peasants were capable of taking action. This notion was strengthened further as the cursillos began to teach the peasants the skills and techniques of organizing. As the peasants actually began to know more, they felt more confident and sure of themselves and of the possibilities of cooperative success.

Those who attended cursillos returned enthusiastic, anxious to tell others and put into practice what they had learned. Attending a cursillo in the pueblo, given by "those in the know," and having had successful experiences solving problems and holding meetings helped overcome their feelings of inferiority and lack of self-confidence. Further, in the eyes of the others in Jaida Arriba, these cursillos conferred special knowledge and abilities on their fellow peasants, knighting them with the mystique of "knowing." One small holder, explaining his motives for entering the cooperative, remembers: "They all gave us their advice. The people that came from other places to speak here. And the people from here that had attended cursillos and who knew more than we did. And they told us what they were told in the cursillos and they convinced us."

The effects of cooperative successes and cursillo education in overcoming peasant lack of self-confidence and deference to the comerciantes' advice were limited in one important way: such efforts took time. Yet the very success of the cooperative depended on getting some peasants to act initially in spite of these obstacles. That some did requires further explanation.

We saw earlier that peasants who could not "see to believe" often depended on the advice and knowledge of "those who know." It was this dependence that the comerciantes tried to manipulate to discourage acceptance of the cooperative. But the cooperative itself was able to turn this way of knowing into an advantage: its leader was himself a sabio. The peasants respected Puro as someone "who knew"; he was someone whose advice could be trusted even if they did not themselves understand or "see." And he was supported by others from the pueblo: the bishop, El Padre, Fidel, and other promotores. It is important to examine the part played by Puro and the others in overcoming these obstacles to the acceptance of the cooperative. But before such an examination, I will first turn to another obstacle to the acceptance of the cooperative against which the actions of Puro, Fidel, and El Padre also proved important: that of distrust and suspicion.

SUSPICION AND *DESCONFIANZA*. Acceptance of the cooperative meant more than the espousal of refrains and attendance at meetings: it meant making a commitment of one's scarce resources, first as pledges and later as coffee for the cooperative to sell. The very ability of the cooperative to create the fund needed to break the compradores' control over coffee hinged on this commitment. Such a commitment, we saw, was hindered by the peasants' lack of knowledge and concomitant lack of self-confidence. They feared that a peasant cooperative might not succeed and that the money they invested or coffee they turned over would be lost. But yet another barrier deeply embedded in the culture and reinforced by everyday experiences was a distrust of each other and of outsiders that was encouraged even more by the comerciantes who turned it into a weapon against the cooperative.[24]

The peasants, we saw earlier, distrusted "big fish" such as the comerciantes.[25] But this distrust also permeated most economic relations among themselves: the day laborers and small holders suspected the coffee growers of trying to get the better of them when setting wages; middle holders distrusted the larger holders who lent money (with interest) or bought coffee a la flor. In any economic transaction there was the fear that the other would act por interés and try to take some unfair advantage.

Past efforts at community action suffered from such distrust. When Pablo organized the building of the chapel and tried to collect money for materials, many hesitated to contribute because they did not trust him to use it honestly. Bundles of clothes sent by Catholic charities in the United States always were suspected of being distributed dishonestly. Even with the most elaborate schemes to assure fairness, deceit and unfairness always were imputed by many. Indeed the assumption of foul play was so strong that "evidence" was needed to disprove it.

Such distrust and suspicion is not simply "pathological" as some observers would have it (Banfield 1967:36). The peasants *have* frequently "been taken"

in economic transactions and there have been incidents where people distributing clothes, milk, or food have pilfered. Many might feel that they themselves would be tempted—so it is natural to suspect others.

Given such distrust and suspicion it is not surprising that the peasants were
hesitant to commit their money and crops to the hands of other peasants in
charge of a cooperative. Some feared saving their money in the cooperative
because it would be loaned to others—and what assurance was there that it
would be repaid, that the fund of capital would not just disappear? Particularly strong distrust was felt by the day laborers and small holders. "Since I
was a poor man—and since I lived the way we used to live here, I didn't want
to hook up with well-to-do people. Because the big fish gobbles up the small.
I was afraid that they were going to gobble me up." The comerciantes played
on this distrust and suspicion, reminding the peasants that "the big fish
always gobbles up the little ones" and warning them that "your money is
going to disappear into the fists of the sabios in charge."

Much distrust and suspicion also were directed toward the "outside
world," where all the promotores came from. "Those in the city are cleverer
than those in the country." the peasants would say. "When these see a
peasant they think that he's just a stupid brute. They think that they can do
whatever they want with us. Because they think we don't know anything, for
sure they'll try to rook us." Those who came to the campo from the pueblo
usually were up to no good: politicians at election times making promises
they never kept; soldiers and foresters coming to prevent peasants from
clearing conucos and extorting bribes for not reporting "offenses"; peddlers
coming to sell them "real" gold chains and other trinkets at "special" prices.
Everyday experiences with the gente del pueblo thus tended to sustain such
orientations of distrust and suspicion. And the comerciantes played on and
reinforced this distrust.

El Padre, Fidel, and the cooperative leaders continually tried to counter
these obstacles of distrust and suspicion. They told the peasants that this time
their money would stay in Jaida Arriba and not be controlled by city folk.
They explained that no money would be loaned unless the borrower could
guarantee it (with savings in the cooperative, an animal, a coming harvest, or
someone else with such guarantees who would vouch for him). They tried to
undermine the warnings of the comerciantes by playing on the distrust and
resentment the peasants also felt toward these middlemen and creating
suspicions about their advice. But such verbal efforts could not possibly
eliminate the roots of distrust deeply planted in peasant culture and experience.

LEADERSHIP

Before accepting the cooperative, the peasants asked themselves important
questions. Before committing their scarce resources to a cooperative they

hardly understood and could not "see" they wanted to know: Were those encouraging and leading the cooperative ones "who knew"? Could they be trusted? The perception of the cooperative as a viable strategy or a dangerous folly thus came to depend heavily on those supporting and leading it. "Being as ignorant as I am, I didn't know anything about cooperativism," explained one peasant. "The only thing I wanted to know was who was going to be directing the whole thing." How did the social position (institutional and class) and the personalities (as expressed by style and actions) of these leaders affect their influence in overcoming the orientations of distrust and inferiority that posed barriers to the acceptance of the cooperative? By what criteria did the peasants judge them?

THE BISHOP AND EL PADRE. The bishop and El Padre might appear to have had great influence in the peasants' acceptance of the cooperative. These men first brought the idea of a cooperative to Jaida Arriba, a campo where religion was an important part of people's lives. And each time they spoke, assembled heads and many voices affirmed all their words. A closer examination, however, reveals that their influence was extremely limited. Why this was true becomes clear if we understand the kinds of orientations the peasants in Jaida Arriba had toward bishops and priests and toward these two individuals.

Only in a narrow religious sphere (mass, marriage, baptism, confirmation, communion, confession, last rites) was the authority of a bishop or priest strong. Attempts to influence the social life of the peasants always had met with little success. The priests declared a son's lying to his father a near-mortal sin; prostitution was decried and those who so sinned were threatened with eternal damnation; couples living together but not married by the church were threatened with severe punishment; for the bodies of unmarried youth to touch while dancing "was enough to go to hell, it was a mortal sin, because those two people are enjoying the concupiscence of their flesh"; and any human interference with conception was strictly prohibited.[26] Nevertheless, these activities continued. Many peasants thought the restrictions too severe. "They depicted God so negatively and harshly, we refused to comply because it was just too much." Prostitution and extramarital relations, never rife in Jaida Arriba, did exist despite the prohibitions and threats. Those who refrained from dancing close to each other were obeying their parents or their partners, not the priests. A few actually challenged the prohibitions against birth control.[27] Indeed, even in more nearly religious matters such as the commands to attend the new adult catechism classes many peasants resisted. "That's kid's stuff," they would say. Or, "Religion is changing so much! Maybe what the priests tell us is good, but it may be bad too."

Because they lacked strong influence in social matters, the urgings of a bishop and priest to join a cooperative had a limited effect. They were not seen as men "who knew" about things beyond the church. Remarked one peasant, "I really didn't take too kindly to the advice they gave us—even though what they said wasn't really bad. In a matter such as that, I prefer to see with my own two eyes. I figured my own advice was the best." Confidence in their economic advice was weakened further by memories of a padre's advice to join an unsuccessful cooperative twenty years ago. "A priest doesn't know anything about cooperatives. He thinks everything's easy. He's there in the pueblo and he thinks the cooperative is as simple as eating bread and butter." And although there was no suspicion or distrust of El Padre, confidence in his intentions did not eliminate the distrust they felt of each other and of the promotores.

Church support was, however, important in overcoming one kind of suspicion: it protected the cooperative from charges of involvement with politics or of being against the government or the president or of being communist. In other regions such accusations created serious barriers of suspicion and fear among the peasants, making organization difficult or impossible. The church, however, was seen as outside of politics and as the antithesis of communism. The strong support it gave to the cooperative thus dispelled what few accusative rumors existed and gave the cooperative a certain protection it might otherwise have lacked.

The particular personalities and styles of the bishop and El Padre widened their influence somewhat. Previous clerics always had been isolated and aloof from the peasants: these men of the city always wore their sacred robes, talked to God in a strange language (Latin), celebrated mass "with their butts out and their faces to the altar," and performed rituals whose meanings were mysterious. "To us, they were like kings." Their advice was assented to quickly, although often ignored later: timid toward these imposing men, fearful of a reprimand, it was far better to say "Yes, yes, padre, we'll do it" than to disagree. But the bishop was different. Born to a peasant family from that same region, he spoke easily to the peasants. Fluent in their sayings and knowledgeable of their lives, he won their confidence with his easy manner and concern for their everyday problems. El Padre was the first priest to say mass in Spanish. Except during mass he wore his street clothes, without a collar. And he even donned and doffed his robes in full view of the congregation. He made it a point to speak informally to the peasants and would smilingly tease someone he liked for being "a naughty, naughty boy." Despite his touches of paternalism and a sometimes stern, rushed manner that hindered frank and open communication, most peasants felt him to be "much kinder," "much more natural," much more "easy to talk to" than any other priest. And he was the first who was really concerned about their problems: "He didn't tell us that God sent us poverty and that we just had to accept God's will. He discovered our problems and sufferings. I never saw another priest like him! He was always looking for ways we could have some progress." Although the bishop and El Padre were unable to overcome the barriers of distrust that existed, their friendly, open, concerned manner and their constant support helped provide encouragement and inspire action. Although most peasants still were hesitant to put their money into a cooperative on the recommendation of the bishop and El Padre, they were willing to listen carefully to what they said and to attend the cooperative meetings they encouraged.

THE PROMOTORES. Fidel and the other promotores from Fenacoop and Idecoop had an important advantage that El Padre and the bishop did not: in the peasants' eyes, their class and institutional positions qualified them as people "who knew." They were educated men, some were agronomists, who worked for official government agencies set up by El Presidente himself. Sporting city accents and flashing facts and figures, they seemed to speak with authority about plant diseases, coffee production, middleman exploitation, and future cooperative profits. To some the whole cooperative seemed plausible simply because "it was agronomists that explained it all to us." But to many these men were also outsiders, gente del pueblo; and their advice was filtered by barriers of suspicion and distrust. Fidel tried to break through this distrust by leaning heavily on church backing: "I exploited religion a bit. I would tell them that I was sent by the parish priest: 'I come here because El Padre sent for me, and El Padre is in this because the bishop came and got him.' And we used to have the meetings in the chapels and priests' houses." But much more important in overcoming these barriers was Fidel's personal style, a style quite rare among promotores. Born in a small pueblo in the region, he spent much of his youth with peasant relatives, learning their sayings and coming to understand the deference and suspicion behind the heads that so easily nodded agreement. In his mild but never patronizing tone he drew on vivid images from the peasants' daily lives: the cooperative was like a junta; the peasants who blindly followed the sabios were like the animals in the mule trains that followed the bell ringing on the lead mule's neck. But perhaps most important for the peasants was the dedication and honesty expressed in his actions—in what they could "see" and thus "believe." They knew he worked for many months as an unpaid volunteer. (Only later did he get an official position as a promotor for Idecoop.) They watched him come day after day to visit them, traveling on mule and on foot, sleeping in their houses and eating their food. In the pueblo, his house was always open to them: they would never be left waiting, hat in hand, outside his door but, rather, were welcomed warmly, seated, and listened to carefully. "A promotor has got to have a great interest in helping the peasants. If he doesn't have this great interest, he may know a lot, but he's not going to do anything. He's got to suffer our problems, feel the pain of always being had. It's almost got to be a vocation—you've got to do it out of love. And that's the way Fidel was." And when conflicts arose between the peasants and Idecoop, Fidel's defense of the peasants at the risk of his job made a deep impression: "He always favored us over institutions. And a lot of times, he even gave us advice that went against the institutions, against Idecoop itself, even though he was working for Idecoop."

Fidel continually sought to give the peasants confidence in themselves, in their own abilities to judge and act and succeed. He discouraged simple trust in his opinions. As one peasant describes him, "The best thing about Fidel was that he'd always say: 'This isn't my cooperative. It's yours. If I start meddling in, throw me out.' And he'd always say: 'I'll give my opinion, but it's up to you. You're the owners.' And now, since we've gone through so much together, now you feel on a friendly basis with him." Further, Fidel took the time to instruct them in beginning to organize a cooperative and making decisions for themselves. The leaders slowly gained the self-confidence, ability, and trust to discuss problems with him, to offer him their own opinions, to disagree rather than nod deferentially. It was thus Fidel's personal style—his actions—that eventually broke down the barriers of initial distrust.

But Fidel's success was largely restricted to the few leaders with whom he worked closely, and even they had certain misgivings about him during the crucial early months of organizing. Nor did whatever confidence these few leaders gained in Fidel eliminate the distrust and suspicion they had of each other.

Despite Fidel's success, then, two central questions still remained in the minds of the peasants in Jaida Arriba: Would outsiders or people from Jaida Arriba be in charge of the cooperative? And if it were to be the peasants themselves, exactly who was going to be in charge?

LOCAL LEADERSHIP. The fact that local peasants and not outsiders would be leading the cooperative proved crucial for many people in Jaida Arriba. "The truth is that the promotores and the church didn't influence me too much. But my compañeros, that was really important. For me, the most important things were that the leaders lived right here. They weren't just going to pack up their families and leave. When they told me that any member could get to be director of the cooperative—that it wasn't going to be run by people from 'outside'—I entered." But the questions still remained in many people's minds: Could these local leaders be trusted? Were they people "who knew" what they were talking about and what they were doing? Although such doubts lurked as obstacles for many months, Puro's initial assumption of leadership proved crucial in allaying both the suspicion that existed despite church backing and the lack of self-confidence still felt despite the support of the promotores.

Important here was Puro's position in Jaida Arriba: socially, he was part of the Las Barrancas group, bound by ties of friendship, kinship, and fictive kinship to these sixteen other coffee-growing families, most of whom came to constitute the initial core of the cooperative; economically, his success with tobacco and coffee harvests and his position as a comerciante were visible proof that he was "an intelligent man." Even before 1967, Puro was someone whose advice was listened to; whose ideas were thought sound. Important, too, was his personal style. He spoke *to* them, not down *at* them. He used their language and sayings, drawing on metaphorical images that made clear and understandable the things he said.

The effect of the confidence in Puro as one "who knew," and his close ties with so many families, was explained to me by one of his compadres: "When the cooperative started, it was Puro who really pushed it ahead. When he was on his way to a meeting we would all follow him like ants. Everybody would go." This faith that so many had in Puro's knowledge also was important in countering the advice of the other comerciantes. One small holder, for example, went to Manuel to ask advice about the cooperative, but he eventually listened to Puro: "I knew that Manuel was more stupid than Puro. I trusted Puro much more."

Although Puro's position as a comerciante helped give plausibility to his advice about the cooperative, it was also a potential barrier: a comerciante was continually suspected of acting por interés. The other comerciantes strengthened such suspicion each time they warned of the "big fish" who were in charge of the cooperative and would "eat" "the little ones." Such suspicion was never completely overcome (particularly among many of the day laborers and small holders), but two factors helped to mitigate its effects. One was Puro's close kinship and fictive kinship ties with the Las Barrancas peasants. But the most important was the personal reputation he had built up. He was considered as un hombre prójimo, not someone who acted por interés. "He always tried to help the poor—he was always in the forefront." And he was considered to be honest and fair in his business dealings: "He didn't cheat others, even if he was a negociante."

As a result, many people had confidence in him as a leader. "I wasn't afraid because I knew the leaders. Puro is a sincere man. You can recognize a sincere person and you can recognize people with evil intentions, those that try to put others down." And, importantly, his position in the cooperative was that of treasurer. Thus a peasant who decided to put his money into the cooperative was not handing it over to this strange new organization, but putting it in Puro's hands where it would be safe. "I heard that Puro was the one that was keeping the money here—that he was the treasurer. And I figured he was a good man, so I entered. I figured we wouldn't lose money."

It was thus Puro's position in the community as well as his personal style and reputation that shaped his importance as a local leader. Such local leadership was crucial in the early months of organizing in overcoming the orientations of inferiority and distrust that posed great obstacles to the acceptance of the cooperative.

CHAPTER 9

BREAKING THE CONTROL
OF THE MIDDLEMEN

INTRODUCTION AND THEORETICAL NOTES

In the early months of the cooperative, "accepting" the movement meant committing money as *ahorros* and rejecting the advice of the comerciantes. "Joining the cooperative" was not yet defined as an act of open defiance or as a challenge to the control of the middlemen. But near the end of 1968, the position of the comerciantes was publicly threatened: the cooperative began to market coffee and urged its members to break their ties with the middlemen. A few months later the cooperative presented a second challenge: it openly threatened Manuel's control over consumer goods by organizing the consumer cooperative. To maintain their control, Manuel and other comerciantes sought to prevent their clients from selling coffee through the Cooperativa Argopecuaria and from buying their goods from the consumer cooperative. From the peasants' viewpoint, the question was one of obedience: whether or not to comply with the comerciantes' demands.

Weber has pointed out that the "causal chain extending from the command [of a ruler][1] to the actual fact of compliance can be quite varied" (1968:947). "In a concrete case the performance of a command may have been motivated by the ruled's own conviction of its propriety, or by his sense of duty, or by fear, or by 'dull' custom, or by a desire to obtain some benefit for himself" (1968:947).

Earlier we touched upon the importance of two of these motivations, "dull" custom and self-interest. The *nonproblematic* orientation the peasants had toward their relationships with the middlemen helped sustain the " 'dull' custom" of obedience to the comerciantes. Despite difficulties with these men, few questioned an arrangement endured by their fathers and grandfathers before them. "Desire to obtain some benefit for himself" helped motivate the peasant to approach the comerciantes when he needed money and food; and this same self-interest was used by the comerciantes to lure the peasants (such as Puro) away from the cooperative. In Chapter 8 we saw how the cooperative leaders frequently succeeded in breaking the bonds of " 'dull' custom" and in identifying the middlemen as problems. We saw, too, how the cooperative used existing orientations and ties of solidarism to undermine motives of self-interest that tempted peasants to stay with the comerciantes. But we have not yet explored two motives for obedience which Weber mentions: belief in the legitimacy of the comerciantes and fear of their economic power.

THE CHALLENGE TO LEGITIMACY

THE STRENGTH OF MORAL OBLIGATIONS. Weber argued that "custom, personal advantage, purely affectual or ideal motives of solidarity, do not form a sufficiently reliable basis for a given domination. In addition there is normally a further element, the belief in *legitimacy*" (1968:213). Man, Weber stressed, must be motivated to obey by a feeling that to act in a contrary way "would be abhorrent to his sense of duty" (1968:31).[2] The duty that the peasants in Jaida Arriba felt to continue dealing with the comerciantes was based on a deeply rooted sense of obligation that took two related forms.

The money and credit advanced by the comerciantes was often defined as ayuda extended by these men out of a sense of projimidad or "charity."[3] Grateful for such help in times of need, many peasants felt verguenza at leaving a particular comerciante. It would seem ungrateful to act out of interés by seeking better prices from the cooperative. The comerciantes played on this orientation of gratefulness and the moral sanction of shame to maintain the loyalty of their clients. They would, for example, remind the peasants of the many times they had given them credit for food or medicine. This moral bond made it difficult for many of the peasants to break from the comerciantes: "Most of the people felt verguenza. Even now there are a lot of people who would like to join but they are too ashamed to do it. That's why a lot of people would go in by the back door—so that Manuel wouldn't see them. It was a hard thing even for me—after all the help Manuel had given me. I felt verguenza at the thought of dropping him."[4]

The peasants' sense of duty toward the comerciantes also took another related form. They were not simply indebted to the comerciantes out of gratefulness for their help but quite literally in debt economically. Such debt was considered a serious obligation: as a "trustworthy," "upright," "honest" person (a *cumplidor*), the peasant felt not only morally obligated to pay, but to pay by selling his crops to the comerciante to whom he owed money.

The comerciantes, particularly Manuel, publicly implied that those who sold coffee to the Cooperativa Agropecuaria or bought goods from the consumer cooperative had no intention to repay debts. Shame at being

considered "untrustworthy" hindered many from taking action. "What verguenza I felt. I didn't want to buy anything in the cooperative as long as I still
owed money to him. If I sold to the cooperative I was afraid he might get the
idea I was not going to pay him." Many also feared that Manuel might remind
them about the debts, or, worse, might demand payment. The latter action
was regarded as a serious insult, which impugned one's honesty and integrity.

These moral obligations were further strengthened by bones of compadrazgo, for if a comerciante was a compadre it was even more difficult to
leave him. One large-holding coffee grower who was a compadre of Manuel
(and after three years still had not joined the cooperative) understood his
losses to Manuel but concluded: "I know I'm losing a great deal of money
with Manuel. But I just can't get around to leaving him. I would like to join
the cooperative. But I'm kind of ashamed to leave my compadre. Manuel has
helped me a lot. He's been like a cooperative to me."

UNDERMINING LEGITIMACY

Using Traditional Notions of "Right" and "Wrong." In spite of the moral
obligations felt toward the comerciantes, the cooperative did have some
advantages. Among the coffee growers many depended upon Puro for credit
and thus owed nothing to Manuel.[5] Further, ten middle holders and nineteen
large holders sold their coffee to comerciantes other than Manuel.[6] Those
who dealt with Puro were free of any moral obligation, and many of the large
holders who dealt with other comerciantes did not feel permanently bound
by gratitude to any particular one. Not only did they not buy their goods
from the same comerciantes to whom they sold their coffee, but some even
tended to "look around" each year for the comprador offering them the best
preharvest deal. Such peasants (usually large holders) saw their relationship to
the comprador primarily as one of "self-interest"—a business deal to be
negotiated for the best price—and only secondarily as one of "gratefulness"
for the preharvest advance. They still owed debts to these compradores and
did feel obligated to pay for preharvest advances in coffee, but if the
cooperative could meet their preharvest needs, they would not hesitate to
leave the middlemen.

The cooperative had another resource: along with felt moral obligations to
the comerciantes was a current of resentment. Most of the peasants were
aware of the "self-interest" and "shady dealings" of these peje grande (big
fish).[7] Many were particularly critical of Manuel.[8] Yet despite the undercurrent of resentment in terms of such traditional notions of "right" and
"wrong," before 1967 the control of the comerciantes was not conceived in
these terms, let alone questioned. The cooperative ideology defined such
control, clearly and publicly, and built upon these notions of right and

wrong. It tapped the peasants' resentment and directed it against the loyalty the comerciantes claimed of their clients.

One important move was the public disclosure of the comerciantes' earnings. Puro and the promotores repeatedly explained how the marketing system worked and how the compradores profited from selling the peasants' coffee in Santiago. Their words were transformed into visible proof when the cooperative members began to receive $34 or $35 per quintal and non-members only $29 or $30 from the compradores. When the consumer cooperative was founded and began selling goods for less than the comerciantes' prices, the peasants again clearly saw the price differences. Their blinders removed, the peasants "saw" what they had been losing: "Before the cooperative, I was completely blind. One year, they paid us $40 or $41 and told us the price in Santiago was $43. Baloney! That year they sold for as much as $56! I always knew that they made a profit, but I never realized they made so much!"

The cooperative leaders used such large earnings to emphasize the resentment already felt against the comerciantes. These earnings were defined in terms of traditional notions of "unfair," "dishonest," and "unjust." The peasants began to see that "he who isn't owner of the coffee earns more than the owner." The lower prices for coffee and higher prices for consumer goods resulted from "self-interest," and this interpretation was aimed at the notion that one should be grateful to the comerciantes. This change in attitude was expressed by one middle holder: "Now I realize that they're not projimistas. They're earning more than you realize. They're earning a lot. In the days before the cooperative, it was true—they were projimistas. If I didn't have money to buy sugar, they'd sell to me on credit. [But why do you think that they were projimistas before, but not any longer?] They're still the same persons. But now we figure that they weren't so neighborly. If they were projimistas, they would have sold the sugar for seven cents and not for eight cents, even if they were selling it to us on credit."

This notion of por interés was used to undermine moral obligations to the comerciantes in other ways. The resentment already felt regarding preharvest selling was sharpened and used to cut away at the gratefulness people felt for preharvest advances. At the first meetings the promotores pointed to the interés that lay behind such "help" and seeming friendship: "I know that you have obligations with those people and that you're grateful to them. But there's no real obligation, no real gratitude. That guy doesn't care when you need $15 to take a child to a doctor. All the comprador is thinking of is that from those $15, he's going to get $30, the original $15 plus $15 of interest. What they're doing is taking advantage of you—playing around with your health and with the health of your children." Puro continually stressed how the profits made by the comerciantes in preharvest deals was proof positive that their advances were not given as help. Such arguments began to have an impact. One middle holder explained: "What 'help'! The cooperative made me see. They were finishing us off! They didn't have our interest at heart, paying us $15 a la flor and at harvest time offering others $29."

The bonds of agradecimiento were further attacked by defining the very giving of credit and money advances as por interés, not projimidad: as exploitation, not help. Credit, Puro would argue, was given por interés to get ahold of a peasant's coffee: "After two or three years of selling, we began to see exactly how much we were losing with those so-called 'friends' of ours. If they're such good friends, let's see if they'll lend us the money so we can sell our coffee on our own. But if that guy wants to lend me money so he can buy my coffee, that's not friendship, that's only interés." Such gratitude, he might add, would be frowned upon by God himself: " 'And you think God is going to be happy with us because we're grateful to those men and let them trick us that way?' And they answered me: 'No, because God loves everyone the same.' And I told them: 'So we have to unite, and find out where the best price is being paid. As long as we're thinking about gratitude, we'll be falling into misery and bankruptcy.' "

The peasants already knew that their debts imposed certain obligations upon them, and many came to accept this redefinition of credit and advances as a form of control based on interés. Credit came to be seen by many as a way in which the comerciante had the peasant "tied up" like an animal, and as a way for the comerciantes to "help" themselves and not the peasants: "They're the ones that are being helped out! They'll let you buy on credit, but also, you'll have to pay them within a fixed time period. And they'll end up charging you more for the merchandise. Or they'll pay you less for your coffee. That's not helping. I mean it's the comerciantes themselves who are getting the most benefit out of this. He's not helping me, he's helping himself!"

A New Notion of Justice. The cooperative thus sought to weaken the bonds of moral obligation by strengthening the already existing currents of resentment against the comerciantes. But it also introduced a new notion of justice (of right and wrong) that further undermined the legitimacy of the comerciantes. The earnings of business, it argued, belonged to everyone and not to one alone. It was wrong that one man should be making a profit. What he earned belonged to all those who sold to and bought from him. In the cooperative the benefits would be divided: one would not gain at the expense of the many.

This new notion "fit" well into existing orientations. It did not call for an equal division of profits among all or for the redistribution of wealth from one group of peasants to another.[9] Rather, it argued for a "return" of the profits to "those who were the rightful owners"—the peasants who produced them and who were "losing" them to these peje grande. In the cooperative, each would be getting his rightful share, according to what he bought or sold. "If another has made himself rich with your products and sweat," one promotor told them, "then you can make yourselves rich too."

At the cooperative meetings, Puro would remind them: "Manuel started with only $500 four years ago, and now he has over $7,000." And then he would ask: "Where did all this money come from?" They would respond: "From us!" Often the comerciante was likened to a pig that was being fattened with the peasants' produce. "The farmers who sell this produce to these middlemen are like a man who has a pig in a pigsty. He keeps tossing them the food he grows so that they'll get fat."

This new notion caught on quickly and provided the peasants with a new way of seeing and judging what previously had been common, traditionally accepted transactions between themselves and the comerciantes. Explained the peasants, "We used to be blind before. They'd buy from us and leave us without any profit. After the cooperative got started, the light dawned. Back in those days, we weren't aware that a guy had a right to live. We were like slaves, working for the good of others, and ending up with hardly anything for ourselves." Now the injustice of "working for them—for their benefit" became clear.

The notion that it was wrong for a comerciante to earn a profit for himself challenged his very right to be a comerciante. It served further to undermine the bond of agradecimiento that existed. All the "help" that the comerciantes were advancing was little more than help for themselves because they were earning all the profits:

> I never earned any profits off the comerciantes, but they sure earned a lot off me. Now I realize that it is out of their own self-interest that they let us buy on credit. Now I realize that what they were doing was robbing us blind. If I go sell them a fanega of coffee they're making money, they're making a profit off me. It's the same thing when I sell them beans, or a thousand plantains, or tobacco. And to make matters worse, I go and buy from them in their store, giving them even more profit. But in the cooperative, the profit belongs to me. If I sell to the cooperative, or buy from the cooperative, the profit belongs to me.

Indeed the whole notion of agradecimiento was turned against the comerciantes: it was they who should be grateful to the peasants for giving them all these profits, not the peasants who should be grateful to the comerciantes.

Manuel's own reaction to the cooperative further weakened his legitimacy. At first he only advised people not to enter. But as his clients began to sell coffee to the cooperative and buy goods from it, he began asking them to pay what they owed and publicly threatened those who left him with no credit in the future. Manuel's actions had some traditional justification: a peasant who left debts with one comerciante to buy and sell at another might be intending not to pay what was owed, and further, was expressing ingratitude for help extended. But the cooperative leaders used Manuel's threats and sanctions as proof that such help was not help at all and only a way to get peasant crops and money. As Puro explained: "People began experimenting, leaving the negociantes. And they saw a difference in the behavior of the negociantes— their friendship vanished, and there were bad feelings. And I'd say, 'Look, because you're not selling them your crops, now they're treating you like enemies. They were just out after your money. They were only doing that por interés.'" People against whom such sanctions were applied, and those who heard about them, began to believe the judgment of the cooperative leaders. Foreclosing was proof that these men were not their friends, that these men were acting por interes, and that one should not feel any moral obligation to continue dealing with them.

Although the cooperative ideology effectively undermined much of the moral obligation of remaining with "one who had helped for so long," most peasants still felt the obligation to pay what was owed before "leaving" the comerciantes and backing the cooperative. Such a course of action demanded money they did not have. There was another serious problem: Manuel would refuse them future cash and credit advances if they sold their coffee to the Cooperativa Agropecuaria or bought from the consumer cooperative. The cooperative thus had to provide them with the money both to repay debts and to survive in the future. The weakened bonds of moral obligation, however, did not undo the economic power of the comerciantes. The peasants could not, Antonio once explained to me, subsist on consciousness alone. They would still have to turn to the comerciantes in times of unforseen need: "Sometimes to have awareness is one thing, but to be in misery is another one. If you harvest 2 fanegas of coffee but you owe $20 to a comerciante who doesn't want to wait any longer, and you're sick, how in the world are you supposed to sell your coffee to the cooperative? What are you supposed to do? You have to sell it to that comerciante. You have no choice. It's not that you're unaware, you have to sell it. It's misery that makes you do it."

ECONOMIC POWER

CONTROL OVER CREDIT AND THE USE OF SANCTIONS. Weber argued that loss of legitimacy might weaken a ruler's control, but he emphasized that there were other, albeit less stable, bases for obedience: custom or habit, self-interest, and fear. The effects of habit and self-interest, we saw, were at least partially undermined by the cooperative, but it still had to confront Manuel's economic power to coerce a peasant into obedience.

Manuel applied two kinds of sanctions to those who deserted him for the cooperative: foreclosing debts and denying credit and preharvest advances. The first sanction was a moral one: he never called government authorities to force debt payment. But the mere threat of this economic sanction prevented many from selling their coffee to, or buying their goods from, the cooperative. The second sanction was strictly economic and posed a severe threat to his clients: they depended on preharvest cash advances to meet production, medical, ceremonial, and travel expenses; they depended on credit to eat in the months when there was no harvest. Such sanctions proved effective. "I want to enter the cooperative," explained one large holder, "but I just can't. I can't buy with cash. I don't dare leave so and so because I owe him money and I'm grateful to him. And the day that I'm broke again, I can never go back to Manuel, to buy on credit because right away he'll say that I am a member of the cooperative. That's the reason I'm afraid to join." In the face of the comerciantes who had both money and know-how, many peasants felt fearful, and this fear was sharpened by stories they had heard of other cooperatives that had been destroyed by the middlemen. And if this cooperative failed, to whom would they turn for food and medicine and production costs?

CONTROL OVER CREDIT AND CONTROL OVER MARKETING. Although Manuel was the only comerciante to resort to economic sanctions, the economic power of all the comerciantes threatened the survival of the cooperative. They had capital, or access to credit, needed for financing the coffee harvests, entering the coffee market, and stocking a comercio with consumer goods. The peasants needed such capital to break middleman control. At harvest time, the peasants needed large amounts of money to pay their pickers. To pay the pickers $8.50 per quintal to pick the approximately 1,000 quintales of the initial thirty members from Jaida Arriba required a cash outlay of $8,500.[10] If the cooperative did not have this money, its members would have to turn to the compradores and obligate their coffee for cash advances. In order to market the harvested coffee, the peasants also needed to buy or rent processing equipment (a huller), drying floors, and a warehouse. Luckily, it cost them only $700 the first year. (They eventually bought a factory for $5,000.) Furthermore, the compradores had the money to make immediate cash payments for the peasants' newly harvested coffee. The coffee grower, in need of cash to pay debts and to meet present expenses, could not wait the one to three months the cooperative would take to process and sell his coffee in Santiago before paying him his share. But for the cooperative to meet the comprador's price of $29 per quintal on even half of the coffee brought in by members (500 quintales) would necessitate having $14,500 available for buying coffee.[11] And the costs of processing even 500 quintales of coffee, at $1.25 a quintal, would be another $625.

THE CREATION OF POWER

CREATING POWER: INDIVIDUAL STRATEGIES. To break the control of the middlemen the peasants thus needed a large cash fund to protect their crops from preharvest obligations, to resist economic sanctions, and to enter the marketplace. A cooperative theoretically provides a way to create such economic power: by forming an organization in which each member invests his savings, the necessary funds can be accumulated. For reasons examined in the following section, this method proved too slow to be effective. Although the small fund the cooperative amassed enabled some to cancel their debts or protect their coffee from preharvest selling, such funds were exhausted quickly. The cooperative, however, was able to survive during its crucial first months for two reasons: the limited use the comerciantes made of their potential power and the ability of cooperative members to mobilize individual resources.

One comerciante, Arturo, could have brought his political power to bear against the cooperative. The failures of other Dominican peasant organizations in the face of police violence and government pressure highlight the importance of Arturo's inaction.[12] Economically, all the major compradores and comerciantes in the region acting together had the potential power to destroy the cooperative in its early months by jointly foreclosing on debts and denying credit and advances to all cooperative members. With the exception of Manuel, however, they did not use their power. Manuel's power alone was limited: about one-third of the middle-holding and two-thirds of the large-holding coffee growers did not depend on Manuel for either credit or advances.[13]

Those who were tied by preharvest obligations to Manuel and afraid of his threats to foreclose on debts needed more money than the cooperative had if they were to break free. A number of strategies were tried. Those large and middle holders with animals sold a cow or a pig for cash. Labor costs (like weeding) often were met by helping each other in juntas. To those in critical need a few members with a little money gave small, personal, interest-free loans to pay debts to Manuel or to avoid obligating coffee to him. One large coffee grower even shared a personal loan he was able to make with the Banco Agrícola (using his forty-odd head of cattle as a guarantee).

Although five of Manuel's clients thus were able to cancel their debts and free at least part of their coffee to sell to the cooperative, such strategies were limited, stopgap measures. By harvest time, as we will see, all the coffee-growing peasants were deeply in trouble: to finance the harvest and enter the marketplace required the thousands of dollars that only the compradores had access to.

Breaking the comerciantes' control over consumer goods presented even greater problems: not only did the peasants first have to free themselves from their debts to the comerciantes, and not only did the cooperative need the capital to acquire and stock a store, but the members needed the money to buy in cash. The consumer cooperative, however, did not have the funds to advance credit. The large- and middle-holding peasants initially were able to get some of the cash they needed from their coffee: the consumer cooperative first opened during the coffee harvest; fortuitously high coffee prices that year (they ranged up to $56 per quintal because a Brazilian frost had created a world coffee shortage) gave them greater resources than usual. As this money ran out, some tried to sell off animals to get cash; others cut their purchases. But such individual strategies proved extremely limited. Indeed in 1970, 1971, and 1972, July through December proved to be months of crises both for the consumer cooperative and its members: the cooperative funds always ran out, and selling livestock (often at great sacrifice) proved insufficient to provide the cash needed. The consumer cooperative survived only because, with the help of Puro, it eventually was able to get credit at a warehouse in Santiago; and it started, under the severe economic pressures its members faced, to give some limited credit.[14]

The difficulties the middle- and large-holding peasants had breaking free of debt and buying with cash were much greater for the small holders and day laborers. Their economic class position gave them few individual strategies to try. Although the debts of these day laborers and small holders were often quantitatively small—$5, $15, $25 (as compared with debts of $50 or $100 or more among the middle and large holders)—for these poor peasants, with limited ways of earning money, they seemed enormous. Daily searching for work that would provide them the "pesito" needed to buy that night's food, these people found paying such debts extremely difficult. A few with animals tried. Colín, for example, sold the cow he had been raising for three years, plus a newly born calf, in order to pay his debts and enter the cooperative. This was a high price to pay: it left him where he had been three years before, with one cow and frustrated hopes for developing a herd. But even if this strategy worked for a few small holders like Colín, there was almost no way they could then get the money needed regularly to pay for food with cash.

The relative difficulty the day laborers and small holders had in breaking with Manuel and entering the consumer cooperative is reflected in the rate of entry of peasants from different economic classes. In Table 9.1, charting the entry by class during the first ten months of the cooperative, we see that of the twenty-six large-holding households, twenty-two or 85 percent joined; of the thirty-eight middle-holding households, thirteen or 34 percent joined; of the ninety-nine small-holding households, only eighteen or roughly 15 percent joined. The only unusual figure is the relatively large percentage of day laborers who joined—nine out of eighteen or 50 percent of the day-laboring households. But only three of these day laborers who joined (that is, paid the dollar membership fee and started investing money) actually began to buy at

TABLE 9.1
Date of Entry into Consumer Cooperative by Economic Class

Month of First Pledge in Consumer Cooperative	Large Holders	Middle Holders	Small Holders	Day Laborers
May (1969)	4	1	1	1
June	4	4	3	2
July	1	–	1	–
August	3	2	2	1
September	6	1	3	1
October	2	2	2	–
November	–	1	5	2
December	–	–	–	–
January (1970)	1	1	1	2
February	1	1	–	–
Totals	22	13	18	9

SOURCE: Cooperative records.

the consumer cooperative. All the others continued to buy their goods at Manuel's store, at least until February 1970.[15]

The severity of the problem faced by the small holders and day laborers highlights the more general problem of the individual creation of economic power in Jaida Arriba: although some of the large- and middle-holding peasants could counteract Manuel's specific sanctions, no individual strategy could enable them to create the economic power needed to break the comerciantes' control over credit and marketing. In order to finance their harvests, enter the marketplace, and build and operate their own store, they needed a fund of capital. What the middle- and large-holding coffee growers had that the small holders and day laborers did not was potential economic power: control over productive land. The cooperative theoretically could convert that potential power into actual power: through organization and savings, power over land and production could be translated into control over credit and marketing, and the control of the middlemen could be broken.[16] How that theory broke down in practice, and what this meant for the cooperative, will be the subject of the next two sections.

CREATING POWER: THE COOPERATIVE STRATEGY. The cooperative ideology held that only through collective action could the peasants "free" themselves from the middlemen: individual earnings at harvest times could be translated into a collective fund for distribution during periods of cash shortage and for use in processing and marketing coffee. Creating power in this way first demanded creating an organization to collect and redistribute money, administer a processing factory, negotiate in the coffee market, and in general handle the problems of both a peasant and a capitalist enterprise.[17]

Creating a viable cooperative organization presented certain serious difficulties for the peasants. Such difficulties often are not perceived by many of the progressive Dominican clergy (nor by many student radicals and political groups) whose major focus among the peasants is concientización, creating consciousness. This task usually implies two things: making the peasants aware of the injustices perpetrated on them, and making them believe that it is desirable and possible to do something about these injustices through collective action. It rarely implies, nor in practice includes, teaching people the skills demanded successfully to mount a collective struggle. The ability to lead, organize, and make collective decisions are among the important skills needed. The peasant in Jaida Arriba knew two basic modes of decision making: deciding for himself or asking "one who knew" to decide for him. But collective decision making was new and strange. Public meetings traditionally took the form of ritual observances (mass) or of receiving "the word" from those above: the priest, the politician, the teacher spoke; the peasants listened. Trujillo's reign had left a thirty-year legacy of autocratic rule on the local as well as the national level. If the peasant felt fearful and incompetent even to speak in public, the notion of publicly discussing, debating, and making an actual decision was not even conceived by most until 1967 when the new adult catechism classes and the cooperative movement began.

Practice in the week-long courses helped many to overcome their fear of public speaking.[18] But there was little sense of agenda or order: speaking in turn, listening to what another was saying, keeping to one subject, defining problems to be dealt with, breaking complex problems into simple, more easily solved problems, and making people responsible for carrying a decision through to action were habits and skills that did not exist. The organization of an election to choose leaders was not only a new experience, but, following national models, elections were not conceived of as the active, free choice of a slate of candidates based on their actual abilities, but as ritual approval of existing officeholders.[19] As meetings shifted from the quiet deference toward Puro and visiting promotores to more active peasant participation, some sessions appeared to border on pandemonium: there were confused, simultaneous discussions of various aspects of different problems, people talking past each other, votes being taken to reach decisions on actions for which no one was made responsible, and a great dependence upon *who* gave a particular opinion rather than *what* the opinion was. These difficulties were partially overcome as peasants attended the special courses. They were taught an agenda that was to be followed in each meeting. Instruction and practice were given in how to raise one's hands and talk in order, how to run a meeting, and how to organize an election.

Certain abilities, however, could not be learned so simply—for example, how to define clearly new problems and break them into solvable pieces. This resulted in inadequate consideration and resolution of certain problems confronting the cooperative. Further, certain forms the peasants learned and practiced were not understood. As a result, they either fulfilled no purpose or were imbued with new meanings. At each meeting, after the ritual reading of the minutes, the issues left pending were ignored, unless someone brought them up again. Often, after a problem was raised, opinions given, and a vote taken, many assumed that this procedure was itself the end; they saw no need to move from the decision to some concrete action that would have solved the problem.

Despite their limitations, the new abilities to speak publicly, conduct discussions, and run elections were important factors in creating the cooperative organization. Public discussions helped turn private problems into public ones capable of collective solution. Although active debate sometimes was limited to a few leaders, such debate at least made public alternative forms of action which people could hear and comment on. These meetings thus gave members a chance to understand more clearly the problems facing the cooperative and to feel that measures demanding sacrifices (greater savings, a tightening of belts, a restriction of credit) were ones they themselves had decided best, not mysterious decisions that had come down to them from above.[20] Meetings also provided a forum where leaders could reach a consensus, often sampling "public opinion" and, if they felt little support for their ideas, dropping them or slowly shifting into agreement with the others. In those (rare) cases where a consensus was not reached among the leaders (Pucho, for example, often would back himself against the wall, leaving no room for compromise, and be too embarrassed to admit he was wrong) the vote often was put off and the issue left temporarily or permanently unresolved.[21]

Leadership and Organizational Skills. The process of collective decision making left a heavy burden on a handful of peasant leaders. To them fell the major tasks of organizing the cooperative, administering this business enterprise, and solving everyday problems. The successes (though limited) that these leaders had in creating a cooperative organization were due to a combination of two factors: the knowledge and abilities that some of them already had in matters of business and the kind of assistance they received from outside *promotores* and priests.

During the first months of the cooperative, there was little organization in terms of structure, personnel, division of responsibility, accountability, records, or rules. There was only Puro and a growing following. Four aspects of Puro's style and abilities seem to have been particularly important: his initiative, his desire to educate others, his ability to handle personality conflicts, and his capacity to think, reason, and analyze.[22]

Everyone in Jaida Arriba was aware of the economic problems that plagued daily life, and many experienced a certain malaise in their relations with the middlemen. But only Puro took a step forward and said: "Let's do something." A certain intranquillity and restlessness burned in Puro—continual debt, low coffee prices, ignorance, and poverty were problems he felt had to be acted upon. He was one of the few who were not like Saint Thomas; he did not have "to see to believe." The idea of forming a cooperative struck him as important, and his support by the bishop on his visit to Jaida Arriba spurred him to try to create a concrete reality from an abstract concept. "In all things, man has to start, and try and see if they're possible or not," he once told me. The intranquillity and faith that fired Puro's initiative and willingness to sacrifice were a source of encouragement and excitement for others.

The encouragement and spirit that Puro continually infused into the early organization was supported by his belief in the importance of education. Rather than striving to be a new patron, maintaining the loyalty and support of his client followers through a monopoly of wisdom and skill, he continually sought to educate others, encouraging them to go to the courses and explaining issues to those who did not understand them. As other leaders began to emerge—his compadres Salvador and Pucho and two of Pucho's brothers—he worked closely with them, often convincing by skillful argument but never insisting that his was the only way.

Personality conflicts were a severe threat to the cooperative organization. One of the major protagonists was Pucho. Dynamic and outspoken, Pucho quickly assumed a leadership position after he returned from New York and finished a month-long course in cooperativism with Puro. Tireless in his dedication, he stubbornly held strong views about *the* right thing to do, and he presented them in a tone and style that often made disagreement difficult without implying a personal attack on his intelligence and integrity (something most would hesitate to do). "I've worked out the perfect plan for. . . ." he would say authoritatively. Or, "I've discovered the solution. . . ." or "the way we must act is. . . ." He would brook no disagreement. One of the peasants remembers: "He'd get violent. When we formed the provisional council of the Cooperativa Agropecuaria, whenever there was some problem and he had an idea, but there was someone else with another idea, he wouldn't feel very good about it. And sometimes, he'd say things like: 'If you don't do it this way, I'm going to leave you.' And once he did leave for a short period." Although Pucho was incorruptible and never sought power for any economic self-interest, he was attracted by the prestige of position. He wanted to be thought of as a leader, a *jefe*. Actively seeking credit and recognition for his efforts, he never publicly could admit a mistake or change his mind; he fought fiercely never to be proved wrong and was bitter if he lost.

Within Jaida Arriba, small conflicts soon developed between Pucho and other leaders. These reached much more serious proportions later when the leaders of Jaida Arriba joined with those of the other neighboring campos to form a central cooperative: there were fewer ties of friendship, kinship, and compadrazgo to smooth over disagreement. Here Puro often played an important mediating role. He rarely lost his temper. Calm, tranquil, and soft-spoken, he had a talent for smoothing over conflicts and for holding the group together.[23]

A final point about Puro's leadership was his innate intelligence: his ability to think, reason, and analyze. Always believing that a problem could be solved, he would think about it carefully, trying out his ideas on others, changing them, refining them. At meetings, he sometimes would listen quietly to a discussion, staring meditatively off into space. Then he might interject calmly: "I have an idea . . . ," and go on to explain a fairly well-worked-out plan. He often approached complex problems by breaking them into more solvable parts. He did it almost unconsciously, and sometimes with difficulty. But few others took this approach. When they felt confused, Puro often could bring back the meandering discussion to the problem at hand. He was aware, as many were not, that decisions should end in action, not simply discussion. He resisted the impulsive nature of some of the other leaders to act without thinking. Further, Puro had learned much from his experience as a comerciante and comprador that was to prove of great value to the cooperative. He had a fairly clear understanding of the system of control in the marketplace. He had experience in the kind of buying and selling the cooperative would have to do. He had some notion of pricing, of profit and loss, of the rudiments of administering a business. He also had experience dealing with the merchants and exporting houses in the cities. Neither timid nor deferential, he was able to defend himself in discussions and bargain for the best deal.

Puro's leadership abilities and rudimentary knowledge of business were crucial to early organizational success and provided him with the foundation for learning quickly; but alone they were insufficient. Puro did not take the initiative to start the cooperative until the church and promotores provided the encouragement and the initial organizational instruction. He had no idea how a cooperative was structured; his rudimentary knowledge of addition, subtraction, and multiplication was matched by an ignorance of accounting and bookkeeping; he knew little of organizing elections and running meetings and less of administering a large-scale capitalist enterprise that would buy thousands of quintales of coffee, process, store, ship, and market it, and make loans, earn profits, and suffer losses that would have to be calculated, explained, and distributed. Further, such organization and administration demanded other leaders. Puro could not manage alone. The cooperative might start with a leader and his following, but to succeed, an ongoing organization had to be created and administered.

The skills needed to create a cooperative organization were taught to Puro and other peasants by men from the world outside the campo: government promotores, Fidel, Padre Miguel. One mechanism for teaching these skills was the official courses sponsored by Idecoop or Fenacoop. These courses had a number of serious limitations. Few peasants could afford the time (away from their crops) or the money (for food and travel) to go to the pueblos. The few who went came back with a special aura of "knowing," and often with more confidence in public speaking, but they had great difficulties in explaining to others ideas and procedures they themselves only partially understood. Further, only the most rudimentary elements of cooperative organization were taught, and most instructors used the same techniques of drill and memorization that had been used to teach the peasants to read, write, add, and repeat their catechism. The cooperative "kit" they were presented came complete with do-it-yourself instructions predefining problems and solutions, but the peasants were not taught the skills needed to solve the new, undefined problems they continually faced.

The courses given by Padre Miguel and Fidel overcame some of these limitations. Because they were held closer to Jaida Arriba, many cooperative members could attend (more than fifteen peasants in Jaida Arriba attended at least one five-day course; four attended all four that were given by Padre Miguel). They taught not simply the standard procedures of cooperative organization, but were geared to the particular problems the cooperative was facing. Further, although Padre Miguel and Fidel often guided the peasants toward particular solutions, their techniques encouraged the learning of rudimentary problem-solving skills. The courses often broke up into small "round-table" groups to discuss the problems facing the cooperative and to recommend solutions; intensive practice was given in running actual meetings dealing with these problems; practice in public speaking helped overcome fears; groups examined constitutions of other cooperatives point by point, discussed them, and reformulated them (working closely with Padre Miguel and Fidel); mock elections were held and the meaning of voting was discussed; peasant secretaries practiced taking minutes, and the treasurers practiced keeping accounts; and the actual conflicts with exporters and government agencies were discussed.

The everyday guidance and advice given by Fidel was also important in teaching the peasants organization and problem-solving skills. Initially the leaders met for bimonthly meetings at his house; later he traveled almost weekly to the campo to attend their meetings, give talks, and assist in organization. The constant guidance the cooperative received was rare in the Dominican Republic: the government promotores were always too thinly spread to give sufficient help to the cooperatives under their auspices; and sometimes these city folk lacked the energy or spirit to endure the hardships of poor facilities and rugged travel in the countryside.

Continual guidance, however, also can be a mixed blessing: in giving the peasants the kind of instruction they need to organize and administer a cooperative, it is easy for a promotor to take initiative and responsibility, creating a dependence upon him. Constantly aware of this problem, Fidel continually sought to make the peasant leaders independent of him. His style was open and not paternalistic; he treated their ideas and arguments with respect, listening carefully and disagreeing delicately. His confidence in them helped them gain confidence in themselves. At meetings of the administrative council, he would try to stay in the background until they asked him for advice. Then he would interject it gingerly, surrounding it with caveats of the importance of their deciding for themselves.[24]

Despite the efforts and successes of Padre Miguel and Fidel, what the peasants learned (particularly during the first years of the cooperative) was severely limited. The cooperative came to face problems that threatened its very existence, but the leaders scarcely understood them. Here the dependence on Fidel became direct and open: not only did they depend on him to define and explain these threats, but his advice was readily and unquestioningly accepted. Thus, as we will see, not only did the creation and maintenance of a cooperative organization depend heavily on men from outside the campo, but the actual survival of the cooperative came to depend on outside brokers. Why this was true demands understanding the severe limits the cooperative faced in creating economic power even after it was able to create an organization.

The Limits of the Cooperative Strategy. Individual strategies, we saw earlier, were woefully insufficient to break the control the middlemen exercised over credit. The middle- and large-holding peasants did not have the resources as individuals to meet household and production costs without turning to the middlemen for the credit and advances that put liens on their production. The cooperative strategy sought to turn the potential power of these individual peasants (given their land and cash crop production) into an actual fund of capital through organization and savings. With talented leadership and exceptional instruction and guidance from Fidel and Padre Miguel, they were able to form such an organization. But they still faced a serious impasse: even acting collectively, the peasants did not have the potential resources to create the cash fund they needed quickly enough to break middleman control. After nine months the first harvest was approaching; and only $2,000 had been amassed. With this fund the members had been able to meet many preharvest cash expenses and to avoid selling a la flor. But there was nothing left in the fund for harvest expenses (which required about $8,500), nor for the costs of renting ($700) or buying ($5,000) a warehouse and processing equipment, nor for buying the members' coffee ($14,500), and processing it ($625).[25] This cooperative strategy was a failure. The middle- and large-holding peasants, living as they did in near-continual debt and experiencing severe demands on what little money they did earn, did not have sufficient surpluses, even collectively, to break the control of the middlemen.

CREATING POWER: THE NEW BROKERS AND THE NEW MIDDLE-MEN. The peasants' ability to create a cooperative organization depended, as we saw, on outside instruction and guidance. But even with such training, the peasants were largely unprepared to deal with the complex, clever, and often corrupt world of large exporters, banks, and government agencies. This problem took on added importance given the failure of the cooperative to amass needed funds through member savings: it was forced to depend on this outside world for the money needed to break the control of the local middlemen.

We saw that Fenacoop advanced this money, contracting for payment with cooperative coffee. This coffee, Fenacoop promised, would be marketed abroad (Fenacoop had a quota from the government) and would command higher prices than even the large exporters could offer the peasants. Fenacoop agreed to charge a 1 percent commission for the marketing. The money advanced ($40,000 to $50,000 were initially promised) would be given, the peasants were told, at 8 percent or 9 percent interest. But these verbal assurances were soon followed by a series of problems.

Most seriously, the money neither arrived in the promised amounts (loans never totaled more than $13,000 that first year) nor at the time agreed upon. Such limitations and delays threatened the cooperative's very existence. [26] There were other difficulties too. When the first $4,000 arrived in the third week of November and Puro went to Santiago to sign a contract for it, he discovered that the marketing commission was set at 2 percent. Further, the price to be paid for their coffee was already specified in the contract, yet Fenacoop had promised them the price received after marketing it abroad. [27] Finally, no mention was made of the interest to be charged on the loan. Puro called the Presidente Administrador of Fenacoop in the capital. Briefly discussing these problems, he discovered that the interest rate would be 11 percent, and received assurances that he should not worry about the other problems. Anxious for the money, Puro signed the contract.

The peasant leaders were dissatisfied and suspicious, but most hesitated to argue or protest. Fenacoop, after all, was helping them with loans, and Fenacoop promotores had helped them initially to organize the cooperative. Further, these were city people: how could they, ignorant peasants, argue? What would they say? But Fidel was furious at such treatment of the peasants. He urged them to protest and helped set up a meeting in the capital with Fenacoop officials. When they arrived they were greeted with great friendliness by the officials who, explained Antonio, "took us by car to a fancy restaurant. That was so they could win us over by filling our stomachs. They treated us like kids, like they were trying to coax us, pretending to pay a lot of attention to us. They thought that, if they treated us that way, we wouldn't figure out what they were up to."

When the meeting opened after lunch, Puro surprised not only the Fenacoop and Idecoop officials, but Fidel and the other cooperative leaders, when he pulled out a prepared list of the problems he wanted to deal with and began to argue them point by point. He protested that the 11 percent interest was high and was not even written into the contract. The auditor of Fenacoop immediately told Puro he was mistaken: the interest was only 8 percent. Puro, turning to the Presidente Administrador of Fenacoop, explained that the Administrador had told him 11 percent on the phone and that one of the Idecoop officials sitting at the meeting was also present during the phone conversation and could confirm this. The auditor then presented the account books, which showed an 8 percent interest. Embarrassing moments followed for the Administrador. "Maybe the administrator was trying to get the 3 percent for himself. I don't know. Even the council of Fenacoop was in the dark, half asleep. That was really an ugly affair—one thing on paper, but another by word of mouth." When the administrador accusingly questioned Puro's intentions, Puro responded politely and sincerely: "No, no. We didn't come here to fight, we came to clarify what our problems are. We came here to solve a business problem, but not for a single moment have we wanted to offend the dignity of anyone." The Administrador explained that there had been an error and asked Puro what he would like in the contract. Puro, again to the amazement of his friends, calmly dictated what he would like written— a statement of the interest at 8 percent. He went on to request and get both the removal of the fixed coffee price and a reduction of the commission from 2 percent to 1 percent. The meeting was a success. It might never have been held without the urgings and assistance of Fidel; it owed much of its success to Puro's rare abilities to think clearly under pressure and to speak and argue in front of gente del pueblo.

This, however, was not the end of the difficulties with Fenacoop. When the cooperative received a statement of its account from Fenacoop Fidel discovered that the cooperative was getting from $1.50 to $2.00 less per quintal than Santiago exporters were offering, despite Fenacoop's promise of higher prices. When the cooperative tried to sell its coffee to an exporter, angry Fenacoop officials arrived in the campo brandishing the contract and threatened to bring the cooperative to court.

Before and during this coffee harvest, the cooperative faced a potentially more serious difficulty with Fenacoop. Fenacoop insisted that the cooperative affiliate with its federation. Five percent of the earnings on coffee sold through Fenacoop would then be held by Fenacoop in a fund that the federation claimed it would use to make future loans to the cooperative. Idecoop (which at that time was funding Fenacoop) joined Fenacoop in putting pressure on the cooperative to affiliate. Fidel, disobeying instructions from Idecoop, warned the cooperative leaders of the danger of giving this money to Fenacoop; keeping the 5 percent in their own cooperative, they could use it when and how they wanted. The leaders, having experienced so many problems with Fenacoop, were convinced not to affiliate. Fidel then openly defended their refusal.

Throughout the 1968–69 harvest, Fidel's criticism of Fenacoop's policies vis-à-vis the cooperative became even more open—despite the fact that his employer, Idecoop, pressured him to lead "his" cooperative into the Fenacoop fold. Fidel came to believe that Fenacoop was in no sense a federation, that it was treating the campesinos unfairly, and perhaps even intentionally trying to deceive them. His criticisms were joined by those of another promotor and the head of the local Idecoop office. The promotor was fired; the Idecoop official transferred. Fidel was warned that he too would lose his job, but he was not quieted. He was probably saved by a special set of circumstances—he was friends with the then director of Idecoop; they once had worked together in politics. Furthermore, at one point the bishop interceded on his behalf. Eventually, the threat to Fidel's job and the pressure on the cooperative to federate lessened: the director of Idecoop was removed and Idecoop's policies toward Fenacoop changed.

The experiences with Fenacoop soured the leaders on any future dealings with this federation. But in the late fall of 1969, as the next harvest approached, the cooperative again found itself in serious straits: it had almost no funds with which to challenge the compradores. The immediate need for a warehouse and a huller was met by buying Arturo's factory with a loan arranged by Fidel.[28] Money the members managed to save in the cooperative enabled them to meet preharvest cash needs. But there was no money for the coffee harvest, for processing, or for advancing to members until the coffee was sold. The leaders had little idea where to get the needed cash. Again, Fidel, this time assisted by fortune, came to their aid. International coffee prices in 1969–70 were rising rapidly as frost attacked and destroyed much of Brazil's coffee harvest, creating a world coffee shortage.[29] Domestically, national production was lagging and exporters were anxious to gain access to the high international prices. Thus when Fidel went for help to friends in Santiago who exported coffee and vouched for the reliability and honesty of the peasants, they were unusually willing to listen. He introduced Puro and left him to negotiate. Puro held his own in a tough bargaining session, and the exporter agreed to advance $4,000 for forty-five days, payable in coffee at the price on the day of delivery. A few weeks later Puro returned and negotiated a $1,500 loan at 10 percent.

This first advance and loan from an exporting house established the cooperative's credit; and this, plus the great demand for coffee by all the exporters, made other advances easily available at a number of different exporting houses. It was still a difficult year for the cooperative. There were

many times when a member, in urgent need of an advance from the cooperative, was forced to sell an animal or turn to a comprador because the
cooperative had no funds. But because the comerciantes took no unified
action to deny credit to the coffee growers, most of the members were able
to manage on the small advances from the cooperative. The cooperative's
survival, however, had come to depend on a new broker, Fidel. Without his
contacts with the exporting houses the cooperative might never have gotten
the money it desperately needed.

In the fall of the following year (1970), access to funding for the coffee
harvest looked brighter than ever before. On 3 October the head of the credit
office at Idecoop visited El Río and told the cooperative leaders that a
$70,000 loan, to be financed with United States AID money loaned to
Idecoop, had been approved for the cooperative and that they could expect
the money within two weeks. Two, three, four weeks passed, but no money.
Anxious requests by Fidel and cooperative leaders brought continued assurances. Finally, at the end of October, Idecoop called a special meeting of the
coffee cooperatives in the region. There would be no AID money.[30]

The situation in Jaida Arriba was growing serious: the small capital in the
cooperative fund (about $7,000) had already been loaned out, many *socios*
needed money for harvesting. More seriously, the consumer cooperative had
just been opened in Jaida Arriba, and members needed cash to buy food. For
the cooperative members and leaders, the situation seemed desperate. The
leaders went back to the exporters, but this time found a reticence to advance
money except at very low prices and in small amounts. The exporter who had
first helped them the previous year could offer no loans or advances, only the
possibility of exporting the cooperative's coffee for a small commission
($1.50 per quintal). In the second week of November, Fidel stepped in to try
himself. He first tried to negotiate a $10,000 loan in Santiago banks, but they
refused.[31]

He then turned to a friend who managed the Dominican offices of a large
European trading house. He explained the situation, emphasizing the immediate need for money if cooperative members were not to be forced back to the
compradores. The manager offered to loan the cooperative the $10,000 from
company funds—and interest-free. He told Fidel that there was also a possibility of interesting his company in Europe in buying the cooperative's coffee,
but there would be no obligation. The cooperative leaders decided to take the
offer, and two days later they walked out of his office with a check for
$10,000.

Finally, after three more weeks, Idecoop (with a loan from the Banco
Central) was able to issue loans to anxious cooperatives in the region. At a
grand ceremony in Santiago, replete with luncheon, photographers, and
smiling government officials, the Jaida Arriba cooperative signed a contract
for a $35,000 loan, at an interest of 1.3 percent a month. The terms were

read to the leaders by an Idecoop official. Based on what they heard (Fidel was also there listening), they signed the contract without reading it themselves. Officials from Idecoop also encouraged the cooperatives to export their coffee abroad through Fetab (Federation of Cooperatives for the Marketing of Tobacco) for a $3.00 per quintal commission. The officials told the leaders they would have difficulty exporting themselves because it would take them at least three months to get an export license. Both Fidel and the cooperative leaders were suspicious.

The $3.00 commission that Fetab was charging seemed strange: it was $1.50 more than the commercial exporting house had just offered the cooperative. Their suspicions were aroused further the next day when the lawyer of the European trading house checked and found that an export license could be obtained in one day.

On 13 December the head office of the trading house in Europe offered to buy 500 quintales of coffee at $40 per quintal—$10 more than the Santiago exporting houses were then offering, based on a sample of the cooperative's coffee. Even reckoning preparation costs, this was still $3 more per quintal than the cooperative could get locally. The cooperative leaders agreed, and the lawyer of the trading house went to work handling the complicated process of exporting. There were to be many obstacles.

The first appeared unexpectedly at an 18 December Christmas luncheon for Idecoop employees in Santiago. When Fidel mentioned that the cooperative had an offer to export directly to Europe, he was informed that this was impossible: the loan contracts signed with Idecoop had committed the cooperative to pay back the loan by exporting through Fetab. Fidel denied this was possible—he had heard the contract read—and a copy of the contract was produced and the clause pointed out. Furious, Fidel denounced Idecoop for having deceived the peasants and immediately contacted the lawyer of the trading house. The lawyer protested directly to the Presidente Administrador of Idecoop in the capital. On 19 December an editorial (written by the lawyer) appeared in the Santiago daily, *Le Información,* denouncing Idecoop (and indirectly Fetab) as new middlemen: "In other words, it should not be permitted, that any type of institution—not even those that exist to encourage cooperatives—should substitute the intermediaries in their role because the situation of the producer continues to remain the same. It is necessary for the producer that he maintain at all times his liberty to sell his own harvest directly to the outside without any supervision." When Fidel, Pucho, and Antonio arrived in the capital two days later to talk to the Administrador they immediately were ushered into his office. Overcoming their nervousness at facing "a fat man ordering people around his office like a dictator" who sat behind his walnut desk amid the plush surroundings of status and power, the two peasants lodged their complaint while Fidel stood to one side. The Administrador calmly explained to them that this clause had been included only to help them; it would take three months, he said, to get an export license, whereas they could export immediately through Fetab. But then Antonio produced a copy of their export license (which the lawyer had gotten in one day) and the Administrador, somewhat embarrassed, agreed to void the restrictive clause.

But the cooperative still faced another problem: getting an export quota. If the peasant leaders had understood little of contracts and the workings of Idecoop, Fenacoop, and Fetab, they understood nothing of the distribution of quotas—except that they needed one to export their coffee to Europe on 12 January. But the lawyer again served as their broker.

At the end of December, he and Pucho went to the Instituto del Café y Cacao to try to obtain 500 bags (seventy-five-kilograms each) of quota. He found that there was no quota available for the cooperative. The second trimester quotas (January through March) already had been distributed. [32] Sixty percent had been divided among the exporting houses and 40 percent among the growers. The peasant growers in Jaida Arriba had not known (indeed had never known) to make applications for a part of the growers' share. But the lawyer discovered that a very small part of this growers' share (5,000 bags, or about 8 percent) had been set aside for grower organizations. Part of this 5,000 bags would be assigned to Idecoop for distribution.

The lawyer and Pucho then went to Idecoop and were able to receive a note from the Administrador authorizing the cooperative to use 500 bags of the Idecoop quota. Back at the Instituto, officials explained that a number of technicalities would make such assignment impossible. At this point the lawyer, quite coincidentally, spotted an old friend of his who turned out to be a high-ranking official in the Instituto. All difficulties were soon resolved.

The shipment went out on time, and the cooperative members proudly celebrated their transformation from peasant coffee growers to exporters by sending a twenty-man delegation to watch the boat sail (and have their pictures taken for the Santiago daily). The cooperative members netted $33 per quintal on this coffee while their nonmember neighbors in Jaida Arriba were receiving about $25 per quintal.

Before the third export trimester, the cooperative filed for a quota (from the portion assigned by exportable coffee in stock) with the Instituto and received 434 bags. Soon afterward, in the middle of March, a new Administrador of Fenacoop and a high official from Idecoop arrived in El Río with a new proposition.

Fenacoop offered to buy 300 bags of coffee from the cooperative at $42 per quintal. The cooperative leaders, suspicious of Fenacoop, were impressed by a price higher than they could earn exporting their own coffee. Idecoop backed the deal, pressuring the cooperative to sell through Fenacoop as a way to pay back some of its debt to Idecoop. Fidel asked whether the Fenacoop price was "with" or "without" the cooperative's quota. Fenacoop, they were all assured, would use its own quota. The leaders accepted the offer.

The following week, the European trading house offered to buy more coffee at $46 per quintal. Confident of their 434 bag quota the leaders accepted.

At the end of March, the deal was closed with Fenacoop. This time the leaders went to the capital to read the contract before signing. But it soon became clear that they had not understood what it had said. Unbeknownst to Fidel, they signed a contract which included a clause agreeing to market all cooperative coffee through Fenacoop.

When the leaders left Fenacoop, they went to the Instituto de Café y Cacao to arrange the necessary export papers for the 434-bag deal with Europe. But officials there told them that only 134 bags were assigned to them. Upset, they immediately went to the Administrador of Idecoop. He assured them he would do everything he could to get more quota and would let them know as soon as possible.

The leaders, however, heard nothing. Not meeting this contract could be serious: under International Coffee Organization regulations, the cooperative could be fined, blacklisted, and lose its Dominican exporting license.

After two weeks, the lawyer went to talk to officials at the Instituto. He discovered that the cooperative had indeed been assigned 434 bags for its third trimester quota, but that 300 of these bags had already been used by Fenacoop to export the coffee it had bought from the cooperative.

The lawyer immediately called the Administrador of Idecoop to protest, and then called a friend at the presidential palace to try to set up a special appointment to se El Presidente.

Two days later, El Padre, walking down a street in the capital, unexpectedly encountered a former priest and old friend. As they talked, he explained the present crisis and the cooperative's attempts to regain the quota that had been "stolen" from them. His friend was a personal friend of the Secretario de Agricultura (the secretary of agriculture). He quickly arranged for a meeting between the secretary and the cooperative leaders.

Four days later, the cooperative leaders, Fidel, the lawyer, El Padre, and El Padre's friend met the secretary in a Santiago restaurant. Upon seeing Fidel, the secretary immediately gave him a warm embrace asking: "Do I look so old you can't even remember me?" To Fidel's surprise, this same high official had once been a low-level government functionary in San Juan de la Sierra and Fidel and he had been friends. El Padre remembered him also and greeted him jovially: "Son, I used to confess you. But don't you worry, I can hardly remember your sins." The secretary, accompanied by the head of the Instituto de Café y Cacao, promised full support.

On the following day, Fidel and the lawyer went to the Instituto. A call was made to the Idecoop official who had given assurances in El Río that the cooperative's quota would not be used to export the coffee through Fenacoop. He produced a contract stating that the cooperative's coffee would be exported through Fenacoop, but there were no signatures on it—the names of

Pucho and Antonio were simply typed in. Fidel claimed that the peasants had never signed such a contract. Further, the Instituto officials pointed out, nowhere did it give Fenacoop permission to use the cooperative's quota. The officials put strong pressure on Idecoop to have Fenacoop transfer 300 bags of the unused quota it still had to the cooperative. The Idecoop official agreed to a meeting with Fenacoop and cooperative leaders.

Fidel and the lawyer, returning to the campo, discovered to their horror that a contract had indeed been signed—although Pucho and Antonio insisted they knew nothing of a clause committing the cooperative's coffee to Fenacoop for export. Worried that the contract might appear at the coming confrontation, Fidel and the lawyer spent hours planning tactics and explaining the situation to the leaders. A series of mock meetings were held: the lawyer, Fidel, and I played stubborn, slippery officials from Idecoop and Fenacoop, and the peasants practiced their arguments. The practice proved useful.

The meeting in the capital opened with Idecoop officials again bringing up the subject of the contract. But a cooperative leader smoothly sidestepped the issue (just as he had done in the practice session): "The contract is not what is really important now. What's important is that we have a serious problem, and it should be worked out together." The contract issue was dropped (and the signed contract never appeared). Within an hour, the leaders (with the assistance of Fidel and the lawyer) had worked out an agreement: Fenacoop would give them back the 300 bag quota.

Again the cooperative had succeeded in overcoming the obstacles to exporting, obstacles this time placed by the very cooperative agencies organized to help them. But their success would have been impossible without new brokers (Fidel, the lawyer, El Padre's friend, the secretary of agriculture, officials at the Instituto) whose friendships and institutional power enabled them to operate in the personalistic, traditional political system of *enllave* (a special "in" or "key"), and *pul* (pull). Further, as El Padre emphasized (thinking of the lost contract and the accidental encounter with his old friend), they had had the help of "the providence of God."

During the 1971–72 harvest, the cooperative again had little trouble getting quotas. These were now available to the cooperative on the basis of having exported the previous year, of having exportable coffee in stock, and of being a grower association. Its quota totaled 2,100 bags. This covered only half of member production, but it enabled the cooperative to gain access to the prices on the international market in a year when high national production drove domestic prices down to $28 per quintal (price paid by exporters to compradores), while the cooperative made contracts in Europe at $42 per quintal.[33]

The biggest event for the cooperative that year came in December 1971. A small exporting house, going out of business, offered its equipment to the cooperative (the owners were friends of Fidel) at about half its actual value. At Fidel's urging, the cooperative leaders bought the equipment (with a loan from Idecoop). Fidel took charge of the contractual arrangements and installation. By January 1972 the peasant coffee growers not only had broken the control of the local middlemen in the campo, but that of the large exporting houses as well. They now controlled their own coffee from harvesting through processing to shipment to Europe. But they continued to lack sufficient funds of their own; and their "control" was still dependent on the help of new brokers.

CREATING POWER: CONCLUSION. In order to break the control exercised by the local and national middlemen over the coffee market, the cooperative needed access to funding, foreign buyers, and quotas. Access to cash funds was the primary barrier to breaking the control of the local middlemen. Although a dedicated and skilled organizer like Fidel and activist priests like El Padre and Padre Miguel could create consciousness and help with local organization, a structural barrier still remained. The cooperative lacked the economic power to break the control of the middlemen: the poverty of its members made impossible the accumulation of sufficient funds through individual savings. Banks and exporting houses were reluctant to make loans or advances. Only national, government-supported cooperative agencies and federations offered them financing. The cooperative turned to them for the funds needed to break the control of the local middlemen and for access to international markets and quotas.

But in providing the cooperative with such funds and access, these agencies and federations themselves became new "middlemen," and their control often proved detrimental. At times, they charged interest rates 2 percent or more higher than the banks; they offered prices lower than the cooperative could get selling directly to exporters; they presented a contract one way orally and then gave another to the leaders to sign; they tried to acquire part of the cooperative's quota, despite verbal assurances that they would not; they tried to discourage the cooperative from exporting directly by lying about the obstacles in obtaining an export license; they promised loans that consistently came late, posing severe individual hardships on peasants in desperate need of cash and threatening cooperative survival by forcing members back to the local compradores; and they continually pressured the cooperative into joining "federations" or selling their coffee through such federations regardless of the economic disadvantages.[34] Except for some exceptional officials and promotores, the guiding philosophy of Idecoop, Fenacoop, and Fetab seemed to be a half-hearted paternalism often bordering on corporativism: the peasants were to be organized into groups whose economic viability remained directly dependent on the knowledge, money, and beneficence of the federation, agency, president, and ruling party.

The cooperative eventually was able to win partial independence from the agencies, federations, local middlemen, and national exporters. But this "independence" depended upon still other brokers who put their abilities and access to power at the service of the cooperative: the lawyer, El Padre, the Dominican manager, and Fidel. They taught the peasants the mixed blessings of agency and federation "help"; they helped educate and organize the leaders to take action; they explained contracts, fought through bureaucratic red tape, arranged for exporting licenses, took care of the complex shipping procedures, and arranged for the buying and installation of processing machinery; they helped the leaders struggle with officials and understand the hidden traps in contracts placed by incompetent, unconcerned, or deceiving officials; and ultimately their access to traditional sources of power gave the cooperative access to the power it needed to gain at least some economic independence.

The cooperative depended most upon Fidel, both in its initial battles with Fenacoop and Idecoop and for its later contacts with exporters, the Dominican manager, and the lawyer. But Fidel was an unusual promotor; and this rarity—this exceptional man in the particular circumstance—throws into serious question the possibilities for peasant cooperative movements in the Dominican Republic. Few promotores have Fidel's good relations with the peasants as well as friends and connections among the wealthy and well-placed. Few would risk their jobs, as he did, to defend the peasants when he thought Idecoop, Fenacoop, and Fetab were deceiving them. Few would resist the political pressures put on them to support the ruling party and encourage the peasants to do so.[35] The promotores who organize peasants in the Dominican Republic are, with few exceptions, employees of government, or government-supported, agencies: Idecoop, Fenacoop, the Institute for Agrarian Development (Land Reform Agency), the Office of Community Development. Some are concerned, dedicated workers; others, incompetent, apathetic political appointees. A few are antigovernment. But almost all are dependent for their livelihood on the small salary they earn. This gives the government agency enormous control over any promotor: he can be promoted, demoted, transferred, or fired. How the government agency chooses to use its power may vary. I have only explored one particular case. And here Fidel's most important actions were taken in spite of, or in opposition to, Idecoop. Few would have done the same. Yet without Fidel, the cooperative might not have survived and certainly would not have gained the independence it did.

CHAPTER 10

CONCLUSION

THE IMPACT OF THE COOPERATIVE

CONCIENTIZACIÓN. The Catholic church—through a bishop, a priest, and a lay volunteer—made a concentrated effort to *concientizar* the peasants of Jaida Arriba. They sought to create the belief that it was the peasants' duty as good Christians to help each other by organizing collectively to improve their present lives and to struggle against those who oppressed them and denied them their God-given equality with all men. Their specific instruments for concientización were catechism classes and a cooperative.

We saw earlier that the acceptance of the cooperative ideology depended only in part on those who encouraged and led the cooperative; and the part played by church officials was extremely limited.[1] Yet the sacred foundations laid by the church through its catechism classes, Cursillos de Cristiandad, and pronouncements in mass and on radio encouraged such important local leaders as Puro. Church efforts also served Fidel, Puro, and other leaders as useful symbolic tools in shaping the meaning given to the cooperative— overcoming obstacles of self-interest and encouraging sacrifice during difficult times.

How deeply did such concientización penetrate? This question could easily form the basis of another study, but this much can be stated briefly. Most of the peasants in Jaida Arriba who were active leaders or participants in the cooperative or in catechism classes have come to believe that it is their Christian duty to struggle collectively, "united" for the "good of the community." They believe that working collectively gives them the strength to improve life in the community: "in union there is strength." They also believe that the only obstacle to the success of such collective action in the community is a continued "lack of consciousness" among others in the community. Finally, such beliefs have been expressed in various forms of action other than the cooperative, many initiated independently of outside organizers: collective efforts to build a community hall, a bridge over the river that divides the community, and a new schoolhouse.

These efforts indicate a certain success in the concientización of the peasants, but they also point up serious limits. The bridge and the schoolhouse were not completed because the peasants had not been taught the collective decision-making, leadership, or organizational skills needed to transform consciousness into successful action.[2] Such concientización was also limited in scope. The consciousness created in Jaida Arriba did not bring into question the class structure and inequalities that existed in the community—indeed the very notion of comunidad (community) excluded a notion of class and conflict. Although such concientización questioned the justice of individual comerciante profits, it did not question private ownership of land. Finally, concientización did not teach most of the peasants anything of the larger national political and economic structures in which their problems were rooted. What the peasants came to see as problematic were individuals (middlemen, exporters, corrupt or incompetent government officials), not "systems" or "structures."

There was a partial exception here. Because of their particular experiences, a few cooperative leaders began to understand the importance of certain democratic principles and realize that their national political system (particularly elections) was far from democratic, and hence was unjust. Further, they began to see that it was a particular kind of marketing and political system, and not simply the individuals within it, that were problematic. Such consciousness was, admittedly, limited. But it does at least indicate that such modest movements as cooperatives have the potential for encouraging a broader concientización than that encouraged in Jaida Arriba.

ECONOMIC CHANGE. The concientización of the peasants in Jaida Arriba was mirrored not simply in their minds and souls but in good deeds as well: the good acts of first organizing and then participating in a Christianlike cooperative effort. But how successful were these good acts in material terms: what kind of economic change did the cooperative bring about for whom?

The cooperative brought about an important shift in the location of economic power in Jaida Arriba. By creating marketing, consumer, and savings and loan cooperatives, the peasants were able to gain the control over credit and marketing formerly monopolized by the middlemen. Their organization helped to force one major comprador out of business and substantially weakened the control of the largest comerciante in Jaida Arriba by depriving him of his coffee-growing peasant clients, upon whom much of his business depended.

But the economic change brought by the cooperative was limited to certain peasant classes. The middle- and large-holding peasant coffee growers no longer had to sacrifice their coffee at extremely low preharvest prices or sell off their scarce livestock to meet urgent cash needs. Freed from their obligations to the middlemen by cooperative funds, they were able to obtain much higher prices for their coffee by marketing through the cooperative, first selling nationally, and then exporting directly to Europe. Furthermore, through the cooperative, they gained access to fertilizers and new coffee-growing technology which, by 1972, had already doubled the yields of some. Finally, they have been able to buy needed consumer goods at lower costs through the consumer cooperative and to earn a share of the profits.

The majority of the peasants in Jaida Arriba did not, however, receive much economic benefit from the cooperative. These small holders and day laborers, lacking the land to grow coffee, received no benefit from higher coffee prices. Their access to cooperative funds to meet urgent cash needs was extremely limited since they had nothing with which to guarantee loans; and the cooperative (a business enterprise in a profit-based economic system) could no more afford to lose money than could a comerciante or a bank. They received some benefit from the lower food prices at the consumer cooperative, but the need to pay in cash limited their access to these benefits, too. The central problem of the day laborers and small holders was their lack of productive land. The cooperative did not solve this problem: it helped only those who had something with which to cooperate. If the middle and large holders often found that their "bootstraps" were too short to "pull themselves up" without outside assistance, the day laborers and small holders who joined the cooperative discovered that they still had no bootstraps at all.

ON THEORY AND METHOD

"CONFLICT-COERCION" THEORIES VERSUS "INTEGRATION-FUNCTIONALIST" THEORIES. In this book I have sought to shed some light on the theoretical debate between the "conflict" or "coercion" theorists and the "integration" or "functionalist" theorists.[3] One cannot, as Dahrendorf does (1966:Chapter 5), simply outline both approaches and then pick one: to explain both stability and change within a particular social order, one cannot decide a priori that what holds that order together is *either* power (coercion, control, force) *or* values (consensus, norms, culture, shared beliefs). An approach is needed that allows for the empirical examination of the relative importance of each in explaining stability and change.

If we conceive of the comerciantes as "functioning" within local economic institutions to "meet the needs of the system," we find that before 1967 the comerciantes in Jaida Arriba did not maintain their social roles through the use of force. Peasants did not continue to pay high prices on consumer goods or accept low prices for their crops because they felt threatened or coerced into doing so. Rather, many believed that the comerciantes were helping them and were grateful; or that this was simply "business," and the comerciante had just as much right to try to get the best price as they. The middlemen were not thought of as "a problem"; their actions were not conceived of as "control." Individuals may have aspired to be comerciantes; but no one challenged the role of comerciante as such. Few even conceptualized an alternative: this was the way things had been since "the time of the old ones." The peasants had been encouraged to accept their lot by the church. Dependence on the comerciantes was a way of life taught by their fathers and supported by certain everyday experiences: the comerciantes helped them get a start in life by financing their first harvests and thereafter helped them meet urgent money needs. Jaida Arriba before 1967 appears, from the vantage point of "integration" theory, to be a smoothly functioning social order, maintained by a consensus of traditional values and norms.

If the middlemen, however, are conceived of as exercising power (control over prices and marketing through control over capital), we are led to ask other questions about Jaida Arriba before 1967: Who benefited and who lost as a result of the comerciantes' economic position? How did middleman control operate? Why were the middlemen not perceived as a problem? Why was no collective challenge aimed at them? Exploring these questions, we found that various orientations that the peasants had toward the middlemen helped support their economic power, legitimizing their control as "help." We also discovered many obstacles to problem definition and the creation of an ideological challenge: a lack of public space and discussion, a lack of knowledge and poor critical abilities, a lack of peasant self-confidence, and a deference to those "who knew." The existence of some of these beliefs and perceptions was consciously encouraged by the middlemen (the agreement not to reveal prices of coffee offered them by the exporting houses, for example); others were not consciously generated or sustained by the middlemen until challenged by the cooperative. But even when those in power were not responsible for such beliefs and perceptions, the "conflict-coercion" approach asks that their importance in helping maintain the control of the middlemen be explored.

This approach also encouraged an awareness of other aspects of the "consensual" acceptance of the middlemen. We discovered that in addition to the norms and values that supported the role of the middlemen, there were elements of threat and sanction: although peasants paid debts because they felt a moral obligation to do so, they also feared being cut off by the middlemen if they did not; peasants sold their crops to the comerciantes in gratitude for the help advanced before the harvest, but they also knew that seeking a better price elsewhere would mean being refused credit the following year. Furthermore, we discovered a certain malaise and resentment against these *pejes grandes* lurking below the smoothly functioning social order.

Both "coercion" theories and "integration" theories are thus useful in exploring the foundations of stability in Jaida Arriba before 1967; they make clear that norms, culture, and shared beliefs were more important than coercion, control, and force in maintaining the existing system; but the existing system also involved inequalities of power and life chances, and the question of why there was no organization to challenge those inequalities needed exploration. Of what use were these approaches in examining the changes after 1967?

The organization of the cooperative clearly created a conflict situation.[4] We would expect "coercion" theories to be useful here in pointing out significant areas for exploration. The cooperative leaders attempted to use ideology as a "weapon" to define the middlemen as a problem, ripping off the existing ideologies that "masked" their true interests.[5] El Padre, the bishop, the promotores, and the local leaders sought to make the peasants "conscious": they were exploited and should organize and struggle collectively against the control of the middlemen. The cooperative ideology put forward a plan for organization.

Here, too, we saw an explicit effort by the cooperative leaders to manipulate cultural symbols to shape the orientations toward the cooperative and the middlemen: building on and strengthening collective and solidaristic orientations, turning deference and mistrust to its advantage, pitting notions of self-interest against "gratefulness" and projimidad, working new notions of justice into existing undercurrents of resentment toward the peje grande.

As the middlemen fought back, struggling to discourage acceptance of the cooperative and maintain their control, they too made conscious efforts to manipulate cultural symbols to orient the peasants against the cooperative: they encouraged the suspicion felt toward outsiders and the distrust the peasants felt among themselves; strengthening the peasants' lack of self-confidence, these "men who knew" advised the peasants against embracing the cooperative; and the comerciantes invoked moral obligations of gratitude for help given out of projimidad in past times of need. In this conflict, culture was anything but the "given" set of norms and values functioning to maintain an ongoing system as it is conceived in integration theories.

"Coercion" approaches would also lead us to look at the use of power and threats by the middlemen to maintain their control. The importance of such power became clear after the initial organization of the cooperative. One comerciante foreclosed on debts, denied credit, and threatened to refuse needed credit and advances in the future to any who sold through or bought from the cooperative. Further, we saw the difficulties the cooperative faced in creating the power over credit and marketing needed to challenge the middlemen: the barriers to creating an organization; the lack of potential economic power, given the class position of the peasants and their lack of resources; and the costs of dependence on the outside "help" of the new national "middlemen."

Finally, such coercion approaches, by emphasizing differences in power and class, lead us to ask who benefits by changes, movements, and struggles. In Jaida Arriba we saw the differential impact the cooperative had on the middle and large holders whose potential resources (land, a cash crop), however limited, were greater than the nonexistent resources of the day laborers and small holders.

Weighing the importance of the factors outlined in the two theoretical approaches in explaining the cooperative's success, we discovered (in Chapter 9) that simply changing values and beliefs (concientización) was not enough to change the economic order; such change demanded creating power. Yet if changing the values and beliefs was not sufficient to change the economic order, neither could power be created without such changes. Here "integration" theories provide important insights: they point up the cultural barriers to change that had little to do with the institutional power of the middlemen. Many of the obstacles to organization were orientations deeply ingrained in the peasant culture, sustained in part through socialization by families, friends, and church: the distrust and suspicion of the outside promotores, the distrust of the poorer peasants for those better off, the belief in change as coming from above, the feelings of incompetence, the lack of organizational skills, the "seeing is believing" way of knowing. Further, some of the obstacles to challenging the economic order were the very "consensual" elements within the culture that had helped maintain it. The norm of moral obligation to the middlemen, for example, made many initially hesitant to break with them. When the cooperative threatened their position, the middlemen did try to strengthen and use certain of these cultural orientations (such as distrust, gratefulness, and obligation) against the cooperative, although it would be misleading to view such orientations simply as "weapons" created by the middlemen to maintain their control. They were able to draw upon them because they already existed. Viewing ideology as a "mask" or a "weapon" used to maintain or challenge the power of a group or class (as a "coercion" approach suggests) might misconceive the complex roots of such orientations, fail to see the barriers to organization they presented, and ignore the difficulties and possibilities of changing them.

Defining and exploring the questions raised in this study thus depended heavily on using both "coercion" theory and "integration" theory; an a priori exclusion of either approach would have missed much of importance. Yet the conclusion here is not simply that one must "use both." What are needed are theoretical frameworks that supersede these two approaches. This was the effort made in Chapter 6 where I developed a framework that went beyond the dichotomy between "interest theory" (drawn from the "coercion" approach) and "strain theory" (drawn from a "functionalist" approach). Although this effort was limited—building as it did only on certain concepts within these two approaches—it would be well briefly to comment on its usefulness in exploring the two questions (in Chapter 7 and Chapter 8) it was designed to illuminate.

AN APPROACH TO IDEOLOGY: THE RISE AND ACCEPTANCE OF "THE COOPERATIVE". The central question in Chapter 7 was this: why did no ideology or movement aimed at collective action either to alleviate existing economic difficulties or to struggle against the control of the middlemen arise in Jaida Arriba before 1967? The theoretical approach in Chapter 6 provided useful guidelines. Positing existing "orientations" as the key link between social situations and the rise and acceptance of new ideologies, it encouraged us to look at how people viewed their social situations, suggesting that new ideologies are most likely to be created and accepted when people both experience a problem orientation toward their situation *and* perceive available institutionalized guides or sets of symbols (or ideologies) to be weak or inadequate as guides to thought or action.

This approach proved useful in understanding why no new ideology aimed at collective action against the middlemen arose before 1967: although many peasants felt a certain malaise, they did not view their relations with the middlemen as problematic. This raised a central question: why did no one transform this orientation of malaise into a clearly defined problem, let alone initiate a collective ideology aimed at struggling against these comerciantes. But we also discovered that the framework suggested at best only a necessary, not a sufficient, condition for the rise of a new ideology: in the one area where there was a problematic orientation (toward basic economic difficulties) there was still no new ideology formed.[6] This raised a second question: why did the peasants not formulate a new strategy? In exploring these questions, we discovered a number of important obstacles to problem definition and ideology formation: most peasants had little conception of "middleman control," there was little public discussion of individual difficulties and problems, the peasants lacked important critical abilities needed to transform a malaise into a problem and to create a new ideology, their lack of self-confidence supported "ways of knowing" that discouraged the creation of new ideological guides, and those few peasants who might have taken some initiative were hindered by a prevailing atmosphere of distrust and suspicion. In each instance, the theoretical approach insisted that we not simply identify the aspect of the culture that discouraged the development of problem orientations and a new ideology, but try to explain them by exploring the life experiences (individual, historical-generational, and social) that helped generate and sustain them.

In Chapter 8, we explored why the cooperative ideology, once introduced into Jaida Arriba, was accepted by some peasants and rejected by others. Here again the theoretical framework in Chapter 6 proved useful. Conceiving ideology as a symbol system, it encouraged us to explore three ways ideologies might be linked to orientations. We saw how the cooperative ideology worked closely with the injustices and difficulties the peasants saw in their relations with the middlemen and transformed the existing private malaise into a public problem, but the ideology was able to undermine the existing strategies traditionally offered by the middlemen for dealing with basic economic problems (credit, preharvest selling). Finally, we saw strong evidence that this new ideology was accepted because peasants saw their situation as problematic (both the old economic problems and the newly created "middleman problem"); viewed available ideologies and strategies as weak or inadequate guides to thought, feeling, or action; and perceived the cooperative as an attractive new possibility: it could solve the problems of money shortage, protect crops from preharvest selling, offer higher prices for coffee and lower prices on consumer goods, and redistribute the profits that were making the comerciantes wealthy.

The importance of the new framework in Chapter 6 was highlighted when we explored the possibility of explaining acceptance of the new ideology by merely looking at objective class situation: class position did not itself determine the reaction to the cooperative ideology. Rather, the relationship that did exist between class and ideology was mediated by the orientations people had toward their own economic situations and toward the middlemen: certain common orientations existing across class lines encouraged an acceptance of the new ideology by some peasants from all classes; orientations that were different among different classes helped explain the predominant acceptance of the cooperative among the middle and large holders; variations in orientations within the same class (such as the different importance of moral obligations of gratitude toward the middlemen) helped explain different reactions to the cooperative among peasants in the same class.

The existence of a problem orientation and inadequacies in available guides to action seemed to have been a necessary condition for cooperative acceptance, but it was far from sufficient: some peasants with such orientations did not accept the new ideology. Here we looked at other orientations that helped explain further why this new cooperative ideology seemed attractive to some but not to others and what the cooperative did to try to overcome these obstacles to its acceptance. The theoretical conception of culture as a symbolic "toolkit" alerted us to the various meanings and orientations available to the peasants for "understanding" and judging the cooperative: orientations toward the means of action (individual versus collective) and the ends of action (instrumental versus solidaristic), the various ways of knowing ("seeing is believing" versus "deference to 'those who knew'"), and the orientations toward outsiders and each other (suspicion, mistrust). We saw, further, that the reactions to the cooperative were not simply "stamped" by the culture, but were the outcome of a struggle between the cooperative leaders and the middlemen to shape the meaning of the cooperative in the two ways the theoretical framework suggested: by reformulating or using existing symbols already within the culture and by formulating new symbols, "fitting" them into the existing symbol system.

These orientations also helped us to understand the importance of leadership in the acceptance or rejection of the cooperative: leaders had to be trustworthy; but furthermore, because the cooperative initially was not something that could be known and judged by being "seen," the leaders also had to be "ones who knew." The peasants judged those who advised and led them both in terms of their social positions (institutional and class) and in terms of their individual personalities. The most important factor in overcoming the barriers of distrust and peasant lack of knowledge and self-confidence appeared to be the quality of the *local* leadership (especially of Puro) and not of the outsiders like El Padre and Fidel. Such leadership, however, was only *one* of the factors in the acceptance of the cooperative: the "masses" did not take action merely because of the leaders whom they followed. Leadership was important only in the context of a particular social situation where economic difficulties and middleman control came to be seen as problematic, where existing guides for action were weak or inadequate, where the adequacy of the cooperative and its leaders were judged in terms of orientations that were part of the existing culture, and where other factors made possible the creation of the power needed to challenge those in control.

PARTICIPANT OBSERVATION: THE LIMITS OF A VIEW FROM THE BOTTOM. I have long argued with close friends doing anthropological research that "theory" was of crucial importance in doing even "community studies": unless a researcher was prepared to explore (test) certain tentative answers (hypotheses) to particular questions, the "facts" gleaned from "participation" and careful "observation" might be disordered, meaningless, or insufficient. Questions and answers do not simply arise out of the everyday experiences of even the most careful participant observer. Thankfully, even the most vocal critics of "theory" unconsciously bring some theoretical baggage on their ethnographic trips, and it may serve as good, if often invisible and vague, aid for their keen empirical observations.

In borrowing anthropological methods but being consciously theoretical, I found I had powerful tools for doing this research project. I had some notions of what to explore to find answers to the central questions I had formulated; and although my theories changed as I gathered data and discovered new answers that sent me gathering yet new information, I never fell into the common trap of simply gathering as many "facts" as I could, hoping to "put them together" when I returned home.

Living and working for eighteen months in Jaida Arriba allowed me to gather information and understand problems that survey questionnaires or even casual short-term interviewing never would have revealed. The peasant attitudes toward the middlemen and toward each other—both crucial factors in their eventual organization for action—were sensitive subjects; it was many months before I observed enough to see—or they trusted me enough to explain—the complex ties that bound and divided the community. Simply comprehending the meaning of "right" and "wrong," "just" and "unjust," took many weeks.[7] And understanding such notions was essential in explaining how the cooperative "created consciousness" and why it was accepted. The everyday peasant problems and deep sense of malaise upon which the cooperative built its support became clear to me only after months of observation and long discussions while working in the fields or sitting around kitchen hearths at night. The lack of peasant self-confidence, the suspicions and mistrust that cut through the community, and the common "ways of knowing" that created such barriers for successful organization became clear only after I worked with the peasants in their actual struggles to organize new community groups. Piecing together the history and causes of a movement that had begun before I arrived—one that was already tempered by struggle and viewed through the newly acquired eyeglasses of the cooperative ideology—took long hours of careful observation and questioning.

The "view from the bottom" implicit in such participant observation does, however, have a serious limitation: one tends to see only the world that is seen by the social actors being studied. But events forced other perspectives upon me. The peasants in geographically isolated Jaida Arriba fought a struggle far beyond their community; they confronted market mechanisms and national and international institutions that decisively shaped their lives and their chances for success. With a view from the bottom, there is much I might never have seen had their struggle not been so wide-ranging. And although I "saw" structures and social forces usually "invisible" to most peasants, I never would have understood them had I simply worked from their perspective; they had little or no idea how the coffee market worked, what the obstacles were to obtaining credit, how a state agency controlled the distribution of coffee export quotas, and what the dangers were of new forms of control being organized by Idecoop and Fenacoop.[8]

Such limitations originally threatened to be reinforced by certain aspects of my theoretical approach. The questions I first asked about power—informed as they were by certain pluralist assumptions—looked only at the obstacles and possibilities for organization and how these were overcome; I did not look at the limits on what could be done even if the peasants did organize successfully. I asked such questions as: What beliefs did the peasants have toward each other, toward outside organizers, and toward action, and how were these changed? What needed organizational skills did they lack and how were such deficiencies overcome? I thus implicitly assumed that the primary problem was how peasants became sufficiently conscious and organized to make demands. It would have been better first to look at the structural limits placed on peasant demands by their *potential* power even if they could actualize it through successful organization. This would have pointed immediately to the crucial fact of *class*: even the large-holding peasants did not have the potential resources to amass a cash fund sufficient to challenge middleman control over coffee marketing. If I had then asked: where can peasants get the resources needed to break local middleman control, I would have been led immediately to an understanding of the system of cash advances in the coffee market (and the power of the national exporters) and the extremely limited possibilities of peasant access to such advances—except through such government agencies as Idecoop. Exploring the purposes for which this agency's economic power was used would have led more directly to the limitations—even dangers—that financing from a state agency poses for a peasant group in the Dominican context (corruption, one-party rule, political control) and how dependency on such state agencies might hinder actions of the cooperative (their ability to control their own funds, their ability to sell on the national market or to export directly). This "view from the top" makes clear the structural limits on and possibilities for peasant action, by forcing an examination of the power of the commercial bourgeoisie in the coffee market: how that economic power is transformed into or reinforced by the political power of certain government agencies and commissions, how the national political institutions use their power for or against the peasants, and which other institutions (the church, certain political parties) or classes are available for alliances with the peasants. This is not to deny the importance of a case study viewed from the bottom: had I not actually followed the struggles of this particular group, I might never have understood the actual boundaries of organized peasant action; the success of any peasant movement to change the marketing system might have seemed a priori impossible. But the structural obstacles and possibilities faced by the peasants would have been clear even before an examination of the immediate problems of consciousness and organization; I would not have had to depend on peasant successes to make the limits of success so painfully clear.

CONCIENTIZACIÓN AND THE CREATION OF POWER. The major emphasis of the Catholic church's social action programs is on concientización: creating the belief that those in power are unjust and that collective action is needed if a community is to improve the life chances of its members. In Chapter 9, we saw how the very successes in "creating consciousness" demonstrated the serious, near-fatal consequences of an approach which, like integration theories, stresses values and norms as the cohesive bonds of a social order and minimizes the importance of power, coercion, and control. The cooperative leaders were able to undermine middleman legitimacy by transforming beliefs of "right" into images of "might," but this still left the economic might of the middlemen untouched. The leaders helped transform an undefined feeling of malaise into clearly defined problems, and they were able to convince the peasants that collective action was needed to bring change, but such concientización was not sufficient to get the people to act, let alone to act successfully. Fear still hindered action; and the sanctions feared were not imaginary ones due to lack of consciousness. The cooperative had to create the economic power needed to break the control of the middlemen.

Fortunately, only one middleman actually used his power over credit and advances to exert sanctions against cooperative members; the failure of the others to act as a group and to use their potential power against the cooperative probably saved it from early destruction. The cooperative, however, still faced the major problem of organizing to create a fund large enough to challenge middleman control over credit and marketing. With the help of promotores like Fidel and local leaders like Puro, the cooperative eventually was able to overcome the serious obstacles to such organization. But successful organization only revealed the greater barrier posed by the very class position of the members: the peasants did not have the potential resources to amass quickly the large cash funds needed to break the control of the middlemen.

To get these resources, the cooperative turned to state agencies and state-supported cooperative federations. The loans they made available enabled the cooperative to break the control of the local middlemen but created a potentially harmful dependency on new brokers: the new control exercised by these agencies and federations came to threaten the cooperative's very survival. The cooperative's ability to overcome these new obstacles depended on the friendly (and, in the Dominican Republic, unusual) support of yet other brokers: a promotor (Fidel), a priest, a skilled lawyer, and an oligarch enabled the cooperative to cope with the patron-client networks, the complex coffee-marketing system, the government agencies, the cooperative federations, and the corruption in the world outside the campo.

The cooperative movement in Jaida Arriba thus emphasizes the severe limitations and dangers of the Church's "social action" orientation: stressing concientización and ignoring the power realities of class position and institutional structures, it gave the peasants little guidance during their most severe struggles.

The peasant struggle in Jaida Arriba has important implications for peasant movements in other areas. The very survival of this movement came to depend on the alliances it made with others outside the countryside. But the experiences in Jaida Arriba also dramatically reveal how the very lack of certain skills and resources that make alliances so important also provide the state with opportunities to capture or preemptively organize peasant movements. The state's ability to provide needed financing, technical aid (legal, organizational, administrative), and legal recognition may enable it to tie local peasant groups and communities so directly to state agencies and bureaus that it can both block independent alliances with urban groups and prevent horizontal class organization across peasant communities. Such direct dependency on the state further gives it the potential to exercise various forms of economic and political control over the peasantry, from extracting surpluses to guaranteeing votes.

There is already evidence in a number of developing countries that increasingly powerful state bureaucracies are following corporatist policies, "penetrating" into civil society in an effort to capture control of existing popular (usually worker or peasant) organizations or to preemptively organize these sectors in order to tie them directly to the state.[9] The possibilities of such action may become increasingly likely as developing countries seek to control the discontent of popular classes who react against being forced to bear the costs of accumulating the capital needed for development. How the state uses its power is a matter of great concern: if the state enters into alliances with already dominant economic groups, it may seek to freeze the existing structures of social inequality. Its success or failure will depend on such factors as the unity among the elites seeking to impose such control, the economic and military resources available to finance or enforce such control, and the prior strength and autonomy of popular sector organizations such as the peasant movement in Jaida Arriba.

NOTES

CHAPTER 1

1. During such singing, each would take a turn leading the song, the others joining in on the chorus or refrain—"there goes Maria, she's leaving," "listen dove." The rhythm often kept time with the work being done: felling trees with axes, driving in fence posts, pounding bean vines with long poles to knock the beans from the pods, picking tobacco, or washing clothes in a stream. But as wage labor replaced exchange labor (with the increasing movement toward a cash economy) exchange labor teams began to disappear. Ownership of radios (once severely restricted by Trujillo) has grown rapidly, further discouraging the singing of décimas by bringing Dominican merengues, Mexican and Argentinian songs, and the Beatles to the kitchens and fields. Jaida Arriba is one of the few places in the country where people still remember décimas. And the neighbor we hear singing is one of the few who still sings, often to himself, as he works.

CHAPTER 2

1. The international politics of coffee in 1972—how the total support quotas and world market prices were set, how power was wielded, how the agreement was enforced, how the percentages of the quota were assigned to each producing country—are beyond the scope of this investigation.

A brief introduction to the world coffee market and the International Coffee Agreement can be found in Grunwald and Musgrove 1970. For an excellent discussion of the politics of U.S. participation in the International Coffee Agreement see Krasner 1973.

2. Such changes may reflect the economic or political power of some of the larger coffee growers. Juan Pablo Duarte, the undersecretary of agriculture who often presides over the meetings, is one of the largest coffee growers in the country. One of the grower representatives on the commission is an important figure in the ruling Partido Reformista and a member of the president's Comision para Desarrollo (Commission for Development), a powerful advisory body often said to have more power than the National Congress.

3. The following table (1960 data) illustrates that the bulk of land and the majority of growers are small growers or peasants: 82.2 percent of the coffee growers who cultivate 54.5 percent of the coffee-growing land have groves of less than 6.3 hectares (16 acres); 95.3 percent, cultivating 79 percent of the coffee-growing land, have groves of less than 18.9 hectares (47 acres) (Instituto de Café y Cacao 1966:5).

Size of Coffee Farm in hectares (1 hectare = 2.471 acres)	Percent of total Coffee Growers	Percent of total area in Coffee Cultivation
Less than 1.9	48.6	18.7
From 1.9 to 6.3	33.6	35.8
From 6.3 to 18.9	13.1	24.5
From 18.9 to 31.5	2.6	7.1
From 31.5 to 62.9	1.4	6.1
From 62.9 to 314.5	0.6	5.2
From 314.5 to 629.0	0.1	1.2
Greater than 629.0	0.0	1.4
TOTAL	100.0	100.0

4. Note that the 1971–72 first and second trimester quotas assigned by production were 0; and the percentage of the total quotas distributed by production thus appears anomalous. These anomalies will be explained in the following footnote.

5. The chart shows a break in the common pattern in 1971–72. None of the quota was divided using the first mechanism of amount exported the previous year; and a large portion was divided up using exportable stock. The reason for this change was the unusually large coffee harvest in 1970–71, which left surpluses of unexported coffee of about 150,000 75-kilogram sacks, which had to be held over until the first trimester of 1971–72. To handle this surplus the commission increased the share of the quota to be divided up by exportable stock to 61 percent.

6. The bulletin of the Instituto de Café y Cacao (1966:5) lists 92,614 farms or plots with coffee cultivation as of 1960, citing as its source the Oficina Nacional de Estadistica (National Office of Statistics). Many of these farms are extremely small, and it is not clear how many of their owners actually sell coffee produced or consume it themselves. Nor do we know the accuracy of the statistics or the changes that have taken place since 1960. But, as pointed out earlier, we do know that the vast bulk of Dominican coffee is produced by peasant growers.

7. This shift from volume to weight is discussed in more detail in chapter 4, in the section "Control over the Coffee Crop."

CHAPTER 3

1. This formulation is presented by Eric Wolf, who writes that a peasantry is "continuously exposed to a set of pressures which impinge on it and challenge its existence. . . . First there are the pressures which derive from the particular peasant ecotype. . . . Second, there are the pressures which emanate from the social system of a peasantry. . . . Third, there are always the pressures which emanate from the wider society in which the peasant holdings form a part" (1966b:77).

2. Much of what I discuss below as forms of production are referred to by Wolf (1966b) as "ecotype" pressures, pressures that derive from a particular form of production applied in a particular environment.

3. Some land may be replanted after letting it lie fallow or using it as pasture land (benefiting from fertilization by manure) for three to five years, but the yields are always much lower than on newly cleared land. Some land becomes so severely eroded, or "tired," that it can not be economically planted again before ten to fifteen years.

4. Circumvention of the forestry law was discussed in Chapter 1. Some peasants also illegally clear and plant in the National Park.

5. Until very recently there was neither the technology nor the capital available for fertilizer, pruning, and so on, making difficult more intensive use of land already under cultivation.

6. Some coffee growers also have the costs of fertilizing, pruning, and controlling shade. But such techniques were only first introduced in late 1969.

7. This period of time between the end of the coffee harvests and the rains in September and October is relatively dry. If weeds are not cut at this time, they will not die before the rains and may reroot or go to seed, reproducing quickly.

8. Coffee must be harvested as soon as it ripens or it will fall to the ground and rot. The coffee grower thus needs a large amount of labor concentrated in a small period of time, and family labor is usually insufficient to pick ripe coffee at peak harvest times.

9. Eric Wolf describes such systems as follows: "Systems based on partible inheritance grant some part of the ancestral homestead, or some claim to its yield to every member of the new generation. Yet by so doing they subdivide the established unit so that each successor receives a combination of resources weaker than the one managed by the departing head" (1966b:73).

10. Analyzing the class structure of Jaida Arriba demands some concept of class. The concept should open theoretical links to other problems of the peasants caused by middlemen and the peasants' attempts to create the power needed to wrest control of credit and marketing from these men in an effort to improve their life chances. Given such a problem, I will identify four economic classes of peasants using criteria based largely on the potential economic power of each. (The notion of class as potential power was first suggested to me by Kalman H. Silvert [1970:15]). My major interest is identifying both the different economic resources and the money and marketing needs of each group: the quality of these peasant resources and the peasants' inability to meet certain needs shape the control the middlemen can exercise as well as the peasants' potential for breaking this control.

My focus will be on the relations of different classes to the central means of agricultural production: slash-and-burn cultivation, coffee cultivation, cattle grazing, and wage labor; and how these relations affect consumption patterns, the ability to get credit, and the quality of life and life chances for the peasants in each class. Of particular importance is not the quantity of land nor the total incomes and expenses of a particular peasant household, but the *quality* of the land and the *seasonal* earnings and expenses. The cyclical nature of money shortages often forces the peasant to accept the mixed blessing of the middleman's kindness and control.

11. These monthly cash flow charts are *not* meant to be complete budgets; they are designed only to provide an approximate illustration of the cycle of debt. As such, they do not include the value of a peasant's labor when he is working his own land, nor do they take account of three types of cash expenses that often increase debt: gambling expenses (local lottery, cockfighting, and the like), drinking expenses (rum), and ceremonial expenses (baptisms, fiestas) other than Christmas. The peasants, of course, do not think in terms of such charts; nor do they remember all their expenses. The prices on the charts are those either given to me by the peasants or estimated by the peasants and me working together. The monthly food costs were calculated by taking the yearly food costs (available at the consumer cooperative where each of the four peasants is a member and buys all his food except meat), dividing by twelve, and adding the approximate monthly expenditure on meat. In reality, the peasant does not spend his money on food in twelve equal parts as the charts indicate. Expenses listed under the heading "Medicine" include not simply the actual medicine, but also visits to doctors (doctors' fees plus travel costs).

12. Their notions are much less rigid and are based on a continuum whose two ends are "rich" and "poor." There are many words for these distinctions: the poor are also "the unhappy ones" or "the undergods"; the rich are "people who live comfortably," "those on top," "those that have," or "those who eat rice and beans every day." How a peasant views others depends very much on his own position. Ramón sees Chaguito and Mamón as people "who live comfortably." But Chaguito sees Mamón as "one who already has a bit" and himself as "a poor one."

CHAPTER 4

1. I will use the term *comerciante* to refer to merchants (usually owners of general stores) who both *sold* consumer goods to the peasants and *bought* their crops. I will use

the term *comprador* (buyer) as the peasants do to emphasize the role of these men as buyers. The label "middleman" (*intermediario*) was first applied to these men by the cooperative. Eric Wolf (1956a) refers to such middlemen more generally as "brokers," stressing the role played by these people as intermediaries between the local peasants and the wider social, economic, political, and cultural system.

2. The compradores could also get one month's interest-free credit on food they bought at the Santiago warehouses, but longer-term credit cost them 2 percent to 4 percent a month. In the rare cases that such sources of capital were insufficient, moneylenders advanced cash at 2 percent to 5 percent a month.

3. The comprador's costs for buying coffee at harvest time were minimal. The money for buying was advanced interest-free from the exporting houses, so there was no cost for this capital. Costs did include the final drying of the coffee; hulling; depreciation of the hulling machine, drying floors, and warehouses; and transportation to the exporting house. Such costs were roughly $1.30 to $1.50 per quintal (the difference due to varying transportation costs depending on the location of the exporter).

4. The exporters calculate their costs using as a rough rule of thumb ten cents per pound or $4 per quintal. This includes all their costs from the time they receive the hulled coffee from the comprador until the time they deliver it ready for shipping in Puerto Plata and receive the F.O.B. price.

The profits of the exporters per quintal (and the corresponding loss to the peasants for having to go through exporters) can be approximated by subtracting about $4 per quintal from the difference between the F.O.B. price and the price the exporter pays to the comprador. Looking at the 1971–72 coffee year, we see the following variations in exporter profits:

	Oct.–Jan.	Jan.–March	March–May
		(price per quintal)	
Price paid to exporter (F.O.B. Puerto Plata)	$37–$40	$41.50	$42
Price paid to comprador "without" quota	$25–$28	$32–$36	$28–$31
Approximate gross profit to exporter	$9–$12	$5.50–$9.50	$11–$14
Approximate net profit to exporter	$5–$8	$1.50–$5.50	$7–$10

It should be noted, however, that much of the coffee bought in May at $28 per quintal will not be shipped until October because of the lack of quota; it must be stored for six months and such costs as interest and insurance paid on it. These alone will probably come to about forty-five cents per quintal per month or a cost of $2.70 for six months. In such a case a $10 profit will, in reality, be about $7.30 per quintal.

These estimates of exporter profits also make clear the difference in buying coffee "with" and "without" a quota—the transfer of profit from the exporter to the grower. Looking at the 1971–72 coffee year we see the decrease in profits to exporting houses when buying coffee from a large grower of comprador "with" a quota.

	Oct.–Jan.	Jan.–March	March–May
		(price per quintal)	
Price to exporter (F.O.B. Puerto Plata)	$37–$40	$41.50	$42
Price to comprador or large grower "with" quota	$32	$37.35	$37.25
Approximate gross profit to exporter	$5–$8	$4.25	$4.75
Approximate net profit to exporter	$1–$3	$.25	$.75

5. This may be calculated as follows. We saw earlier that the comprador made about $7.30 per fanega of coffee bought at $29 per fanega. If we add to this the $9 difference

($29–$20) we find an increase of $16.30. If we then subtract the interest of 2 percent a month on $20 for six months ($2.40), we get $13.90.

6. Thinking of a la flor buying in terms of a cash loan, a six-month loan of $17 to $20 is costing $9 to $12, and the comprador is earning an equivalent yearly interest rate of 90 percent to 140 percent. Coffee growers who had to sell coffee only three months before the harvest, and were paid $21 a la flor, were losing $8 for this three-month loan and the compradores were earning a yearly interest of 152 percent.

7. Arturo held no formal institutional position in politics, but he was always consulted by the alcalde and local political leaders. Decisions, such as who was to be appointed alcalde, were usually dependent upon his request.

8. A good summary analysis of *compadrazgo* is provided in Mintz and Wolf (1950). Anthropologists have recognized that such fictive kinship ties as compadrazgo are a way of gaining patrons (and maintaining clients). Foster, for example, writes: "Exploiting the compadrazgo system is one of the most obvious ways of gaining a patron, and wealthy city relatives, local ranchers . . . and storekeepers . . . with whom one may have commercial relations are common targets" (1967:223). Compadrazgo ties are, however, only one way that patron-client ties are created, maintained, or strengthened. Others include kinship ties, friendship ties, and imbalances of social, economic, and political power or influence. What existed between the middlemen and the peasants was a patron-client relationship. There is a growing literature, largely but not exclusively among anthropologists, on this subject. See, for example, Boissevain 1966; Foster 1967; Kenny 1960; Pitt-Rivers 1961:137ff; Wolf, 1966. Interesting comments are also found in Huizer (1972:188–92).

9. Manuel was a nephew of Pedro's wife.

10. Three other very small general stores, all operated by large-holding coffee growers in various parts of Jaida Arriba, picked up the remaining day laborers and small holders—often their neighbors or relatives. These general stores could, however, offer only very limited credit. Each owner, of course, bought goods from his own store, accounting for the three large holders shown in the table as buying from other small comercios.

11. Most of the coffee grown in Jaida Arriba, it should be remembered, ultimately passed through the major compradores (Arturo, Francisco, Isidro). They were the conduits through which the cash advances of the large exporters passed to the small compradores, and this latter group reaped the largest profits.

CHAPTER 5

1. El Padre (used as a proper name) will be used as the pseudonym of the parish priest who was active in helping to initiate the cooperative.

2. Such beliefs in curanderos and in the protective or curative powers of religious symbols were an important part of the culture of Jaida Arriba. But not everybody accepted such beliefs. Three of the major coffee-growing families, for instance, had been raised by parents with strong beliefs in the saints, but with little faith in curanderos or brujos. These families viewed such beliefs with skepticism and sometimes with scorn. But such widespread beliefs do reflect the current of fear and mystery that surrounded the peasant as he faced unknown and uncontrollable forces of God and religion, of sickness and death, of bad luck and misfortune.

3. The bishop found support among some of the Jesuits who already had been experimenting with attempts at *promoción social.* One group of Jesuits, for example, was giving courses to peasant groups emphasizing their equality before God with the rich and the powerful and their basic nature as subjects of their own development who had a duty and responsibility as Christians to organize and act to improve their material lives against those who would exploit them as objects.

4. I will examine the effects of this attitude in Chapter 9.

5. The following answers were gathered only after I had known Puro for over a year. They are the result of many long interviews and much hard reflection on Puro's part.

6. At the time the cooperative in Jaida Arriba was formed, directors of both Idecoop

and Fenacoop were personal friends. Most of Fenacoop's working capital was loaned from Idecoop.

7. He had gone to New York and had been washing dishes and working as a janitor to try to earn the money he needed to pay large debts he had accumulated.

8. Fidel discouraged the cooperative leaders from getting involved in a consumer cooperative. He argued that too much work was still needed to strengthen the first cooperative, yet they did not have enough funds to pay cash. Finally, Fidel argued, the small profits to be made in a consumer cooperative were not worth the greater risk of failure.

9. This administrator later moved to New York and was replaced by another. In early 1971, Puro was chosen to replace the second administrator.

10. This loan came from the Comité de Cuidadanos in the capital, one of the few groups willing to loan peasant organizations the money they urgently needed.

CHAPTER 6

1. See Marx and Engels 1962:363. It should also be noted that interest theories are very much a part of the historical theoretical tradition which Dahrendorf labels "co-ercion theories" (1966:159ff), Rex calls "theories of conflict and change" (1963:115ff), and Lockwood refers to as "conflict theories" (1964:246ff).

2. They may recognize, for example, that groups of men within the proletariat may, at a particular historical moment, accept the bourgeois ideology or a utopian socialist ideology or an anarchist ideology or a communist ideology.

3. Gerrit Huizer, for example argues: "It does not seem to be the traditional *status quo* which provokes peasants to start organizing. The situations where organizations have sprung up tend to have in common what could be called an 'erosion of the *status quo.'* A change for the worse in peasants' conditions of living can awaken them to defend the little they have" (1970:397).

4. Marx himself, for instance, saw the importance of creating consciousness among the workers, rather than merely waiting for it to occur. And interest theory, in holding that ideology is a "weapon" that can unmask interests, implies that the way people see their interests can be changed independently of change in class position.

5. For example, at the end of their article, "Agrarian Radicalism in Chile," examining the relationship between the peasant class structure and voting choice (which at least implicitly is seen as the acceptance of the FRAP party's political ideology), James Petras and Maurice Zeitlin add that "political culture" may be an intervening factor between class position and ideology (1970:527).

6. Strain theory is part of a theoretical tradition very different from that of interest theory. Referred to commonly as functionalism, this tradition is what Dahrendorf discusses as the "integration theory of society" as opposed to "coercion theory" (1966:159). For a good example of the use of strain theory see Sutton et al., 1956.

7. A word I will often use instead of "meaning" to refer to the perceptions and judgments people have about a particular event or situation is "orientation." I will thus speak of the orientations people have toward the middlemen or toward the cooperative.

8. A recent example is provided by Teodor Shanin. He applies this theoretical stance in his analysis of the Russian peasantry during and after the Russian Revolution. He argues, for example, that the "specific peasant culture" is one of the important factors in understanding "the full impact of socio-economic differentiation on the political consciousness of the Russian peasantry and the possible division of the peasantry into conflicting classes" (1972:140).

A number of authors who have dealt with social mobility have made similar points, suggesting that the impact of particular kinds of social mobility depends on the particular orientations people have toward that mobility (Germani 1966:369; Lipset 1959:263–66).

9. Barrington Moore also stresses this point (1966:480). He then goes on to warn of the conservative bias that occurs if "cultural continuity" is assumed to require no explanation: one tends to overlook whose interests are served by a particular culture and

the possible ways that the culture has been recreated anew in each generation: "To maintain and transmit a value system, human beings are punched, bullied, sent to jail, thrown into concentration camps, cajoled, bribed, made into heroes, encouraged to read newspapers, stood up against a wall and shot, and sometimes even taught sociology" (1966:489). (In *Fanshen,* Hinton explicitly discusses how "tradition" is maintained by those in power (1968:47–48)). Moore also suggests the importance that culture may have as "an intervening variable, a filter . . . between people and an 'objective' situation" (1966:485). But he insists on linking such perceptions to how people reached them, to the historical context: "The problem is to determine out of what past and present experiences such an outlook arises and maintains itself" (1966:489).

10. The basic limitation of such an approach, as Goldthorpe et al. point out, is "that the attempt to provide explanations from the point of view of the 'system' entails the neglect of the point of view of the actors involved" (1968:183–84).

11. This metaphor was first suggested to me by Sidney Mintz.

12. I will briefly discuss some of these barriers in Chapter 7.

13. I did treat it to a limited extent in Chapter 5 in trying to understand how Puro came to accept and promote the cooperative ideology. I will again return briefly to discussions of personality in Chapter 7, and again in discussions of leadership in Chapter 8.

14. See note 13 above.

15. Chapter 7, the section entitled "Obstacles to Problem Definition and Ideology Formation"; Chapter 8, the section entitled "Shaping the Meaning of the Cooperative: Further Struggles"; and Chapter 9, the section entitled "The Creation of Power."

16. Chapter 8, the section entitled "Shaping the Meaning of the Cooperative: Further Struggles."

17. Chapter 7, see sections entitled "The Economic Situation: Many Problems, Few Solutions," and "Relations with the Middlemen"; Chapter 8, see first five sections; and Chapter 9, see "The Challenge to Legitimacy."

One of the few authors writing on peasant movements who does this particularly well is Teodor Shanin. In dealing with the sense of communal solidarity and internal cohesiveness felt by the Russian peasants, for example, he does not merely take such orientations as givens with which he can explain the peasants' reactions to the revolutionary ideology, but rather seeks to show how these orientations were sustained by certain experiences. See, for example, Shanin 1972:141, 177.

18. At times, Sutton et al. recognize this formulation for "felt" strain (1956:306–7), but their basic concept of strain is that of "emotional energy" generated by conflicting demands, tensions pent up inside individuals and in need of an outlet or release. Ideology then becomes a "symbolic outlet" for this energy and not primarily a set of guiding principles. This notion of strain is of limited use since it reduces the complexity of meaning men give to their social situations—how they see and wrestle with conflicting demands—to an all-encompassing but flabby notion of "emotional energy."

19. I found Mills's distinction between "troubles" and "issues" useful here. He uses these to indicate the public-private aspects of what I call a "problem" orientation. Mills goes on to distinguish troubles and issues from "indifference" and "uneasiness." He writes that it is possible that people "are neither aware of any cherished values nor experience any threat" (1959:11). This is "the experience of *indifference,* which if it seems to involve all their values, becomes apathy. It is also possible that "they are unaware of any cherished values, but still are very much aware of a threat." This is "the experience of *uneasiness,* of anxiety, which, if it is total enough, becomes a deadly, unspecified malaise" (1959:11). This "uneasiness" is similar to what I have called malaise—inchoate difficulties, undefined anxieties, unspecified frustrations. But I have not adopted Mills's exact terminology because a "bad" situation for me is one in which people do very much feel some cherished value as threatened—or at least feel something is wrong, bad, or evil—but the threat is not clearly defined as a problem.

20. A fine literary description of the transformation of private malaise into a public problem is found in Zola's novel of the lives and struggles of the French mineworkers, *Germinal* (1969). See especially pages 162–72.

21. This section avoids certain important theoretical issues by joining sets of concepts that derive from very different theoretical stances: "class position" and "social role" are joined under the heading "social situation"; "interest" and "strain" are brought together as particular "orientations" people can have toward their social situation, and then refined into categories of "malaise" and "problem," "public" and "private." But "class position" and "interest" are integral parts of a theory first made explicit by Marx and more recently referred to as "interest theory" (Sutton et al. 1956:12,13; Geertz 1964:52), "coercion theory" (Dahrendorf 1966:159), and "the theory of social conflict and change" (Rex 1963:115). The concepts of "social role" and "strain" have wholly different theoretical origins that go back at least as far as Talcott Parsons's functionalist theory, more recently referred to as "integration theory" (Dahrendorf 1966:159). Behind each of these theoretical frameworks are very different assumptions (about man, society). The important task of building a wholly new framework is beyond the scope of this chapter.

22. This theoretical approach appears–although never explicitly–in certain treatments of peasant ideologies. Gerrit Huizer, for example, argues that "people become restless and 'organizable' " when "à well conserved, more or less benevolent paternalistic *status quo* . . . starts to take on aspects which create acute frustration" (1970:397). See also Hobsbawm's analysis of why an anarchist ideology was accepted in Andalusia but not in Sicily although similar social conditions existed in the two areas (1959:81,94); and Robert White's explanation of why Mexican peasants turned to Zapata's movement (1969:131–32).

23. This will be the basis for part of my argument in Chapter 8, the section entitled "The Cooperative versus the Middlemen," and in Chapter 9, the section entitled "The Challenge to Legitimacy."

24. Thomas Kuhn suggests this possibility in his discussion of scientific revolutions. His basic argument is analagous to the one I have presented above. He argues that the crucial, though not only, condition for the acceptance of new scientific paradigms and the rejection of those which exist is a crisis in the ability of the paradigm to provide solutions to problems, a "breakdown of the normal technical puzzle-solving activity" of the paradigm (1964:69; see also p. 76). But, Kuhn argues, men do not first come to reject the validity of one paradigm and then go looking for another. Rather, people will only declare one theory invalid "if an alternative candidate is available to take its place" (1964:77).

25. It should be noted that no clear distinction has been drawn between an "orientation" (or the "meaning" of a particular situation) and an "ideology." Both are symbol systems that give meaning to events or situations, yet I conceive of an ideology as more systematic than an orientation; it is a more explicit definition of a problem and a more explicit guide to action in a problematic situation.

Because no explicit, systematic definition of peasant economic problems nor guide for action existed in Jaida Arriba before the cooperative, I refer to a "lack of ideological activity" there before 1967. Those institutionalized guides for action or explicit symbolic guides that did exist in situations that people experienced as problematic I usually refer to as "strategies."

26. This approach will provide the foundation for part of the analysis in Chapter 8, "The Cooperative versus the Middlemen." The notion of ideology as a "creator of problems" or a transformer of meanings situations have for people is implicit in a number of studies. Goldthorpe et al., for example, imply the importance that cultural prescriptions (such as ideologies) have in molding and defining existing tensions (1969:189). Hobsbawm talks briefly about the role of ideology in providing centralized expression for aspirations and needs and in converting "inchoate strivings" into defined problems and struggles when he discusses the different impacts anarchism and communist ideologies have on Andalusian and Sicilian villages (1959:6, 10, Chapters IV and V).

Paul Friedrich (1970) also emphasizes this possible formative role of ideology. In the Mexican community he studied he argues that although the material preconditions for revolt were indispensable, "they did not generate revolt in isolation as 'objective facts,' or even when mediated by the attitudes and traditional value systems of the popula-tion. . . . The material conditions had to be not only apprehended and verbalized by the peasantry but critically evaluated and persuasively tied to an ideology" (1970:137).

27. Wolf writes: "Peasants often harbor a deep sense of injustice, but his [sic] sense of injustice must be given shape and expression in organization before it can become active on the political scene; and it is obvious that not every callow agitator will find a welcome hearing in village circles traditionally suspicious of outsiders, especially when they come from the city. The social scientist used to viewing the peasantry from the vantage of national level may often be tempted to forget that social or economic or political mobilization of a peasantry involves contact with many small groups not always eager to receive guidance and leadership from the outside. How this resistance is overcome, if indeed it *is* overcome, is not always a foregone conclusion" (1969:xii–xiii).

28. I will explore this problem of leadership in Chapter 8.

The central point here is not simply that leaders are important. Rather, I am arguing that our very ability to understand why and how they are important is made possible by the particular way this theoretical approach conceives of the relationship between social situation, orientation, and ideology. It is because the meanings (such as strain) that social situations have for people are not deterministically linked to class position or social role that we can talk about the malleability of meanings by leaders and ideology (on this point see also Goldthorpe et al. (1969:189); it is because of the distinction made among different forms of one kind of orientation, that of strain, that we can explore the role leaders may play in using ideologies to transform the experience of malaise to the experience of problems; it is because problem orientations are conceived of as situations in which men need explicit symbols to give meaning and direction to their thought, feeling, and action that we can talk about how leaders can intensify doubts people already have about the adequacy of existing sets of symbols and convince people of the usefulness of a new ideology.

29. This will be discussed in further detail in Chapter 8 in the sections entitled "Shaping the Meaning of the Cooperative: Further Struggles" and "Leadership."

30. More recently a number of other social scientists have made similar points about the importance of the consistency of new political beliefs with the existing beliefs for a person's acquiring this new belief (Lane and Sears 1964:44ff; Dahl 1971:175–76). Dahl adds the importance of "consistency with experience" in the acceptance of a new belief (1971:177–80).

31. That men may not use such logical criteria in relating new symbols to existing ones is also suggested by Philip Converse in his article, "The Nature of Belief Systems in Mass Publics" (1964:Chapter VI).

32. Particular emphasis will be given to these orientations in Chapter 8, in the section entitled "Shaping the Meaning of the Cooperative: Further Struggles."

One of the few authors writing on peasant movements who gives even passing attention to these questions regarding the culture into which a new ideology is intro-duced is White 1969:104, 123.

33. He mentions philosophers such as Pierce, Wittgenstein, Cassirer, Langer, Ryle, and Morris; literary critics such as Coleridge, Eliot, Burke, Empson, Blackmur, Brooks, and Auerbach; and linguists such as Whorf and Sapir.

34. See, for example, the discussions of the use of the image of junta by the cooperative ideology in Chapter 8 in the section entitled "Shaping the Meaning of the Cooperative: Further Struggles." It should be mentioned that an alternative approach to stylistics for understanding how and why symbols carry the meanings they do is through the use of linguistic analysis. For an important pioneering work in this area see Douglas Bennett 1976.

CHAPTER 7

1. Many afternoons day laborers, friends, or neighbors of mine came to my house hoping to find a way to feed their families on the morrow. They would rarely ask for money. They would come in, often awkwardly, hat in hand. Their greeting might be

warm–an outstretched arm, a half embrace. It depended on how close we were. Their eyes said to me what they had been unsuccessfully asking others all day: "Pay me a day so we can eat tonight." But often their lips could not say these words. They were embarrassed to ask, ashamed of their poverty, and embarrassed to come to a stranger from another country. But hunger was stronger than shame.

During my first months in the campo, worried that all would descend on me if I gave work to one, I waited for them to say: "Pay me a day." I hoped that if I played naive they would just chat about their problems and leave. But I soon came to know who had come to chat and who had come to me in desperation looking for a way to eat. I came, too, to suffer with them and could no longer hope that shame would keep these words out of their mouths. So I invented work (house repairs, a vegetable garden) and "paid a day."

2. One of Morse's central points here is that the belief system in a Catholic society "militates against the formation of perception of rigid castes or classes or solidary ethnic groups" (1969:13). Indeed Weber points out in his *Sociology of Religion* that Catholics, unlike Protestants, do not achieve "grace" through individual endeavor, excellence, or personal abilities. Rather, grace is institutionally dispensed: "Salvation (which we can secularize as achievement or social mobility) cannot be attained outside an institution vested with the control of grace. . . . In addition, the personal qualification of the individual requiring salvation is a matter of indifference to the institution which distributes grace. In a Catholic society, then, people's positions and their hopes for improving them (or of achieving salvation) are determined by institutions or authority figures–not vice versa. This militates against the formation or perception of rigid castes or classes or solidary ethnic groups" (Morse 1969:12–13).

3. See, for example, Friedmann 1967:324, 330; Miller 1967:190–92; Banfield 1967: 36–37; Foster 1967:315–21.

4. In exploring peasant resistance to change, Huizer criticizes Banfield, Foster, and Erasmus for deemphasizing "the repression and struggle that bring perspective into the resistance to change of the peasant communities they studied" (1972:317).

5. In an article (written after the completion of this chapter), James Scott presents an interesting discussion of peasant notions of justice and legitimacy in terms of two moral principles: "the norm of reciprocity" and "the right to subsistence." Aspects of these principles appear in the following discussions of Jaida Arriba although, unlike Scott, I am dealing with middlemen-peasant (not landlord-peasant) relations. See Scott 1975.

6. The notion of a "gift," and the obligations that gifts incur, are often discussed in anthropological relations that are involved. See, for example, Mauss 1966 and Bailey, ed. 1971.

7. This is well illustrated by an incident that happened to me. For many Sundays, I had been drinking coffee at midday at one of the small kitchens operated near the church. Maria, the cook, often would beckon me in to have some coffee and dessert. Payment in the kitchens is done informally: Maria never "charges" anybody. Rather, when they leave, they talk quietly with her to settle accounts. If they leave without paying, or merely give her something less than she might have expected as they leave, nothing is said. I had always felt uncomfortable about "paying" for the coffee within this informal system. But having in mind that I really did owe her money, when I encountered her alone one day as she swept out the church, I decided to give her a peso. I said: "Maria, I have something for you. I've been drinking a lot of coffee and eating a lot of rice candy in your kitchen. I'd like to pay you." As I produced a peso from my pocket, she shook her head no and wagged her finger disapprovingly at me. "No, no, no, no, no! Absolutely not. I didn't do that por interés. It was my own pleasure. I'd be ashamed to take this. I can't accept it." Good-naturedly, and joking, we argued back and forth, I trying to insist. "I know you didn't do it por interés. But I want you to take this." But she continually refused, even when I tried to put it in her hand. At one point I said: "But I know you weren't doing it por interés. And I'm not giving you this as a form of payment. This is like a gift from me. I want you to accept this gift." To this she replied: "Oh, all right, if it's like a gift, then it's O.K. But if it were payment, I couldn't

accept it." And she took the peso, folded it twice, and tucked it safely into her ample bosom.

8. That this relationship was supported by economic power—the continued need for help from the comerciantes and the fear of losing it if one did not reciprocate—as well as by such consensual beliefs will come clear when I discuss the cooperative's efforts to break the control of the middlemen in Chapter 9.

9. Wolf discusses how capitalism has, throughout the underdeveloped world, turned traditional relations governing human interactions into commodity relations defined by land, labor, and capital (1969:276–80).

10. Wolf indicates that such dual feelings of gratitude and resentment may not be uncommon in patron-client relations (1966a:12–13).

11. Indeed that such criteria as projimidad and por interés still existed alongside the profit criteria of capitalism might be peculiar only to traditional highland mountain communities such as Jaida Arriba. Such notions were far weaker in some of the flatland rice communities I studied. Middlemen-peasant relationships were more openly cash-based; it was accepted that a comerciante or rice factory owner was "naturally" out for his own interest.

12. A sense of bitter but undefined resentment felt against the rich, the bosses, the foreman, and others is not an uncommon phenomenon among peasants, sharecroppers, wage laborers, migrant workers, and other lower-class groups. Things are "bad," men are "evil," life is filled with hardships. Transforming such resentment into public awareness and anger, getting men to see evils as public problems or to see causal relations between their poverty and wider institutions and structures is a difficult task. Actually, organizing them to do something is often even more difficult, as we will see in Chapter 9. This resentment of the poor, and the difficulties of creating consciousness and organization, are graphically drawn by Steinbeck in his early novel *In Dubious Battle* (1972).

13. The Palabra de Dios, which brought people from all over Jaida Arriba together each Sunday, was not started until early 1968, after the cooperative had started to organize.

14. Analytical discussions of gossip are found in some of the anthropological literature. See, for example, Bailey (1971), Heppenstall (1971), Foster (1967: Introduction). A beautiful scenario of the gossip relationship is painted by Zola in *Germinal* when three women successively meet in separate pairs, each time confiding their dislike and suspicion of the other (1969:102–14).

15. Politicians did talk of the need to give land to the landless and of the injustice of land distribution in the Republic. But the big landowners in the flatlands who had all this land seemed far away from Jaida Arriba. And, too, this was all "politics": the personal struggle of those in the city; promises that were never fulfilled. In 1967 the priests had only just begun to take to the air waves and talk of the importance and benefits of cooperatives and the evils of comerciantes, intermediarios, and compradores. The prices exporting houses were paying the compradores for coffee were not announced.

16. It is this type of education (not uncommon even in the United States) that Freire criticizes as a "banking" type of education where knowledge is simply deposited in the peasant's head (1970).

17. The effect of ignorance on lack of self-confidence, and this in turn on the failure to speak or act is something that most of us are familiar with in our everyday lives, but we may not normally think of it as politically significant. For a fascinating description of how this phenomenon affects a young French coal worker see Zola's *Germinal* (1969: 164–65).

18. The ambiguity between these two ways of knowing is not without its effect on the peasants themselves. Fidel first pointed this out to me. The peasants often will go along with, or follow, the advice or suggestions of someone "who knows"; but they often will do so with reticence—ready to pull back at the slightest difficulty. This presents serious problems for organizing a movement.

19. It is interesting to note here that Puro had not been familiar with marketing or consumer cooperatives; he had only heard of the savings and loan cooperative in the

pueblo. Yet he extended the idea of a cooperative to cover these other possibilities. On a number of occasions during his struggle to organize the cooperative Puro used or manipulated existing cultural notions and ideas, applying them in different ways to new situations. Geertz mentions such an ability as one important to an entrepreneur: "The function of the entrepreneur in such transitional but pretake-off societies is mainly to adapt customarily established means to novel ends" (1968:152).

20. Pucho also had some notion of exactly how the control of the comerciantes worked because he once had worked for two years as the manager of a small comercio.

21. This atmosphere of mistrust and suspicion will be discussed further in Chapter 8, in the section entitled "Shaping the Meaning of the Cooperative: Further Struggles."

CHAPTER 8

1. Organization started formally in May 1969, when the first peasants began investing money in a fund for the Cooperativa de Consumo. The actual store, however, was not opened until September 1969.

2. Some of the day laborers and small holders who initially entered perceived and judged the cooperative in terms of certain "Catholic" orientations: they saw the cooperative not as a way in which one helped oneself, or each helped all through saving pennies and creating a loan fund, but rather as an organization that had been formed (by the government, the church, or those peasants with money) to help them. They expected to be granted loans as soon as they joined, independent of such criteria as the amount they already had saved or their ability to pay. They expected that the cooperative would divide the profits of those with coffee equally among all members. And when the consumer cooperative began to give credit they saw this cooperative as providing them with desperately needed credit often denied them by the other comerciantes. Given such a perception of the cooperative, it indeed seemed to these day laborers and small holders like a solution to many of their problems. And they entered. When their expectations went unfulfilled, many became disillusioned with the cooperative. Where was the union and community? Many who had so perceived the cooperative left.

3. See Chapter 7, the section entitled "The Economic Situation: Many Problems, Few Solutions."

4. See Chapter 5, the section entitled "The Cooperative Organizes."

5. I first asked open-ended questions regarding motives for entering, then probed specific motives.

6. It is interesting to note here that the very conception of the middlemen as a problem was in part due to the presentation of the cooperative as an alternative. Without the notion of the cooperative alternative, even if the control of the middlemen had been made clear and the peasants dissatisfied with it, they still might have accepted it as something about which they could do nothing. Also, it seems that the fact that the cooperative revealed this control, presenting it in a framework that made sense to the people, helped reinforce the image of the cooperative as a good alternative: because the definition of middleman control was presented by the cooperative, accepting the definition also may have encouraged acceptance of the cooperative. It may have made sense to the peasants that if what the cooperative said about the middleman was right, then one should join the cooperative.

7. How the cooperative ideology functioned to bring about a new view of the relationship with the middlemen will be discussed extensively in Chapter 9 in the section "The Challenge to Legitimacy."

8. See Chapter 7, the section entitled "Relations with the Middlemen."

9. The idea became permanently fixed in their minds in March 1968, when they took the month-long course in San Cristobal. The group at the course had set up a consumer cooperative for the time they were there, and through this practice they learned not only the mechanics but saw the "profits" that could be made by all. The impact of this experience was strengthened by the previous experience both had already had working in comercios.

10. In Chapter 9, in the section "The Challenge to Legitimacy," I will discuss more fully how the cooperative ideology functioned to shape the peasants' judgment of the "right" and the "wrong" of the comerciantes' actions.

11. In Chapter 9, I will deal more thoroughly with how the different economic power among various classes affected their ability to break with the middlemen.

12. When Puro and Pucho first insisted upon forming a consumer cooperative, Fidel strongly discouraged them, arguing that it was not in the store that the middlemen made their profits but in the buying of crops through their control of capital. A consumer cooperative, he argued, was not worth the time and risk. They simply needed a savings and loan cooperative that could provide the capital needed to avoid the control the middlemen exercised over crops through credit and advances and a marketing cooperative to avoid their control over the coffee market. But Puro and Pucho were not to be dissuaded. One of the reasons was their identification of the wealth of the comerciantes with what was visible: their stores and merchandise. The comerciantes' real source of wealth could not be seen; and thus it was difficult to understand why a consumer cooperative—which would then give the peasants all this visible wealth—would not also be highly beneficial to the peasants. But Fidel seems to have been right. Although the consumer cooperative had the effect of bringing prices down, the actual savings were minimal as were the earnings (except perhaps for a few large holders) compared to the sacrifice and suffering caused by having to pay cash. Further, the capital that was actually tied up in the store could have been used to buy in cash from the comerciantes, avoiding their control through credit. To make matters worse, the consumer cooperative, under pressure from its cash-short members, began giving credit on a limited basis after nine months of operations. But the limited basis quickly expanded, and in two years, with almost $3,000 credit extended to members, the cooperative was having a difficult time paying its bills in Santiago; and the members were having a difficult time paying what they owed.

13. The "scale" questions I used are listed below. The first three were adopted from Cantril's "Self Anchoring Striving Scale, question #3 using a drawing of a ladder with ten rungs (each numbered) as he does with his "ladder device" (1965:22–24). The first three questions were always asked in the same order with the same wording; there was some variation in #4 and #5 depending on the course of the discussion after #3. I asked the questions quite casually (having memorized them beforehand). The questions in parentheses are probes that I used after people had either responded or failed to respond to the initial question.

(1) We all want a number of things out of life. Thinking of what is most important to you in life, what wishes and hopes do you have for the future? In other words, if you were to imagine the best possible future, what kind of future would it be? (In order to consider yourself happy, what kind of life do you wish for in the future? Which are your hopes for the future? What are you missing now to be happy? Anything else?)

(2) Let's look at the other side for a moment: what fears and preoccupations do you have about your future? In other words, if you were to imagine the worst possible future, what kind of future would it be? (What things could make you unhappy? What are your fears and preoccupations about the future? Anything else?)

(3) Here's a drawing of a ladder—like the type you use to climb up the roofs. Let's suppose this is the lowest part (here I pointed with my finger to the rung labeled #1) and also the worst possible type of life, as you just explained to me. The top is here (here I pointed to the top rung labeled #10); this highest part is the best possible type of life.
a. Where in the ladder do you think you are right now? (Here I ran my finger rapidly up and down the ladder.)
b. And in what part of the ladder were you four years ago?
c. And where do you think you'll be five years from now?

(4) (If they saw a change in the future, I asked:) How do you think you'll get there (and here I mentioned the number they had said in 3c).
(If they saw no change, I asked:) Why do you think you aren't going to change?
(If they saw a downward change, I asked:) Why do you think you'll go down?

(5) Four years ago, when you were here (I pointed to the rung mentioned in 3b), what kinds of problems did you have? Which were your main problems and preoccupations? (Economic problems? Lack of money? Sales a la flor? Debts?)

a. At that time, did you think you would be able to solve those problems?

b. How did you go from here (pointing to the rung mentioned in 3b) to here (pointing to the rung mentioned in 3a)?

14. It is important to note that I never mentioned the cooperative during the course of the questioning. Nor did I ever administer these questions in the context of a discussion about the cooperative; indeed, in almost every case, these questions were the first ones I asked in a particular interview, precisely to avoid triggering thoughts of the cooperative. There are, of course, still methodological problems. For example, it is possible that people identified me with questions about the cooperative because I so often asked them. But this method was the only way I felt I could come close to seeing how people placed the cooperative within the context of their present and future lives. I found, for example, that any direct question about what they thought of the cooperative invariably would enlist a positive, often laudatory response. And I thought it possible that people who were members would hesitate to criticize it, or would assume that I was looking for a positive answer and give it to me, or that their telling me that it was important to them would mean little more than "it was a good thing." I adapted Cantril's scale to my purposes to see how they placed the cooperative in their lives without any hints from me.

15. It should be noted that the late arrival of outside loans to the Cooperativa Agropecuaria—loans many members needed to buy in cash during the difficult months before the harvest—and the later consumer cooperative's policy of extending credit began to create debts to the cooperative that were a new source of worry by 1972. In a sense, then, the cooperative seemed to have "solved" the problem of continual debt through credit buying for about a year, but slowly recreated the problem in a new form. In 1972, however, most of the middle and large holders still felt their situation to be different and better: owing money to their own cooperative seemed better than the former debts to the comerciantes.

16. A similar point is made by Henry A. Landsberger and Cynthia N. Hewitt. They write that "Altruistic motivation . . . is essential during the early stages of peasant (and many other) organizations, since few other (individualistic) rewards are offered by the environment. No material rewards are attached to the activity; very limited rewards in terms of exercising power over others, certainly at the beginning; some rewards in terms of personal recognition and prestige, but hardly enough to offset the severe frustrations and dangers of the activity, etc." (1970:567). For a more general discussion of this topic see Olson 1973.

17. See Chapter 5, the section entitled "The Cooperative Organizes." The lure of individual mobility at the expense of the group is discussed as one of the major sources of weakness and cleavage in Latin American peasant movements in Landsberger and Hewitt (1970:566–77).

18. Such instrumental orientations are the basis of the hypothesis of "amoral familism" that Banfield finds to hold in the Italian peasant community he studied: "Maximize the material, short-run advantage of the nuclear family; assume that all others will do likewise" (1967:83).

19. See Chapter 7, the section entitled "Relations with the Middlemen."

20. I have invented this label for reference purposes. The peasants had no name for this group.

21. This fact is explained by their historical position as the children of the first settlers of Jaida Arriba who claimed large tracts of virgin forest land suitable for growing coffee. (Rafael's family bought their land from another one of the original settlers.) It should be noted, however, that there were many more middle and large holders in Jaida Arriba who were not in the Las Barrancas "group." In this sense, economic class and felt solidarity were independent.

22. This table takes into account only godfathers in Jaida Arriba. It does not include godfathers drawn from neighboring communities.

23. They often dared not enter on the advice of the comerciantes not only because the comerciantes were reinforcing doubts they already had, but because they feared going against these men—they feared rejecting the "friendly" advice of those on whom they depended for help. They feared being embarrassed in front of them, alienating them, and perhaps even losing their help. Such fear as an obstacle to cooperative acceptance will be discussed in Chapter 9.

24. Many observers of peasant social life have commented on the suspicion and distrust in the communities they have studied. See, for example, Banfield (1967:Chapter 5), Cotler (1970:537), Friedmann (1967), and Foster (1960–61).

Most of these observers argue that such peasant distrust is an obstacle to development and change. For a thoughtful critique of this position, emphasizing the causes of such distrust and how it can be converted into a source of political activity, see Huizer (1972).

25. See Chapter 7, the section entitled "Relations with the Middlemen."

26. The rhythm method, although allowed by the church, was rarely if ever mentioned to the peasants.

27. When one peasant (a future cooperative leader) was told he should stop having contact instead of practicing the withdrawal method he said to the priest: "Look Padre, if you cannot pardon me this, I cannot come to confession anymore. It is better that I follow what my own conscience tells me is right. You don't seem to realize that this is one of the few joys a poor peasant has in his life—that this is one of the few moments in his life when he feels that he is equal to the rich guys. A poor man toils and sweats all day in his fields. He comes home exhausted. And this is the only pleasure he has. What do you expect him to do: come home in the evening and sit around the house with his arms folded! And after I told him that I would not come to confession anymore, he gave me absolution and did not say anything more of this."

CHAPTER 9

1. There are certain limitations in using Weber's schema to explore the relationship between obedience and domination. The comerciantes in Jaida Arriba were not "rulers" giving "commands" in the sense that Weber meant. But because they did exercise a particular form of control and expect certain kinds of obedience—that their clients would negotiate with them and not go to another, that debts not only would be repaid, but repaid with coffee—Weber's discussion of the motivations for obedience may prove useful in helping us to examine the obstacles to disobedience. It should, however, be noted that the disobedience we are discussing is of a particular and limited kind: the peasants are challenging the control of the middlemen not by trying to overthrow them nor eliminating their class or institutional positions, but rather by setting up parallel, alternative institutions.

2. Weber further argued that the failure of a ruler or an institution to gain or to maintain legitimacy does not mean that the ruler will "lose" control nor that the institution will break down: other motivations for obedience may still exist. (Fear, for example, proves to be important despite the breakdown of legitimacy in Jaida Arriba.) Yet in such situations there would be a breakdown in *authority*: the control exercised by the ruler no longer would be based on a belief that he had a right to rule. The meaning of obedience to the ruled would have changed. Weber saw such a loss of legitimacy as weakening the rule of institutions in control. An obedience "to an order imposed by one man or a small group," that is, "derived . . . from fear or from motives of expedience" or even on a "purely customary basis through the fact that the corresponding behavior has become habitual" is still "much less stable than an order which enjoys the prestige of being considered binding, or, as it may be expressed, 'legitimacy' " (1968:37, 31).

3. See Chapter 7, "*Projimidad* versus *Por Interés*" in the section entitled "Relations with the Middlemen."

4. The influence of such moral pressure became real and understandable to me as even I came to find it painfully uncomfortable and embarrassing to pass in and out of the cooperative in full view of Manuel standing behind his counter. Sometimes I, too,

used the back door, or split my purchases between Manuel and the cooperative, or overcame my embarrassment and forced myself at least to go in and chat.

5. There were eleven large holders and seven middle holders in this situation. See Table 4.5.

6. See Table 4.5.

7. See Chapter 7, the section entitled "Relations with the Middlemen."

8. See Chapter 4, the section entitled "The Middlemen: Who Controlled What in Jaida Arriba."

9. In the first months of the cooperative, at least some day laborers and small holders understood the cooperative to be a redistribution scheme. They expected that the profits of those who had coffee would be divided equally among all. When they discovered that profits were to be divided according to how much coffee each had sold through the cooperative, many left the cooperative feeling that it was no more than an organization to help those who already had.

10. About four to six months before the harvest, money was also needed for weeding. At $1.50 per tarea, the approximately 2,200 tareas of the initial members would cost $3,300 to weed. Many, however, could meet part of the weeding cost with family labor.

11. It is reasonable to estimate the need of cash for only half the coffee since the peasant continually brings in his coffee during the months of the harvest, and the first coffee he has brought in can be processed and sold by the time his other coffee is harvested.

12. In one campo, for instance, a comprador was able to use his political influence to turn the guns of the local rural police against the promotor who was attempting to organize a cooperative group. The bullet holes in his door and windshield discouraged him from returning again. In the rice-growing campo of Los Canales, arrests of peasant leaders organizing a strike of day laborers against rice growers quickly put an end to such "communist" activity. And a later attempt to organize a Liga Agraria there was thwarted when the peasant leader was arrested by the rural police and the following day found hanged in his cell. Such use of political-military power against peasant attempts to organize appear frequently in Dominican newspapers.

13. See Table 4.5.

14. This policy of giving credit—completely forbidden when the cooperative was formed—eventually got out of control. Although the cooperative officially discouraged its members from seeking credit except in the cases of most dire needs, such dire need was commonplace when there was no harvest. As the money out on credit grew from a few hundred dollars in late 1970 to $1,300 in mid-1971 to $2,900 in mid-1972, the cooperative continually tried to make rules to limit credit. But in the face of the real economic needs of its members, and the continual shortages of capital in the Cooperativa Agropecuaria (and later in the savings and loan cooperative), such limitations always proved unworkable. Until the Cooperativa Agropecuaria and the savings and loan cooperatives have enough liquid capital to finance some food costs for at least four months for eighty families (at least $30 per person per month, or a total of about $9,600), it remains questionable whether this consumer cooperative can make a profit, let alone survive.

15. The cooperative records showing date of entry only go to February 1970. It is important to note that in late 1970, when the cooperative began to give at least limited credit, many of these day laborers and small holders began to buy their goods there, and a few more entered. But even as late as February 1972, more than sixty-five day laborers and small holders still bought from Manuel.

16. This notion of potential power was first formulated for me by Kalman H. Silvert. It is a useful notion for distinguishing between those who are actually using power (usually through some institutional arrangement) and those who might be able to use the power resources they have. By making the distinction it also allows exploration of the process by which potential power is transformed into kinetic power, the ways in which power can be created and applied. This is indeed one of the central problems for the peasants in Jaida Arriba. See Silvert 1970:15. On the translation of power from one kind to another see also Franz Neuman 1957:11-14.

17. In the following discussion of some of the obstacles to creating a peasant organization, I am focusing on a very particular kind of organization: a cooperative, replete with a given structure and set of rules "brought into" Jaida Arriba. This structure may not be an "adequate" organizational form for peasants. Perhaps it is too "Western," too "Anglo-Saxon"; perhaps another mode of organization might be better suited for such peasants. Generalizations from this case should be made cautiously with an eye toward understanding those obstacles which might be similar in any peasant organization and those which are peculiar to cooperatives of this kind.

18. See Chapter 5, the section entitled "The Cooperative Organizes," and Chapter 8, "Shaping the Meaning of the Cooperative: Further Struggles."

19. The general problem here is, as Wolf has noted, that one of the obstacles to peasant organization and action is that his past exclusion from action has deprived him of the knowledge needed to articulate his interests with appropriate forms of action (1969:290).

20. By 1972, the fourth year of the cooperative, attendance had dropped off markedly at the weekly cooperative meetings; some were canceled. The everyday administrative problems of running a cooperative did not have the same excitement and sense of urgency that consistently drew the membership to earlier meetings. Despite continued faith in the leaders, such lack of participation had in it the seeds of future difficulties: many began quietly to disagree with decisions they no longer understood (having missed the meetings) and which they felt were being made from above. If future crises demand great sacrifices this growing distance of members from the organization could cause difficulties in mounting collective action.

21. I was never present when a vote was taken in the face of a severe split among the leadership. Such cases would raise serious difficulties because voting is public and a leader might consider a vote against him as a personal affront or rejection. In one case that occurred before I arrived, strong opposition by Pucho to the choice of an administrator for the consumer cooperative was overridden by a vote of the administrative council. In protest, Pucho temporarily stopped buying in the consumer cooperative. In my discussions with Pucho it was clear that the notion of "majority as right" made sense to him only when he was in that majority. In any decision which a large number of people opposed, those in opposition probably would not go along with the majority in any case. It seems that most of the cooperative leaders realized that a decision not reached by near unanimity would have been unworkable and thus put off decisions in such cases rather than force them to a vote. In such cases, what the outside observer may see as failure to take action on an important issue may actually be the rational thing to do.

22. Puro's personal background was discussed in Chapter 5, in the section entitled "A Peasant Leader."

23. I also discovered that Puro often was able to eliminate conflicts before they occurred through premeeting politicking with Pucho and others. In meetings, Puro consciously used certain tactics that allowed Pucho to change his mind without losing face. I once asked Puro how he planned to deal with the possible opposition of Pucho at an upcoming meeting, and he explained to me: "What I have found often works with him, is to start out agreeing with his idea and backing it up. Then when he thinks that I am on his side and we are both working together, I will slowly begin to change my mind. And as I change, because he thinks we are in agreement, he will begin to change too. And I will carry him with me until I arrive at the plan [that Puro was in favor of] and he will end up agreeing—without ever having disagreed."

24. The ability to educate peasants may be one of the crucial determinants shaping the quality of their social or political movements as at least partially autonomous and self-directed, or as mere instruments of governments, urban intellectuals, political parties, and the like. Paulo Freire gives much attention to this problem (1970). But he merely sets the problem: understanding the importance of educating the oppressed to be thinking subjects rather than manipulated objects still leaves largely unexplored the question of how, if at all, such education can be accomplished.

25. See Chapter 5, the section entitled "The Cooperative Organizes."

26. See Chapter 5, the section entitled "The Cooperative Organizes."

27. The contract, like those of exporting houses, fixed the amount of coffee to be given to Fenacoop in return for the advance.

28. See Chapter 5, the section entitled "The Cooperative Organizes."

29. Given Brazil's large percentage of total coffee production, the International Coffee Organization's attempts to stabilize prices were of only limited success.

30. AID eventually was willing to let its loan to Idecoop be used for technical assistance to coffee growers and improvement of their production but not for financing the harvest.

31. They explained that the cooperative first would have to present its accounting records so that its financial status could be analyzed. The cooperative leaders, with no knowledge of accounting, had left this job to Idecoop accountants who, despite many months of "working," in reality had not yet started the books. Over a year later, they still had not finished an accounting of the cooperative's first year—thus effectively eliminating banks as a source of funds for the cooperative.

32. See Chapter 2, the section entitled "Who Controls What," for more details regarding the quota distribution process.

33. The fall of 1971 again saw a money crisis: a loan promised by Idecoop for the beginning of October did not arrive until November. Again banks refused to loan money because the cooperative still had no accounting records (Idecoop accountants were still "working" on them). And again the Dominican manager of the European trading house bailed out the cooperative by guaranteeing a $10,000 loan that allowed the members to subsist until the Idecoop money finally came.

34. Although the cooperative leaders, Fidel, and the lawyer saw indications of corruption and personal interest on the part of public officials, and believed these factors to be behind many agency actions, it was difficult for me to get conclusive evidence. In addition to corruption as an explanation, two other possibilities are plausible: the government agencies might have wanted to maintain national control over all cooperatives to prevent the movement from developing autonomously; or the government officials might have wanted to control peasant coffee because they did not trust the peasants to pay back what they owed.

35. During the 1970 election campaign, all employees of Idecoop (and of most other government agencies) were expected to campaign actively for the reelection of President Balaguer and the ruling Partido Reformista. Fidel refused. In November 1970, all employees of Idecoop received a letter requiring them to pay a 2 percent levy for the coffers of the Partido Reformista; Fidel was the only one in his office who did not.

In 1971 the Presidente Administrador of Idecoop was accused in a newspaper article of misuse of Idecoop funds. A press conference was called for all employees of Idecoop at which they were publicly asked to sign a letter of support for the Administrador to present to the press. Fidel refused to sign, claiming that he had no idea whether the allegations were true or false since he had never seen Idecoop's books. Four days later he received a mimeographed sheet in the mail from Idecoop. Entitled "Loyalty," it suggested that all those who could not support "their institution" and "leaders" should leave. Fidel did not.

CHAPTER 10

1. See Chapter 8, the section entitled "Leadership."

2. I witnessed some of these difficulties when I was asked by a newly formed Consejo de la Comunidad (community council) to help and "advise" them. After thirteen months as a member of the community, it was difficult to refuse. I struggled to keep a "low profile," refusing to take a leadership position or to make any decisions. I spent many weeks teaching peasants who already trusted me and were anxious to learn; I read Paulo Freire at night and tried to work out ways to teach these men and women how to think and organize for themselves and be independent of me. While I was there, the Consejo successfully organized an effort to complete the bridge over the river dividing the community (it had been left unfinished for three years), established access to a CARE milk program for the children, and made an unsuccessful effort to get the

government to establish fourth and fifth grades in the local school. In the ensuing months I came to understand the real limits that peasants who were clearly "socially conscious" still faced when it came to actual organization and administration. Their lack of success in creating a self-sustaining, autonomous community group taught me the limits of the concientización effort in the community. What I learned from this practical experience also helped inform many sections of this book.

3. Such theoretical stances were discussed briefly in notes in Chapter 6. See in particular: Sutton et al. (1956:12, 13), Geertz (1964), Dahrendorf (1966:Chapter 5), Rex (1963), Lockwood (1964:246ff), and Cohen (1968).

4. A functionalist might refer to this as "deviance" from established norms and point to a failure of existing institutions of "socialization." The middlemen's reactions would be seen as "social sanctions," natural and necessary in such situations where the functioning of the system was threatened.

Quite clearly what might seem like similar phenomena are sometimes referred to with different terms in each approach: "conflict" in one approach is "deviance" in the other; "socialization into society's norms and values" is "deception by the ideology of the ruling class." What makes them "different" phenomena is the different emphasis deriving from the different theoretical frameworks in which these concepts are set.

5. For a discussion of this conception of ideology as a "mask" or a "weapon," see Chapter 6.

6. The discussion here also suggested that we should be more precise about the kind of problem orientation involved. The particular way the peasants viewed their economic problems may have been an important obstacle to the rise of a new ideology: they were seen as private problems, not public ones; and these economic problems were all seen as unrelated—there was no well-defined problem orientation that gave any coherence or connection among the individual problems.

7. See, for example, Chapter 7, "Relations with the Middlemen."

8. For an important discussion by a sociologist of some problems similar to those raised here see Gouldner 1973.

9. There has been much discussion of such state activity in recent social science literature. See, for example, Schmitter 1974, Malloy 1976, Huizer 1972:188–89; Erasmus 1968:73; Stepan forthcoming; Hansen 1971; and Pike and Stritch 1974.

GLOSSARY

a la flor Literally, "at the flowering"; refers to coffee sold before the harvest to meet cash needs. Such coffee was sold anywhere from eight to nine months before the harvest (when it was first flowering) to a few weeks before the harvest. Often coffee sold only one or two months before harvest was referred to as coffee sold *a la cosecha*.

a medias Splitting the gross earnings on an animal or piece of land, half going to the person who raised the animal or tilled the soil, and the other half to the person who put up half the original price of the animal or who owned the land.

abrazo Embrace; a common, affectionate greeting in the *campo* among close friends.

agradecimiento Pertaining to agriculture and cattle raising; the Cooperativa Agropecuaria in Jaida Arriba was essentially a coffee processing and marketing cooperative that also made loans and advances to its members to meet costs of coffee production.

ahorros Savings.

alcalde Mayor; justice of the peace; and in the *campo*, something of a sheriff, often armed with a revolver.

alegría Joy, happiness.

ambiente Ambience.

amor Love.

avergonzado Ashamed.

ayuda Help, aid, assistance.

brujo Sorcerer, witch.

cadena Chain.

campesino Peasant.

campo Countryside.

carajo A local expletive.

caridad Charity.

chisme Gossip.

colerín A gastrointestinal illness.

colín What North Americans commonly call a machete. It is so named because of the manufacturer's name (Collins) printed on the label stuck to the blade.

comerciante Merchant, dry goods store owner. See also *comprador.*

compadrazgo Ritual coparenthood; spiritual affinity between the godfather and the parents of a child.

compadre Ritual coparent; name used to express kinship between the father and godfather.

compañero Companion.

comprador Buyer. In Jaida Arriba, usually a coffee buyer. The compradores were most often also *comerciantes,* dry goods store owners. The credit they offered the peasants on merchandise obligated the peasants to sell their coffee to these buyers at harvest time.

comunidad Community; used by the church to indicate spiritual (rather than geographic) community.

concientización The creation of consciousness.

concientizar To create consciousness; to make conscious. A common term among progressive elements of the Dominican clergy used to mean making people aware of exploitation or oppression and the need for collective action to change the situation.

confianza Trust; reliance; confidence.

conuco A small cultivated plot of land.

coño Cunt; used as an explanation, although much less frequently in the more traditional backland mountain region of Jaida Arriba than in urban centers or the heavily populated rural flatlands of the Cibao.

cooperativa A cooperative.

Cooperativa Agropecuaria The Agropecuarian Cooperative. Originally also a savings and loan cooperative open to all peasants in Jaida Arriba, it was later restricted to growers of coffee. Today it is essentially a coffee marketing and processing cooperative, making loans and advances to its members.

Cooperativa de Ahorros y Crédito Savings and Loan Cooperative.

Cooperativa de Consumo Consumer Cooperative, a cooperatively owned food and dry goods stores.

cumplidor One who complies with his obligations; a trustworthy person.

curandero Curer, healer, witch doctor.

cursillos Short courses.

Cursillos de Cristiandad Christianity courses (see Chapter 5).

décima a song-poem, often telling a story like a ballad.

desconfianza Distrust.

dueño Owner.

echar días To sell a day's labor; literally, to "throw out" or "throw away" a day.

El Presidente The president of the Dominican Republic.

El Rio Small village located where the foot trail from Jaida Arriba meets the jeep road.

engañador Deceiver; cheat.

engañar To cheat.

enllave A special "in" or "key."

espiritu comunitario Community or communal spirit.

fanega A unit of volume in which a peasant's coffee traditionally was sold. One fanega of coffee was equal to approximately one *quintal* (100 pounds) of coffee, but in Jaida Arriba, a *fanega* often contained 105 to 110 pounds of coffee.

Fenacoop Federacion Nacional de Cooperativas Agropecuarias. The National Federation of Agropecuarian Cooperatives.

Fetab La Federacion de Cooperativas para el Mercadeo del Tobaco. Federation of Cooperatives for the Marketing of Tobacco.

fia'o Fiado, or credit; from the verb *fiar.*

gente del pueblo Townspeople; people of the city.

gente grande Powerful people.

gente que sabe Clever or wise people.

grande Big, large; *los grandes* is likely to refer to those who are wealthy or powerful.

guardia Rural police.

güira A musical instrument made of a cylindrical tin tube about a foot and a half long and two or three inches in diameter, whose rough surface is scraped with a metal rod. A traditional merengue group is composed of a *tambara, güira,* and accordian.

hola Hello.

honrado Honest.

Idecoop Instituto de Desarrollo y Crédito Cooperativo. Institute of Cooperative Development and Credit.

intermediario Intermediary; middleman.

jaida The local pronunciation for the word *halda,* meaning steepness.

jefe Leader, chief, head.

junta An exchange labor team.

La Banda The band, group; used to refer to a vigilante group active in 1971 and believed by the press to be supported by the National Police to eliminate those who actively opposed the government.

La Loma A small village about two hours by mule from Jaida Arriba; the scene of the first meeting held by cooperative organizers called in by El Padre.

Las Barrancas A section of Jaida Arriba.

lucha Struggle, fight.

macuteos Bribes; from the word *macuto,* a woven sack with a shoulder strap used for coffee picking or carrying food.

machete A broad-bladed tool for weeding. The tool the peasants in Jaida Arriba called a machete is not the slender, long-edged knife for slashing brush and trees which we commonly call a machete. Rather, it has a much wider blade (4 to 5 inches) with a still wider curved end (6 inches across) used for cutting under the roots of weeds when weeding. What we call a machete, they call a *colín.*

mal Bad.

malestar Malaise, uneasiness.

negociante Dealer; businessman; tradesman. The peasants often used the word *negociante* as a synonym for *comerciante.*

Nueva York New York, often used to mean the United States. New York *is* the United States for most Dominicans who go there.

padre Priest; or father, depending on context.

Palabra de Dios A special church service designed for the peasants and given by the Presidente de La Asamblea; often abbreviated as La Palabra by the peasants.

peje grande Big fish. Peje is the local slang for *pez* (fish).

peso The Dominican peso is the smallest denomination in paper currency. The official exchange rate in the Dominican Republic is 1 peso = 1 U.S. dollar. On the international market the value is somewhat less. Unless otherwise noted, the sign $ means peso and not dollar.

por interés Literally, "for interest." A person acting *por interés* is acting out of self-interest, often for monetary gain, and not out of *projimidad* or *caridad.* (See also Chapter 7, the section entitled "The Middlemen: Just or Unjust?")

Presidente de la Asamblea President of the Assembly; lay head of religious functions in campos like Jaida Arriba. The position was often referred to by the peasants as the *Jefe de la Comunidad* (head or chief of the community).

problema Problem.

projimidad Neighborliness; (see Chapter 7, "The Middlemen; Just or Unjust?" for detailed discussion).

prójimo Neighbor.

projimista Neighborly.

promoción social Social promotion.

promotor Promoter; organizer.

pueblo City or town. Used by the peasants to refer to either the small municipal capital or the provincial capital.

pul Pull, influence.

pulperia A general store, usually smaller than a *comercio*.

quintal 100 pounds.

rezar la primera To pray the morning prayer.

rico Rich, wealthy; *Los ricos* was a term often used to characterize the rich and powerful.

sabio clever, wise; skillful at taking advantage of another.

San Juan de La Sierra Municipal capital of municipality in which Jaida Arriba was located.

Santiago The provincial capital of the province in which Jaida Arriba was located; the second largest city in the Dominican Republic.

socios Members; members of the cooperative.

tambora Drum.

tarea Approximately one-sixth of an acre.

temor Fear.

tostones Flattened plantain slices fried in oil.

un campesino bruto A stupid, ignorant peasant.

uno que sabe One who knows, one who is clever.

verguenza Shame, embarrassment.

vicios Vices; forms of gambling (dice, billiards, cockfighting) or drinking.

víveres A term used to denote such foods as plantains, bananas, yucca, etc. Its origin might be from *vivir*, to live, *víveres* being the local pronunciation of *viveres*.

yuca Sweet manioc; nonpoisonous manioc, yucca; cassava.

BIBLIOGRAPHY

Adames, Roque. 1966a. *Carta Pastoral.* 29 de Julio. (On file at the bishop's office, Santiago, Dominican Republic.)

———. 1966b. *Escritas de Monseñor Roque Adames.* (On file at bishop's office, Santiago, Dominican Republic.)

Bailey, F. G. 1971. Gifts and Poison. In *Gifts and Poison,* ed. F. G. Bailey, pp. 1–25. New York: Schocken Books.

Banfield, Edward C. 1967. *The Moral Basis of a Backward Society.* New York: Free Press.

Bennett, Douglas C. 1967. The Observation of Meaning: Presentational Analysis as an Alternative to Content Analysis. Ph.D. dissertation, Yale University.

Berger, Peter L., and Luckmann, Thomas. 1967. *The Social Construction of Reality.* New York: Doubleday.

Bernstein, Eduard. 1967. *Evolutionary Socialism.* New York: Schocken Books.

Boissevain, Jeremy. 1966. Patronage in Sicily. *Man.* 1:18–33.

Bosch, Juan. 1970. *Composición Social Dominicana* Santa Domingo: Impresora Arte y Cine, C. por A.

Cantril, Hadley. 1965. *The Pattern of Human Concerns.* New Brunswick: Rutgers University Press.

Cohen, Percy, S. 1968. *Modern Social Theory.* New York: Basic Books.

Converse, Philip E. 1964. The Nature of Belief Systems in Mass Publics. In *Ideology and Discontent,* ed. David E. Apter, pp. 206–61. New York: Free Press of Glencoe.

Cotler, Julio. 1970. Traditional Haciendas and Communities in a Context of Political Mobilization in Peru. In *Agrarian Problems and Peasant Movements in Latin America,* ed. Rodolfo Stavenhagen, pp. 533–58. New York: Doubleday, Anchor Books.

Dahl, Robert A. 1971. *Polyarchy.* New Haven: Yale University Press.

Dahrendorf, Ralf. 1966. *Class and Class Conflict in Industrial Society.* Stanford: Stanford University Press.

Erasmus, Charles J. 1968. Community Development and the Encogido Syndrome. *Human Organization* 27:65–74.

Foster, G. M. 1960–61. Interpersonal Relations in Peasant Society. *Human Organization* 19:174–78.

_____. 1967. The Dyadic Contract: A Model for the Social Structure of a Mexican Peasant Village. In *Peasant Society: A Reader,* ed. J. M. Potter, M. N. Diaz, and G. M. Foster, pp. 213–30. Boston: Little, Brown.

Freire, Paulo. 1970. *Pedagogy of the Oppressed.* New York: Herder and Herder.

Friedmann, F. G. 1967. The World of *La Miseria.* In *Peasant Society: A Reader,* ed. J. M. Potter, M. N. Diaz, and G. M. Foster, pp. 324–36. Boston: Little, Brown.

Friedrich, Paul. 1970. *Agrarian Revolt in a Mexican Village.* Englewood Cliffs: Prentice-Hall.

Geertz, Clifford. 1957. Ritual and Social Change: A Javanese Example. *American Anthropologist* 59:32–54.

_____. 1964. Ideology as a Cultural System. In *Ideology and Discontent,* ed. David E. Apter, pp. 47–76. New York: Free Press of Glencoe.

_____. 1968. *Peddlers and Princes.* Chicago: University of Chicago Press.

Germani, Gino. 1966. Social and Political Consequences of Mobility. In *Social Structure and Mobility in Economic Development,* ed. N. J. Smelsar and S. L. Lipset, pp. 354–75. Chicago: Aldine.

Goldthorpe, John H., Lockwood, David, Bechhofer, Frank, and Plat, Jennifer. 1968. *The Affluent Worker: Industrial Attitudes and Behavior.* Cambridge: Cambridge University Press.

_____. 1969. *The Affluent Worker and the Class Structure.* Cambridge: Cambridge University Press.

Gouldner, Alvin. 1973. "The Sociologist as Partisan: Sociology and the Welfare State. In Alvin Gouldner, *For Sociology,* pp. 27–68. New York: Basic Books.

Grunwald, Joseph, and Musgrove, Philip. 1970. *Natural Resources in Latin American Development.* Baltimore: The Johns Hopkins Press.

Handelman, Howard. 1975. *Struggle in the Andes: Peasant Political Mobilization in Peru.* Austin: University of Texas Press.

Hansen, Roger O. 1971. *The Politics of Mexican Development.* Baltimore: The Johns Hopkins Press.

Heppenstall, M. A. 1971. Reputation, Criticism and Information in an Austrian Village. In *Gifts and Poison,* ed. F. G. Bailey, pp. 139–66. New York: Schocken Books.

Hewitt, Cynthia N. 1969. Brazil: The Peasant Movement of Pernambuco, 1961–1964. In *Latin American Peasant Movements,* ed. Henry A. Landsberger, pp. 374–98. Ithaca: Cornell University Press.

Hinton, William. 1968. *Fanshen.* New York: Vintage Books.

Hobsbawm, E. J. 1959. *Primitive Rebels.* New York: W. W. Norton.

Huizer, Gerrit. 1970. Emiliano Zapata and the Guerillas in the Mexican Revolution. In *Agrarian Problems and Peasant Movements in Latin America,* ed. Rodolfo Stavenhagen, pp. 375–406. New York: Doubleday, Anchor Books.

_____. 1972. *The Revolutionary Potential of Peasants in Latin America.* Lexington: D. C. Heath.

Huntington, Samuel. 1968. *Political Order in Changing Societies.* New Haven: Yale University Press

Instituto de Café y Cacao. 1966. Mimeo Pamphlet. Santo Domingo n. p. (Much of the data included is based on the National Agropecuarian Census of 1960.)

International Coffee Agreement, 1968. 1968. Washington: World Coffee Information Center of the Pan-American Coffee Bureau.

Kenny, Michael. 1960. Patterns of Patronage in Spain. *Anthropological Quarterly* 33:14–23.

Krasner, Stephen D. 1973. Business Government Relations: The Case of the International Coffee Agreement. *International Organization* 27:495–516.

Kuhn, Thomas S. 1964. *The Structure of Scientific Revolutions.* Chicago: University of Chicago Press.

La Información, 5 January 1971. Santiago, Dominican Republic.

_____. 14 January 1971. Santiago, Dominican Republic.

Landsberger, Henry A., ed. 1969. *Latin American Peasant Movements.* Ithaca: Cornell University Press.

_____, and Hewitt, C. N. 1970. Ten Sources of Weakness and Cleavage in Latin American Peasant Movements. In *Agrarian Problems and Peasant Movements in Latin America,* ed. Rodolfo Stavenhagen, pp. 559–83. New York: Doubleday, Anchor Books.

Lane, Robert E., and Sears, David O. 1964. *Public Opinion.* Englewood Cliffs: Prentice-Hall.

Lewis, Oscar. 1959. *Five Families.* New York: Basic Books.

Lipset, S. M., and Bendix, R. 1959. *Social Mobility in Industrial Society.* Berkeley: University of California Press.

Lockwood, David. 1964. Social Integration and System Integration. In *Explorations in Social Change,* ed. George K. Zollschan, and Walter Hirsch, pp. 370–83. Boston: Houghton Mifflin.

Malloy, James ed. 1976. *Authoritarianism and Corporatism in Latin America.* Pittsburgh: University of Pittsburgh Press.

Marx, Karl, and Engels, Friedrich. 1962. *Selected Works.* Vol. 1. Moscow: Foreign Languages Publishing House.

Mauss, Marcel. 1966. *The Gift.* London: Cohen and West.

Miller, Soloman. 1967. Hacienda to Plantation in Northern Peru: The Process of Proletarianization of a Tenant Farmer Society. In *Contemporary Change in Traditional Societies,* ed. Julian Steward, 3:133–225. Urbana: University of Illinois Press.

Mills, C. Wright. 1959. *The Sociological Imagination.* New York: Oxford University Press.

_____. 1967. *Power, Politics, and People.* New York: Oxford University Press.

Mintz, Sidney, and Wolf, Eric. 1950. An Analysis of Ritual Co-Parenthood (compadrazgo). *Southwestern Journal of Anthropology* 6:341–68.

Moore, Barrington, Jr. 1966. *The Social Origins of Dictatorship and Democracy.* Boston: Beacon Press.

Morse, Richard. 1969. Comments on Carl N. Degler's Paper, "Slavery in the

United States and Brazil: An Essay in Comparative History." 62nd Annual Meeting of the Organization of American Historians, 17 April 1969.

Neumann, Franz. 1957. *The Democratic and Authoritarian State.* Glencoe: Free Press.

Olson, Mancur. 1973. *The Logic of Collective Action.* Cambridge: Harvard University Press.

Petras, James, and Zeitlin, Maurice. 1970. Agrarian Radicalism in Chile. In *Agrarian Problems and Peasant Movements in Latin America,* ed. Rodolfo Stavenhagen, pp. 503–32. New York: Doubleday, Anchor Books.

Pike, Fredrick B., and Stritch, Thomas, ed. 1974. *The New Corporatism.* Notre Dame: University of Notre Dame Press.

Pitt-Rivers, J. A. 1961. *The People of the Sierra.* Chicago: Chicago University Press, Phoenix Books.

Potter, J. M., Foster, G. M., and Diaz, M. N., eds. 1967. *Peasant Society: A Reader.* Boston: Little, Brown.

República Dominicana en Cifras, vol. 4. 1969. Santo Domingo: Oficina Nacional Estadistica.

Rex, John. 1963. *Key Problems of Sociological Theory.* London: Routledge and Kegan Paul.

Schmitter, Philippe. 1974. Still the Century of Corporatism? *Review of Politics* 36:93–98.

Scott, James. 1975. Exploitation in Rural Class Relations: A Victim's Perspective. *Comparative Politics* 7:489–532.

Shanin, Teodor. 1972. *The Awkward Class.* Oxford: Clarendon Press.

Silvert, Kalman H. 1970. *Man's Power.* New York: Viking Press.

Sorokin, Pitirim. 1959. *Social and Cultural Mobility.* Glencoe: Free Press.

Stavenhagen, Rodolfo, ed. 1970. *Agrarian Problems and Peasant Movements in Latin America.* New York: Doubleday, Anchor Books.

Steinbeck, John. 1972. *In Dubious Battle.* New York: Bantam Books.

Stepan, Alfred. Forthcoming. *The State and Society: Peru in Comparative Perspective.* Princeton: Princeton University Press.

Sutton, Francis X., Harris, Seymour, Kaysen, Carl, and Tobin, James. 1956. *The American Business Creed.* Cambridge: Harvard University Press.

Weber, Max. 1968. *Economy and Society.* ed. G. Roth and C. Wittich, vols. I, II, and III. New York: Bedminister Press.

White, Robert A., S. J. 1969. Mexico: The Zapata Movement and the Revolution. In *Latin American Peasant Movements,* ed. Henry A. Landsberger, pp. 101–69. Ithaca: Cornell University Press.

Wolf, Eric R. 1956a. Aspects of Group Relations in a Complex Society: Mexico. *American Anthropologist* 58:1065–78.

———. 1956b. San José: Subcultures of a "Traditional" Coffee Municipality. In *The People of Puerto Rico,* ed. Julian Steward, pp. 171–264. Urbana: University of Illinois Press.

———. 1966a. Kinship, Friendship, and Patron Client Relations in Complex Societies. In *The Social Anthropology of Complex Societies,* ed. Michael Banton, pp. 1–22. New York: Praeger.

———. 1966b. *Peasants.* Englewood Cliffs: Prentice-Hall.

_____. 1969. *Peasant Wars of the Twentieth Century.* New York: Harper and Row.

Womack, John, Jr. 1970. *Zapata and the Mexican Revolution.* New York: Vintage Books.

Zola, Emile. 1969. *Germinal.* Baltimore: Penguin Books.

INDEX

Library of Congress Cataloging in Publication Data

Sharpe, Kenneth Evan.
    Peasant politics.

    (Johns Hopkins studies in Atlantic history and culture)
    Bibliography: pp. 251–55
    Includes index.
    1. Peasantry–Dominican Republic–Haina Arriba.
2. Coffee trade–Dominican Republic–Haina Arriba.
3. Cooperative marketing of farm produce–Dominican
Republic–Haina Arriba. 4. Power (Social Sciences)
I. Title. II. Series.
HD430.H34S47   301.44′43′097293   770 77-4782
ISBN 0–8018–1952–0